M

Overboard, Situ
Without Saying, Nina, That's Something Else,
A Smile on the End of the Line

Overboard: 'Combines Shakespearian tragedy, Aristophanic farce and a Chekhovian drama of lives consumed and memories that fade.' *Le Progrès*

Situation Vacant: 'The play builds to a climax which powerfully captures a mind under siege, bombarded by a cacophony of voices and tormented by guilt.' *Independent*

Dissident, Goes Without Saying and *Nina, That's Something Else*: 'These two plays bring to a summit the art of suggestion . . . Two fables in which prosaic everyday life is captured, at times fraught with pathos, often compassionate.' *L'Humanité*

A Smile on the End of the Line: 'A six-part invention which interweaves half a dozen plot lines to bring life and speed into the manufacturing sector.' *Daily Telegraph*

Michel Vinaver was born in 1927. For nearly thirty years he was an executive with Gillette International and this inside experience of the workings of a multinational corporation has provided material for many of his plays. In the 1950s he was labelled a political dramatist, especially after his play *The Koreans* provoked right-wing demonstrations and was subject to government censorship. In the 1960s he suffered from prolonged writer's block, but overcame it with the writing of *Overboard* (1969). Since then he has written eleven more plays and is known as the leading 'dramatist of the everyday'. His work has been produced by every leading director from Vitez to Lassalle; he was the first chairman of the Theatre Commission of the Centre National des Lettres, and is generally acknowledged as France's major living dramatist.

by the same author

Michel Vinaver Plays: 2
(High Places, The Neighbours, Portrait of a Woman,
The Television Programme)

MICHEL VINAVER

Plays: 1

Overboard
translated by Gideon Lester

Situation Vacant
translated by John Burgess

Dissident, Goes Without Saying
translated by Peter Meyer

Nina, That's Something Else
translated by Peter Meyer

A Smile on the End of the Line
translated by Peter Meyer

edited and introduced by David Bradby

METHUEN DRAMA

METHUEN CONTEMPORARY DRAMATISTS

This collection first published in Great Britain 1997
by Methuen Drama
Random House, 20 Vauxhall Bridge Road, London SW1V 2SA
and Australia, New Zealand and South Africa
and distributed in the United States of America
by Heinemann, a division of Reed Elsevier Inc.
361 Hanover Street, Portsmouth, New Hampshire
NH 03801 3959

ISBN 0-413-71780-1

Random House UK Limited Reg. No. 954009

A CIP catalogue record for this book
is available from the British Library

Typeset by Deltatype Ltd, Birkenhead, Merseyside
Printed and bound in Great Britain by
Cox & Wyman, Reading, Berks

Contents

Michel Vinaver:
Chronology

1927   Born in Paris of Russian-born parents of Jewish origin,
        his father an antique dealer and expert in Russian art,
        his mother a civil lawyer, later head of the Section on
        the Status of Women at the Secretariat of the United
        Nations. Early schooling in Paris. His first play, *The
        Revolt of the Vegetables*, written at the age of nine: all the
        vegetables in the kitchen garden get together to
        overthrow the tyrannous regime of the gardener, which
        is only achieved with great sacrifice on the part of the
        artichoke.

1940   On the German occupation of France, the family
        moves, first to the 'Free Zone' in the South. Then, in
        1941, they sail for the USA. Secondary schooling
        completed at the Lycée Français of New York.

1944–5 One semester only at Wesleyan University, Middletown,
        Connecticut, followed by one year spent in barracks in
        France after volunteering for the Free French Forces.

1947   Completes his BA in English and American literature at
        Wesleyan. Returns to France; goes to England for a
        spell with his uncle (Eugène Vinaver, Professor of
        French Literature at Manchester University), where he
        translates T. S. Eliot's *The Waste Land* into French.
        Desultory studies in the humanities at the Sorbonne.

1948   Completion of his first novel, *Lataume*, published in 1950
        by Gallimard on the recommendation of Albert Camus.
        Start of a lifelong friendship with Roland Barthes.

1951   Publication of a second novel – it will be his last –
        L'Objecteur, reflecting the Cold War which was then
        raging, and his experience of the absurd in the army:
        awarded Fénéon prize. Translates Henry Green's novel
        Loving into French for publication by Gallimard; this will
        be later a source for his play *Iphigénie Hôtel*.

1953   Decides against living by his pen and advertises for a
        job in the *International Herald Tribune*. Although lacking in
        education or experience in either business or the law, is

taken on by Gillette, then moving its French
headquarters from Paris to Annecy. Moves from Paris to
live in a house near Lake Annecy that had been
acquired as a summer residence by his maternal
grandfather in 1923 shortly after he emigrated from
Russia, fleeing the Soviet Revolution. Is put in charge of
Gillette France's legal and administrative service.

1955   Becomes involved in a new summer theatre festival run
by Gabriel Monnet in Annecy. At Monnet's request, he
writes his first play (since childhood), *Aujourd'hui*.

1956   Retitled *Aujourd'hui ou Les Coréens*, it is performed by
Roger Planchon's young company in Lyon, where
political disturbances are caused by right-wing groups
outside the theatre.

1957   Monnet plans to produce the play for a theatre festival
at Serre-Ponçon, where a vast temporary town has been
erected for the workers on the hydro-electric dam under
construction, but the Minister for Youth and Sports,
who is sponsoring the festival, censors Monnet's choice
of play. In its place, Monnet stages Sophocles's *Antigone*,
with new choral passages written by Vinaver, performed
in the costumes for *Les Coréens*. Vinaver writes his second
play, *Les Huissiers* (*The Ushers*) – an attempt to dramatise
the texture of French political life at the height of the
Algerian war and through the agony of the Fourth
Republic, following events week by week as they
happen. Planchon has plans to produce the play but
these fall through.

1958   Adapts (on commission) Dekker's *The Shoemaker's Holiday*
for Jean Vilar's Théâtre National Populaire. Vinaver is
attracted by the Elizabethan play's unvarnished
presentation of the life of ordinary city dwellers, but the
TNP production by Georges Wilson upsets him by
giving the play a 'Merrye Englande' treatment.

1959   Writes *Iphigénie Hôtel*, ostensibly about the struggle for
power below-stairs in a Greek tourist hotel, but also
dealing with the theme of power in general, and in
particular with the generals' attempted putsch in Algeria
and their attempted coup in France which culminated in
de Gaulle's coming to power. Gillette sends him to
Britain for one month as an apprentice salesman and

then to Imede, an international business school in
Switzerland, on an intensive nine months' general
management training programme.

1960   Appointed managing director of Gillette's sales subsidiary
in Belgium (forty employees) and moves to Brussels. This
is the time of the marketing revolution in Europe, with
the engineering of mass consumer product promotions to
stimulate desire rather than merely push the goods out.
Distinguishes himself with the triumph of the launch of
Toni and Prom home perm kits on his market.

1964   Transferred to Milan as managing director of Gillette
Italy (300 employees). Rapid expansion of the core
business – blades and razors – along with the launch of
a line of toiletries.

1966   Appointed managing director of Gillette France, one of
the three manufacturing subsidiaries of the company in
Europe (1000 employees), which brings him back to
Annecy. In the course of five years, launches the
Techmatic ribbon razor, the Teflon-treated Gillette
Extra Blue Blade, the stainless steel long-life Super-
Gillette blade, the Right Guard deodorant.

1967   Overcomes seven years' writer's block, and begins to
work on *Par-dessus bord*, a vast Aristophanes-inspired epic
concerning the fortunes of an old-fashioned family-
owned French toilet-paper-manufacturing firm caught in
the transatlantic competition of the boom years of the
sixties, and ultimately taken over by an American
multinational corporation.

1969   *Par-dessus bord* (*Overboard*) completed: it runs to 250 pages,
and would take about eight hours to perform. It is
turned down by Gallimard.

1970   Negotiates the acquisition by Gillette of the French
family-owned company S. T. Dupont, makers of luxury
lighters and 'Cricket' disposable lighters. Is appointed
managing director of this firm and will run it for eight
years, diversifying the luxury operation with a line of
writing instruments, and extending the distribution of
'Cricket' worldwide.

1971   *Par-dessus bord* accepted for publication by L'Arche. After
writing a chronicle of exceptional dimension, feels the
need to treat the same subject matter in microcosm: the

result is *La Demande d'emploi* (*Situation Vacant*), centring on an out-of-work sales executive, his wife and his daughter.

1972   Becomes involved with the Théâtre Eclaté, a young, politically active group in Annecy.

1973   First productions of *La Demande d'emploi* and *Par-dessus bord*. The latter is directed by Planchon in an abridged version and a glitzy style reminiscent of Hollywood musicals.

1976   Writes two short 'chamber plays', *Dissident, il va sans dire* and *Nina, c'est autre chose*. An industrial plant he is managing at Faverges (near Annecy) goes on strike and workers occupy the factory.

1977   *Iphigénie Hôtel* produced (eighteen years after it was written) by Antoine Vitez with his Théâtre des Quartiers d'Ivry at the Pompidou Centre in Paris. Writes *Les Travaux et les jours*, inspired by the previous year's events in the factory and by the effects of the advent of the computer in the office world.

1978   Production of *Dissident* and *Nina* at the studio theatre of the Théâtre de l'Est Parisien, directed by Jacques Lassalle – the start of a long and fruitful association between author and director. (Lassalle was to become head of the Théâtre National de Strasbourg in 1983, where he stayed until being appointed director of the Comédie-Française on the death of Vitez in 1990.)

1979   Writes *A la renverse* (*Falling Over Backwards*), centred on the cosmetics industry, and the manipulation through advertising of mass fears and obsessions; it contains some televised sequences and a preliminary reflection on the function of television in society, later given a more thorough treatment in *L'Emission de télévision* (*The Television Programme*, 1988). At the end of the year, leaves Gillette.

1980   Adapts Erdman's *The Suicide*, working from a literal translation done with his father. Production of *Les Travaux et les jours* by Alain Françon, director of the Théâtre Eclaté of Annecy. Production of *A la renverse* by Lassalle at Théâtre National de Chaillot. Publication of a children's book, *Les Histoires de Rosalie*, based on the stories of his grandmother's childhood in late nineteenth-century Russia.

1981   Writes *L'Ordinaire* (*High Places*), sparked off by the story of a plane crash in the Andes several years before, which some passengers survived by eating the flesh of the dead – a play about the cannibal tendencies of big business.

1982   Commissioned by the Comédie-Française to write an adaptation of Gorki's *Summerfolk* for a production by Jacques Lassalle. Begins teaching at the University of Paris III (Censier). Publication of his collected writings on the theatre. Appointed to chair the newly established drama committee of the Centre National des Lettres.

1983   Vinaver's first (and last) venture into stage directing: in collaboration with Alain Françon, he directs *L'Ordinaire* at Théâtre National de Chaillot. First unabridged production of *Par-dessus bord* by the Théâtre Populaire Romand in Switzerland, directed by Charles Joris.

1984   Writes *Les Voisins* and *Portrait d'une femme*. *Les Voisins* traces the intermingled lives of two families who are neighbours in semi-detached houses. *Portrait* is based on the newspaper reports of the trial of a woman who murdered her ex-lover. His version of *The Suicide* is staged by the Comédie-Française, Jean-Pierre Vincent directing. Begins a series of playwriting workshops at the University.

1986   Production of *Les Voisins* by Françon at Théâtre Ouvert in Paris, and on tour at a number of Centres Dramatiques. Awarded Ibsen prize. *Théâtre Complet* in two volumes published by Actes Sud. *Dissident, Goes Without Saying* and *Nina, It's Different*, a translation of the chamber plays by Paul Antal, published in *Dramacontemporary France*, PAJ Publications, New York.

1987   Publication of a report, *Le Compte rendu d'Avignon*, written by Vinaver as chairman of the Drama committee of the Centre National des Lettres, on the current crisis of play publishing and the state of the playwright in the French theatre industry. This report triggers a number of initiatives, particularly in the area of national educational programmes. First production of his work in Britain: *Les Travaux et les jours*, translated by Peter Meyer as *A Smile on the End of the Line*, directed by Sam Walters at the Orange Tree Theatre, Richmond.

1988   Appointed titular professor at the University of Paris VIII (Saint-Denis). Writes *L'Emission de télévision*.

1989   Production of *Situation Vacant* (John Burgess's translation
       of *La Demande d'emploi*) by Sam Walters at the Orange
       Tree. A second UK production of *Les Travaux et les jours*,
       in a new translation by Ron Butlin under the title
       Blending in, staged at the Traverse Theatre for the
       Edinburgh Festival. Vinaver is commissioned by Vitez to
       write *Le Dernier Sursaut*, an impromptu for the yearly
       celebration of Molière's birth at the Comédie-Française.
       Publication of *Portrait of a Woman* (Donald Watson's
       translation) in *New French Plays* (Methuen) and, in the
       US, by the Dramatic Publishing Company.

1990   Translation of Shakespeare's *Julius Caesar*, commissioned
       and produced by the Comédie de Genève, directed by
       Claude Stratz. Production of *L'Emission de télévision* at the
       Odéon, by the Comédie-Française, directed by Jacques
       Lassalle. Staged reading of *Portrait of a Woman* by Di
       Trevis for the RSC at the Covent Garden International
       Festival.

1991   Translates *Time and the Room* by Botho Strauss: a
       commission by Patrice Chéreau, who directs it at the
       Odéon.

1992   Production of *The Television Programme* (D. and H.
       Bradby's translation) at the Gate Theatre, London,
       directed by Kim Dambaek.

1993   After extensive restoration works, the Vieux Colombier
       Theatre reopens in Paris as the second home of the
       Comédie-Française, to be devoted to the work of living
       playwrights; one of the two opening productions is a
       revival of *Les Coréens*. Publication of Vinaver's *Ecritures
       Dramatiques*, a new approach to the analysis of dramatic
       text, founded on the research and teaching he had
       developed in the University. Production of *Situation
       Vacant* (*La Demande d'emploi*) by the Public Works
       Company in Sydney, Australia, in a new translation by
       Paul Dwyer and directed by him.

1995   Production of *Portrait of a Woman* by Sam Walters at the
       Orange Tree, and simultaneously in New York by Peter
       Sylvester at the Synchronicity Theatre. Production of
       Overboard (Gideon Lester's translation of *Par-dessus bord*)
       by the Institute for Advanced Theatre Training at
       Harvard University, American Repertory Theatre,

Author's Foreword

How does a painting come to get started? An adventure: one doesn't know where it will take you. The interest for the artist would be low if he had foreknowledge, if he had to execute a picture pre-existing entirely in his mind. Nothing of the kind; the artist is harnessed with chance; he doesn't dance alone, there's two of them; chance, his partner, pulls here and there, while the artist leads as best he can, but in a supple manner, employing himself to take advantage of all that is fortuitous along his way and making it serve his aims, allowing himself to deviate from them and take an oblique course at any moment. But strictly speaking, here, one shouldn't talk of chance. Neither here nor anywhere else. There's no such thing as chance. Man names chance anything that stems from this great big black hole of little-known causes. It isn't exactly with any kind of chance that the artist deals, but with chance of a particular sort, proper to the nature of the material employed. The word chance hardly applies; one should rather talk of the inclinations and aspirations of the material which rebels.

How does a play come to be started? As far as I am concerned, the description of the process given by Jean Dubuffet,[1] talking of his work as a painter, expresses it exactly. Granted that my material is not shape and colour but words – more specifically, words spoken and exchanged – there's no difference.

There's no difference but there are differences. Two of them. Unlike shape and colour, words are loaded with meanings (they are a transit for communication). Unlike a painting's, a play's reception takes place not in an instant but in a stretch of time with a beginning and an end.

As a finished product, a play, like a painting, has to provide

[1] Jean Dubuffet, *L'Homme du commun à l'ouvrage* © Editions Gallimard, 1973.

pleasure, i.e. take hold of the spectator's interest, move him, surprise him, give him unforeseen insights into the world and himself. The condition for this to happen is ease of access, preferably immediate, short of which boredom creates a barrier.

Close as I stand to the creative process described by Dubuffet, the act of writing a play and bringing it to completion (not just starting it) is one where there is a ceaseless negotiation between opposing forces: abandonment of the pen to random happenings, and a push towards a construction as orderly as a Doric temple, in which meanings, characters and events coalesce.

Negotiation is not the appropriate term, as it implies intentions and strategy. Call this, instead, a tension, primordial in the act of writing, in which the necessities of form (sound, rhythm, verbal accidents: chasms, collisions, echoes, repetitions, variations, etc.) and the need for the whole thing to make sense after all, clash and are jointed.

Michel Vinaver
December 1996

Introduction
A Modernist Theatre

The duality that is the hallmark of Vinaver's life is also a key to understanding his innovative use of dramatic techniques. His method is a juxtapositional one and his inspiration is drawn from poetry, painting and music rather than from other playwrights. The translation he made of T.S. Eliot's *The Waste Land* at the age of twenty convinced him of the value of a method which brings together disparate elements, not integrating them, but challenging readers to relate them in their own imaginations.

Eliot's juxtapositional technique is characteristic of much modernist poetry, and it was precisely the techniques of modernism that Vinaver came to adapt for dramatic purposes. The features that he picks out as valuable in *The Waste Land* can equally well be applied to his own plays:

> The primacy of rhythm from which meaning may emerge; the contrapuntal treatment of a multiplicity of autonomous themes; the pre-eminence of themes over elements of plot; the movement given to the themes so that they collide or scrape up against one another, even to the point of fusion, rather than a movement of causal links. ('La Terre Vague' (Vinaver's introduction to his own translation), *Poésie*, 31, 1984, p. 4)

As can be seen from this list, considerations of rhythm, theme, language precede those of plot, character and meaning in Vinaver's conception, and he uses terms such as rhythm and theme much as a painter or a musician might use them. By adopting a fragmentary, discontinuous method of composition he is able, like T. S. Eliot, to achieve startling, often ironic and humorous effects by the jointing of disparate elements.

Among the many painters he admires, he has been especially inspired by the Cubists, by Dubuffet and by

Rauschenberg. Just as the pictures of Rauschenberg juxta-
pose images of different kinds, playfully allowing for happy
coincidence, or the surprise of the unexpected, so Vinaver
juxtaposes different linguistic registers, from high culture to
low, from learned to familiar, from mythical to modern. In
the texture of the completed dramatic dialogue, they do not
lose their quality of difference, but acquire new resonances by
virtue of other uses of language against which they reverber-
ate.

The thematic material from which he builds up his plays is
as vast and, initially at least, as shapeless as everyday life.
This central concern with 'the Everyday' was reflected in the
title of Vinaver's first play *Aujourd'hui* (*Today*) and he has
described his relationship with the Everyday as follows:

> My relationship with the Everyday is one going back
> unchanged to my infancy and which is at the very centre
> of my creative work. I recall that as a child I was
> astonished when permitted to do the simplest things, such
> as open a door, run, stop running, etc. I was both
> astonished and enraptured at being given these rights; I
> was always afraid that they would be withdrawn and that I
> would be thrust back into non-existence. In this way the
> Everyday was something highly charged, on the brink of
> transgression, at all events precarious, undeserved. (*Ecrits
> sur le théâtre*, Lausanne: L'Aire, 1982, p. 123)

Because he had a sense of standing somehow *outside* reality,
creative writing became, for him, not an exercise in imitating
reality, but rather a constant attempt to capture or penetrate
a domain never perceived as given in advance: 'In other
words, for me, as a writer, nothing exists before I begin to
write, and the activity of writing becomes an attempt to give
consistency to the world and to myself within it' (ibid.).

The experience of the world as something not given in
advance, but constituted in and through the act of writing,
provides an essential key to understanding Vinaver's work.
Almost obsessively, he insists upon the banality, the absolute

flatness of the material from which he begins the compositional process. The situations depicted are intensely *ordinary*: a
man looking for a job (*Situation Vacant* and *The Television
Programme*), the routine workings of a secretarial office (*Smile on
the End of the Line*). Even where the situation is exceptional (as
in *High Places*, depicting the aftermath of a plane crash in the
Andes, with the survivors turning to cannibalism), Vinaver
emphasises the ordinariness of daily life, underlined by the
play's title in French: *L'Ordinaire*.

Vinaver sees the work of the playwright as being to empty
all these situations of their dramatic potential in the common
sense of the word, to prevent the usual presuppositions and
interpretative grids from falling easily into place.

> At the start of the play there is no meaning. But as soon as
> the play is begun there is a thrust towards meaning, a
> thrust towards the formation of situations, themes, charac-
> ters. Beginning with a shapeless nucleus, the product of the
> initial explosion, the play constructs itself bit by bit. At the
> end, if completed successfully, it will appear as rigorously
> structured as if there had been a pre-existing plan. (Ibid.,
> p. 130)

Writing, for Vinaver, is thus a process of *composition*, not of
interpretation. The result aims to surprise, stimulate, and
question its readers/spectators, not to teach them a lesson.
The author does not claim to know something which he can
then pass on through his writing. In fact, his intention in
composing the play is to create a work that will, to some
extent, resist interpretation, in the sense of not being easily
expressed in different terms, not reducible to paraphrase or to
a 'message'. Writing is a process of research and discovery. It
is (as for Václav Havel) a journey, starting from an attempt to
penetrate the terrain of the Everyday and discovering along
the way points of articulation between experiences of different
orders.

Because of the political nature of much of the action in his
plays, and because all of French theatre was subject to a very
strong Brechtian influence in the 1950s and 1960s, Vinaver

has sometimes been blamed for not coming out with clear ideological statements in his plays. In reply, he argued that the writer's commitment must be of a different kind:

> It is sufficient for the creative artist to apply himself to his work, to avoid being distracted by what he wants to say, to dare to commit himself (or abandon himself) completely to his material. (Ibid., p. 12)

The nature of this material is, in the first place, linguistic, and he is fond of describing language as his 'raw material'. The playwright's job, he considers, is to assemble the building blocks of our everyday speech in such a way as to reveal how we construct our images and understandings of the world. In his plays different linguistic idioms confront one another, shift, break up, and re-form, attuned to the characters and the situations in which they find themselves.

Because he refuses to submit the events of his plays to a single narrative line of causal links, but is constantly breaking them up into discontinuous fragments, his dramatic technique clearly has points in common with the Brechtian epic. Like Brecht, Vinaver strongly rejects the Aristotelian unities (something which goes against the grain in France, with its neo-classical tradition, more than in Britain, where we look back to Shakespeare). But Vinaver rejects the didactic element which is present, to a greater or lesser extent, in most of Brecht's work. He shares Brecht's concern to demystify and show up the contradictions of the social structures generated by capitalism, but believes that the playwright must always remain a marginal figure, like a court jester, paid to say the unsayable, to expose the cruelties and absurdities of the system that are taken for granted, rather than to identify himself with a given political philosophy.

In the late 1950s, when the French theatre was torn in two between the supporters of political theatre, inspired by Brecht, and the defenders of the Absurd, inspired by Ionesco and Beckett, Vinaver developed his own middle way. On a visit to New York in May 1958, he attended some working sessions at the Actor's Studio, directed by Lee Strasberg, and wrote an account of them. This concluded with a comparison between the seemingly opposed methods of Brecht and of Stanislavski. He expressed the view, uncommon in 1958, that 'it would be the greatest nonsense to imagine that Brecht substitutes reflection for emotion. No work of art can dispense with emotion: it has to affect the whole person, not just the mind, and Brecht's plays certainly have their effect on the spectator's emotions.' The function of theatre, he concluded (and he found this in the work of both Brecht and Stanislavski) was 'to change men, to liberate them from the imprisoning present and to open up a new field of vision and of action' (ibid., p. 75).

This vision necessitates dynamic, rapidly changing dramatic action, in which relations between characters are constantly shifting. In drama, character is always presented through a process of interaction. Vinaver's approach leads him naturally to exploit this as a strength: the characters in his plays are not pre-defined but gradually acquire their substance through their relationships with one another. Just as Braque claimed that the important thing in his pictures was not so much the objects depicted as the space between them, so Vinaver's characters can be seized only in the actions that take place between them. His fragmented, juxtapositional method deliberately disrupts the traditional or received patterns of relationships, whether they be between parent and child, husband and wife, or boss and employee. Each of his plays affords a wealth of insight into how what we term 'character' is composed of a constantly shifting network of interactions: between persons, between groups, between the individual and the group. An effect of this compositional method is to question the given existence of patriarchal structures, whether in the family or in the work-place.

There is practically no monologue in Vinaver's theatre: speech is always part of a process of action and reaction with others. Here again a fundamental duality or multiplicity can be seen as the underlying principle of his creative vision. The layering of many different voices, which drama inevitably entails, is fundamentally congenial to him. He welcomes the fact that the playwright, unlike other writers, cannot speak with his own voice, but only through the orchestration of other voices: 'Dramatic writing suits me because in it I make others speak, and because its language does not describe, nor comment, nor explain, but acts' ('Mémoire sur mes travaux', *Les Cahiers de Prospéro*, 8 juillet 1996, p. 17). The absence of punctuation in the written texts of his plays only serves to reinforce the active quality of this language, which is not tied to a static, fixed form on the page, but asks for a reader to give it life, rhythm and hence meaning.

This makes for plays in which the audience is never able to settle back into a comfortable emotional identification with any given character, since the perspective is constantly shifting. The viewpoint of one character is contradicted by that of a second, or a third, often overlapping in the same scene. A similar tension characterises his use of dramatic situation. Every one of his plays can be seen as an ironic exposure of the gap between the expectations of the characters and the situation in which they are placed. This is where the social and political dimensions of Vinaver's work emerge most clearly. The plays restlessly explore the discrepancies between the characters' own limited appreciation of their situation and the realities of that situation. The author has gone so far as to suggest that such irony is the necessary condition for the emergence of meaning:

> Irony – that is to say the brutal discrepancy between what is expected and what occurs – is the equivalent in writing of an electric discharge: all at once the current flows. A current of meaning. (*Ecrits sur le théâtre*, p. 125)

Vinaver's achievement lies in his having abandoned a theatre of linear narrative for one of multiple perspectives: he suggests that it may be impossible to make sense of our lives as linear sequences, but that we can at least get a partial grip on them by establishing connections between ordinarily discontinuous situations. In this way a new form of epic theatre is created, opposed to the Aristotelian theatre, but differing from Brecht's in that the 'distancing effect' is obtained by a continuous stream of microtextual fractures rather than by the systematic discouragement of empathy. It is the first authentically modernist theatre, succeeding in 'transforming the most uninteresting raw material into an object of enjoyment and knowledge' (ibid., p. 132).

The Plays

Overboard (Par-dessus bord), 1969

'*Overboard* was begun as an act of exorcism' (*Ecrits sur le théâtre*, p. 309). In 1967, when Vinaver began to write his longest play, he was at the height of a successful career as managing director with Gillette in a number of European countries. Added to this, he had fathered four children between 1959 and 1963. His last play (*Iphigénie Hôtel*) had been completed over seven years earlier; amid the demands on his time of work and family, he doubted if he would ever be able to write again. But then the idea came to him that perhaps the solution lay, not in keeping the different areas of his life apart, but in refusing to go on 'playing at hide and seek with myself' and instead to put himself into his writing:

> To do my own portrait in a great burst of laughter. I am Passemar. I am also Benoît, and Alex and Jack. My reference point was a series of portraits of the artist and his model painted by Picasso. (Ibid.)

He decided that the play would attempt to stage the world of big business, but through the eyes of a manager (Passemar) who is also the author of a play. As the action unfolds, it soon becomes clear that Passemar's play is the one the audience is watching. By this device the very process of dramatic creation, especially the near-impossibility of staging the complex movements of a large commercial enterprise, become a significant element in the play, both structurally and thematically. The audience is invited to join the playwright in a meditation on the central question of how we may best make images, or tell stories, or recreate the world in which we live, so as to understand and act upon it.

The play interweaves a number of different stories, but they all share some connection with the central struggle which provides the context for all the action. This is a fight to the death, pitting an American Goliath against a French David. The American company is a paper products giant in search of new outlets; its prey is an old-fashioned French family business with a monopoly on the sales of toilet paper. In the first stage of the combat, the American giant seems sure to be able to outmanoeuvre the French company: it launches a new brand of soft paper which rapidly outsells the more Spartan French brand. This leads to a radical shake-up in the hierarchy of the French company, and its rapid adoption of modern marketing methods. As a result, in a second stage of the contest, the French regain the advantage. Finally, the third stage produces another unexpected result: just when the French company has established its commercial viability and seems sure of the independence it has fought so hard to retain, it appears that it will, after all, be absorbed by its former adversary.

In order to prevent the play from becoming too exclusively led by the commercial plot, Vinaver decided to impose upon it the discipline of Ancient Greek comedy: he used the six-part structure of all Aristophanic plots (as interpreted by Cornford) – Transgression, Combat, Agon, Counter-transgression, Feast and Marriage. He also introduced the Norse legend of the conflict between the Aesir and the Vanir, seeing its incomprehensible reversals as typical of the equally baffling developments in the fortunes of any commercial organisation. In line with his attempt to 'exorcise' his writer's block, Vinaver refused to limit himself to the normal constraints of a three-hour play with no more than six characters. The complete text contains fifty characters, twenty-nine different settings and took over seven hours of performance time on the only occasion when it has been presented in its entirety (at the Théâtre Populaire Romand in 1983). The text included in this volume is a version

abbreviated by the author and translated by Gideon Lester
for a production by the American Repertory Theatre of
Harvard University in 1995.

Despite its outsize length and concern with commerce,
however, the play retains a focus on intensely felt private
emotions. Within the different phases of the struggle, and
inside each of the six 'movements' borrowed from Aristophanes, the audience's interest is engaged by a variety of
interwoven personal dramas. There is, for example, the
drama of Lubin, the salesman whose regular visit to one of his
retailers provides the opening scene of the play. With the
character of Lubin, Vinaver has captured with deadly
accuracy the peculiar relationship that develops between two
parties trying to strike a deal. Part of the dialogue is extremely
personal: each one asks after the others family with apparent
(perhaps real) sincerity. But at any moment this is liable to tip
over into a different kind of dialogue, one in which each
speaker adopts a self-conscious role (recognised by the other)
in which the attempt to make a sale becomes a trial of
strength or jousting match.

Overboard marks a watershed in Vinaver's development as a
playwright: it contains within it the source of all the
subsequent plays he was to write. In it he also sets the pattern
for his treatment of myth and of other literary material. Just
as the different themes, stories, and characters of the play
come into collision, fuse and separate again, achieving effects
by juxtaposition, so the play's mythic reference points are
drawn from many different sources and are made to interact
in unexpected ways. As well as Aristophanes and Norse
legends, the play contains material drawn from St Augustine,
Shakespeare, Montaigne, Rabelais, the Marquis de Sade,
Madame de Pompadour, Freud, Nietzsche, Max Weber and
the 'happenings' of Oldenburg. Most important of all, these
reference points do not appear in self-consciously literary
fashion, but are used to enhance the documentary reality of
the period: *Overboard* provides a wealth of insights into the
cultural and commercial life of the 1960s. This was, in reality,
the period in which French companies had to face up to new

predatory behaviour of US capital, and when the multi-national corporations were coming to dominate world markets; it was also the period when 'happenings' were born – Claes Oldenburg's *Washes* took place at New York's Riverside Plaza Hotel in 1965 exactly as Jiji describes it in the third 'movement'.

But more interesting than the range of sources from which Vinaver draws his material is the variety of uses to which he puts it. There is a group of dancers, for example, who are attempting to use the Norse myths as the basis for new choreography, while a professor attempts to establish their reality from a scholarly point of view. Seeing the same myths treated so differently, the audience is led to reflect on other myths, and the uses to which they are put. Similarly, the play includes a group of jazz musicians: through their efforts to arrange a 'happening', the playwright is able to introduce reflection on the 'Aktionen' inflicted on Polish Jews by the Nazis. These were 'real-life happenings', similar to 'snuff movies', in which sadistic excitement was generated through the knowledge that the tortures and deaths being witnessed were genuine and final. In the underlying struggle between French and American commercial interest, each side makes use of the myths that suit it. The French exploit the myth of European culture and the Americans similarly exploit the myth of New World modernity. The image consultants Jack Donohue and Jenny Frankfurter initially rely on the myth of the brash but commercially brilliant American to justify their presence (and their outsize fee). More importantly, their whole sales strategy depends on appeciation of the mythical associations surrounding defecation: first they aim to remove the guilt induced by potty-training, then persuade the customers that a new brand of luxury toilet paper will be the passport to guilt-free anal eroticism. The final choice of name for the product ('Moss and Heather') is taken because of its ability to encapsulate the myth of cleanliness and release associated with nature.

In its full version, *Par-dessus bord* takes its place in the history of modern drama as the complete modernist play, worthy to stand beside such 'monsters' as James Joyce's *Ulysses*. It is a work in which all the established conventions and expectations of theatre are thrown overboard and the most fundamental principles subjected to critical scrutiny. It succeeds better than any other play in the contemporary French repertoire in mobilising conflicting registers of discourse and in showing how their rival claims to explain or express reality also carry hidden implications of power and control. It tests the old, mythical structures which claimed to give a unified explanation of the world and finds them wanting. But it does not, for all that, reject them entirely, accepting that the twentieth-century world view must of necessity entail the fragmentary awareness of our ruined cultural inheritance. It documents the 1960s accurately and with affection but not with sentimental nostalgia. It maintains its affirmation of human pain and joy, loss and profit, struggling for expression in a world where all the old certainties have been overturned.

Situation Vacant (*La Demande d'emploi*), 1971

In the course of writing this play, the author fancied that it might turn out as a set of exercises for actors, similar to the Book of Anna Magdalena Bach for pianists. After completing it, he realised that it was more like another musical paradigm: the set of variations on a given theme. Although they are sparse and fragmentary, elements of a story line are unmistakeably present, recurring in different combinations and configurations. More than a linear development, however, the play has the circular development (in spiral form) of a set of variations on a theme, where the composition keeps returning to elements which are, at one and the same time, familiar yet strange. Vinaver identified the basic theme as:

> Birth / initiation / transition / acceptance–rejection / self-affirmation–guilt–loss of self-esteem / who I am. (*Ecrits sur le théâtre*, p. 246)

The play turns on an experience shared by many of Vinaver's characters: that of losing one's job, hence one's place in

society and ultimately one's identity. There are four characters: Fage; his wife Louise; his daughter Nathalie; and
Wallace, the recruiting director of a specialist tour operator.
The play's thirty 'variations' all relate in one way or another
to Fage's experience of a mid-life crisis, though the different
scenes do not necessarily occur in chronological order.

Each different scene presents Fage in a new perspective,
but each scene also includes scraps of dialogue which do not
relate to the situation in which Fage currently finds himself:
an interview scene with Wallace, for example, may be cross-
cut with dialogue between Fage and his wife, or his daughter,
or both. This technique casts an ironic light on affirmations of
principle or value judgement by abruptly shifting the
perspective. In Scene Ten, for example, Fage appears to
Wallace as a self-possessed individual, who imposes his will
on the world around him, at the same time as his will is
shown to break down in a scene with Louise. He lectures
Nathalie on her responsibilities at the same time as his own
behaviour gives him the lie. The last two lines of the scene
illustrate well the ironic humour generated by this cross-
cutting. Wallace says: 'You build your life' and Fage follows
with: 'On the King's Road'. These statements are parts of
two separate conversations, but their juxtaposition creates a
third meaning, one which provokes laughter because of its
incongruity, but which then goes on to cause a secondary
smile of ironic recognition on the part of the audience, as they
realise that Fage's behaviour towards his daughter on their
trip to London has indeed contributed to shaping his life.

This compositional method requires considerable agility on
the part of the actor, who has to establish a character *and*
show it in different lights, without the benefit of sequential
development. Vinaver's only stage direction specifies that
'they are on stage throughout'. The fact that a conversation
taking place in London may intersect with another in Paris,
or on a mountainside in the Alps, makes it impossible to
present each location separately on stage. Each of the
characters inhabits a kind of virtual reality, managing to be in
several places and times simultaneously. Vinaver imagined

that the staging would present a multiple performance space, in which several locations could be seen to overlap or collide with one another, rather in the manner of a collage. In other words, to stage the play involves placing more emphasis on the actors' movements and voices than on the visual setting. For this reason it was successful when staged in the round by Sam Walters in 1989 at the Orange Tree Theatre in Richmond. The fact that each member of the audience had a different perspective on the actors fitted perfectly with the style of dramatic composition.

The impression one receives from watching *Situation Vacant* is of a number of different dialogues proceeding simultaneously, like so many musical lines, and constantly cutting across one another in such a way as to provoke harmonies or dissonances. In a musical composition such as a string quartet, the different intruments can play simultaneously without harming the listener's ability to distinguish each separate melodic line. In a stage play, this is hardly possible, though it is sometimes a feature of experimental performances to have everyone on stage talking at once. Rather than adopt this method, which involves each separate line being drowned in noise, Vinaver interrupts one dialogue with a second, returns to the first, continues with a third, etc. Part of the success of this interweaving technique in the theatre derives from the surprise effect of cuts when audiences expect continuity. Every time a dialogue is interrupted by another, there is potential for the mood or the meaning of one to colour the other and provoke the emergence of other moods or meanings. A sort of echo-chamber effect is set up, resulting in the themes resonating beyond the precise situations in which they arise.

Dissident, Goes Without Saying (*Dissident, il va sans dire*) and *Nina, That's Something Else* (*Nina, c'est autre chose*), 1976

These two short plays, published together as *Théâtre de chambre* in 1978, are constructed on the same principles as *Situation Vacant*, but they are less complex, involve fewer characters, and follow a chronological story-line. *Dissident* presents fragmentary snapshots of the relationship between a single mother and her adolescent son; *Nina* depicts a threesome: two brothers living together, who cope with the arrival of the unpredictable but compelling Nina, her brief period of living with them, and her subsequent departure.

The dialogue in these plays is more typical of what is known as Theatre of the Everyday (*Théâtre du Quotidien*) than most of Vinaver's works: it is halting, inarticulate, emotionally hesitant. It is filled with all the bric-à-brac of life in France in the late 1970s: office automation, industrial crisis, go-slows and strikes, the new Renault 5, traffic congestion in the cities, military service in North Africa, etc. Unlike *Situation Vacant*, whose scenes could, theoretically, be performed in a different order, these plays both explore a brief episode in the lives of their characters, following an irreversible time sequence.

The twelve scenes of *Dissident* portray a separated mother, Hélène, and her teenage son, Philippe, as they work through the permutations of parent–child behaviour, ending up with the disappearance of the child, followed by a reconciliation when he returns. In the course of the play the two characters move from one stage to another in their mutually dependent relationship. At the beginning this relationship is circumscribed by the normal division of roles between the parent as provider and the child as object of care and attention. In the course of the action we see both trying out different roles, though they remain dependent on one another, and so each new variation involves an attempt by one to coerce the freedom of the other. At the end, the strains and blocks in their relationship dissolve, and they are able to share a moment of tenderness. As so often in this play, the emotional mood is expressed through an object: Hélène offers to put on one of Philippe's records, the very records which had been a major source of arguments between them earlier in the play.

Nina, while similar in structure to *Dissident*, introduces one extra character and reverses the balance of ages and sexes: the two brothers, Charles and Sebastien, are in their early forties and Nina is twenty-four. Like *Dissident*, it consists of twelve short scenes, but here each scene carries a title which refers to an object that plays a key role in the scene. Charles and Sebastien are both characters who define themselves primarily in relation to objects. Sebastien, the elder of the two, works in a factory, where he is about to be promoted to charge-hand; Charles is a hair stylist and works in a hairdressing salon.

The brothers are depicted through their dependence on one another and on the memory of their defunct mother. When Charles instals Nina in their shared flat, these dependencies shift. Charles expects his brother to befriend Nina, but is upset when she finds it only natural to share her favours equally between both of them. Both brothers experience a conflict with their hierarchy at work: Charles overreacts, is fired, and turns to alcohol, while Sebastien shows himself more resilient and prone to compromise. The audience's understanding of what is happening to each character is built up kaleidoscopically, through the juxta-position of their own accounts and the reactions of the other two characters. The last scene echoes the opening: in both, we see Sebastien opening a packet of dates, a special gift he receives once a year from a girl he spent one night with under a palm tree in Tunisia twenty years before.

The box of dates offers a good example of how Vinaver uses the most banal objects to create echoes going far beyond the detail of the scenes. Sebastien is in the habit of comparing national traits. When trying to decide what to do with the dates in the first scene, he says: 'Mother used to love them we could send them to help the victims of the disaster in China they put out a press release to say that they were not in need of help from anyone that's what I call pride the Algerians too are a proud people not like the Tunisians what you notice about the Tunisians is their flexibility.' Later in the play he has to make a decision (as charge-hand) about whether an Algerian worker in his factory should be sacked. Having had no choice but to accept the promotion to a position of (minimal) responsibility, he then finds himself obliged to sack

the Algerian worker, suspected (wrongly, it seems) of pilfer-
ing.

A Smile on the End of the Line (*Les Travaux et les jours*), 1978

This was the first of Vinaver's plays to be produced by Sam
Walters at the Orange Tree Theatre (in 1987); it was later
performed in a new translation as *Blending In* at the Traverse
Theatre, Edinburgh in 1989. Set in the after-sales office of a
manufacturing business, it develops the innovative dramatic
method of *Situation Vacant*, showing how the repercussions of
take-overs, strikes, increased or diminishing commercial
successes affect the lives of a small number of the firm's
employees.

In this play Vinaver investigates the ties that bind people to
their work, as well as to the other people and to the objects
which make up their lives. In the course of his professional life
as a business executive, Vinaver observed that the two most
powerful forces at work are, on the one hand, the eagerness
to belong, to resist change (or, when necessary, to espouse it),
and, on the other hand, a terror of being excluded as a result
of the new economic order: 'Comic situations arise from this
dialectic in our everyday lives: we act and think as autono-
mous producer-consumers, while simultaneously we are
consumed, annihilated' (*Ecrits sur le théâtre*, p. 286).

The play achieves many humorous effects from the shifts
and jumps between the formal, company phrases employed
by the secretaries to answer customers on the line, and the
gossipy chatter they keep going amongst themselves in-
between times. Often the two are intercut, and the very
discrepancy between the two speech idioms makes it seem as
if they are able to inhabit two different worlds at once,
keeping the private and professional aspects of their lives well
apart. But, as the play progresses, it becomes clear that they
have invested their own private emotions in aspects of the
firm's life, and so its changes affect them as private
individuals, not just as corporate employees. Anne has taken
emotional involvement to the point of having an affair with

Jaudouard, which places her at his mercy. Nicole is in a permanent relationship with Guillermo, at least so she thinks until her exclusive place in his affections is challenged by Yvette. The 'rationalisation' of the office as a result of automation, and Guillermo's enforced departure, alter the personal destinies of both Nicole and Yvette and change their whole conception of life.

In the end the company is bought up, sweeping cost-cutting measures are implemented and the factory goes on strike. The three female employees in the after-sales office cope heroically with the increasing number of calls from anxious customers, convincing them that normal service will be resumed as soon as possible. But once a settlement is reached, it transpires that the after-sales office will be the first victim of the economies. Now there will be no one to answer the callers; instead a computer will be installed to send the customers one of a range of sixty-four standard replies drawn up in advance.

Here the dramatic techniques first employed in *Situation Vacant* are exploited to the full, since the play explores not one but five different life trajectories. The dialogue is fragmentary: questions and answers do not meet. They are interrupted by other lines of discussion or argument. Through these shifting perspectives, five different worlds are built up, each with a point of intersection in the office, but also reaching beyond it, into the characters' emotional lives. The method avoids all the usual traps of melodrama, sentimentality and didacticism by its subtle interweaving of themes and languages. It avoids pathos by refusing to focus all the dramatic attention onto one story alone – for example, the story of Nicole, first having to share her lover with and then losing her job to a younger woman – but by showing the network formed by all the different stories, so that we understand how Nicole's story cannot be isolated from the take-over of the firm, the experience of Anne, the political struggles of Guillermo, etc.

Vinaver controls this complex material in masterly fashion, and the overall experience for an audience is that of sensing the interdependence of all the play's apparently disparate elements. Michel Cournot, drama critic of *Le Monde*, commented on the unusual dramatic structure of this play as follows:

> After a few moments of acclimatisation, the spectator has the feeling that he holds within his grasp the multiple series of causes and effects contributing to a given event, whereas classic, linear dialogue reduces these series to a single thread. From this grasp there arises in the audiences a profound emotion, stemming no doubt from the fact that life itself seems to be captured in the fullness of its flux and all its mystery. (14 March 1980)

David Bradby
Royal Holloway
University of London, 1997

Bibliography

1. Works by Michel Vinaver:

Théâtre complet (2 vols.), Arles: Actes Sud & Lausanne: L'Aire, 1986. [Volume 1 contains: *Les Coréens*; *Les Huissiers*; *Iphigénie Hôtel* (shortened version); *Par-dessus bord* (shortened version); *La Demande d'emploi*. Volume 2 contains: *Dissident, il va sans dire*; *Nina, c'est autre chose*; *Les Travaux et les jours*; *A la renverse*; *L'Ordinaire*; *Les Voisins*; *Portrait d'une femme*.]

L'Emission de télévision, Arles: Actes Sud, 1989.

Le Dernier Sursaut, Arles: Actes Sud, 1990.

Ecrits sur le théâtre, Lausanne: L'Aire, 1982.

Théâtre de chambre [Three plays (*Dissident, il va sans dire*; *Les Travaux et les jours*; *Les Voisins*) edited with an introduction in English by David Bradby], London: Duckworth ('Bristol Classical Press' French series), 1995.

2. Critical works on Vinaver's plays:

David Bradby, *The Theater of Michel Vinaver*, Ann Arbor: Michigan University Press, 1993.

Kevin Elstob, *The Plays of Michel Vinaver: Political Theatre in France*, New York: Peter Lang, 1992.

Anne Ubersfeld, *Vinaver, dramaturge*, Paris: Librairie Théâtrale, 1989.

Overboard

Par-dessus bord

a play in six movements

translated by GIDEON LESTER

Characters

Fernand Dehaze, *president and managing director, Ravoire et Dehaze*

Olivier Dehaze, *director and vice-president in charge of manufacturing*

Benoît Dehaze, *business manager*

Madame Alvarez, *administrative manager*

Passemar, *sales administration manager*

Madame Bachevski, *purchasing manager*

Cohen, *chief accountant*

Grangier, *production planning manager*

Dutôt, *sales manager*

Lubin, *sales representative*

Saillant, *controller*

Battistini, *market research manager*

Peyre, *product manager*

Madame Lépine, *wholesaler*

Professor Onde

Father Motte

Dr Temple

Toppfer, *antique dealer*

Ausange, *banker*

Margery, *Benoît's wife*

Alex Klein, *jazz musician*

Jiji, *Lubin's daughter*

Rendu, *lawyer*

Etienne Ravoire, *Benoît and Olivier's uncle and a director of Ravoire et Dehaze*

Yvonne Ravoire, *Benoît and Olivier's aunt and a director of Ravoire et Dehaze*

Jack Donohue, *marketing consultant*

Jenny Frankfurter, *marketing consultant*

Reszanyi, *psycho-sociologist*

Ralph Young, *vice-president, United Paper Company*

De Panafieu, *advertising agency account manager*

Jaloux, *agency copy-writer*

Pianist

Three Dancers

Nude Model
Two Black Musicians
Servant
Ravoire et Dehaze Employees

Overboard was first performed in the UK at the Orange Tree Theatre, Richmond, on 2 October 1997. Members of the cast played several parts and the company included:

David Antrobus, Robert Benfield, Joss Brook, Prue Clarke, Britta Gartner, David Gooderson, Emma Gregory, Dilys Hamlett, Pascal Langdale, Ben Livingstone, Robert McBain, Brian Miller, Joanne Mitchell, Michael Poole, Helen Ryan, Michael Sherin, Auriol Smith, Timothy Watson, Tim Welton and Philip York.

Directed by Sam Walters
Designed by Lorna Marshall

First Movement

Cards on the Table

Lépine Bros., **Passemar's** *office,* **M. Dehaze's** *studio, the canteen at Ravoire et Dehaze, a classroom at the Collège de France.*

Lubin Got something sensational for you

Mme Lépine Everything's always sensational

Lubin Yes but today it's something truly sensational

Mme Lépine As always

Lubin My company has thought of you Madame Lépine

Mme Lépine Maybe so but everything's fine

Lubin An incredible bargain an unprecedented offer designed by my company for your customers because times are hard

Mme Lépine Don't I know it

Lubin Springtime soon Madame Lépine

Mme Lépine And?

Lubin In spring business picks up and to help you make money

Mme Lépine To make money you have to sell

Lubin To help you sell we've put together this unbelievable special offer which will find its way onto every one of your retailers' shelves

Mme Lépine I tell you everything's fine

Lubin An offer which is advantageous to you and enticing for the customer it's a winner one million eight hundred thousand French women are going to jump at it

Mme Lépine   I've still got aisles full of your special offer from six months ago customers aren't buying today when they buy I'll buy

Lubin   I understand your point of view you want to be sure the goods will move

Mme Lépine   Well?

Lubin   And move fast well that's exactly what our promotion will achieve bringing you a nice fat profit with no effort on your part I'm putting myself in your place

Mme Lépine   You can have it

A pianist appears with his piano and three masked **Dancers** – *two men and a woman – dressed as lorry drivers, carrying a box.*

Mme Lépine   Put it over here unstrap it for me

Lubin   Let's limit it to six cartons plus one free

Mme Lépine   Cheque on delivery two per cent discount

Lubin   And I'll leave you two flyers for your salespeople how's the little girl doing? Already taller than her mum

Mme Lépine   Still growing you're from Johnson Wax?

Lorry driver's song; they dance as they open the box.

Three Dancers   Ah yes oh but yes – but of course

First Dancer   Ah yes

Second Dancer   Oh but

Third Dancer   Yes but of course

Three Dancers   Ah yes oh but – yes but of course

First Dancer   But of course yes

Second Dancer   Of course oh but

Third Dancer   Yes but oh

Three Dancers   Ah yes oh but yes – but of course –

ah yes oh but – yes but of course

Passemar *emerges from the box wearing a mask. He is caught up in the wake of the* **Dancers** *whose movements become more convulsive. The dance increasingly centres on* **Passemar** *and the* **Dancers** *bump him, knock him to the ground, step on him, lift him up again, throw him in the air, quarter and dismember him and perform acts of great vulgarity on him, then they piece him back together, place him on the lid of the box as if on a throne. They strap the lid back on the box.* **Lubin** *and* **Mme Lépine** *have disappeared. The* **Dancers** *lift the box and,* **Passemar** *on top, put it onto their shoulders, carrying it in a procession.* **Passemar** *has raised his mask – and the audience discovers that he looks like the mask's brother. He puts on his glasses, straightens his clothing.*

Passemar That's a little free-form masked entertainment composed in Aristophanic form which I thought could possibly serve as prologue to this play I am the author of this play I lead a somewhat fractured existence my gift for writing appeared at a very young age at nine I wrote a one-act play called *The Vegetable Revolt* it was about the garden rising up against the tyranny of the gardener but you have to live so I put a notice in the classified section of *Figaro* not expecting too much a bottle at sea up-and-coming young graduate able and confident and they hired me at Ravoire et Dehaze they needed someone right away to replace a fellow who had committed suicide for no apparent reason he was in charge of the billing department until then I hadn't really stopped to think about what goes into an invoice living as I did with my head in the clouds so at first it was sort of panic and then and then no but what's very important in all that is to enter into real life to mix your life with the lives of other people I was no longer on the sidelines I was taking part I was making decisions and ta-da the young graduate got married he had children (*The* **Dancers** *place the box on the ground.* **Passemar**, *without realising it, is down from the box and continues his procession alone, walking.*) up-and-coming no more (*The* **Dancers** *remove their*

lorry-driver masks and dance out with the box, masks in hand.)
they knew nothing of my literary bent at Ravoire et
Dehaze to them I was just one of umpteen middle
managers doing their jobs reasonably well I reported to I
still report to Madame Alvarez (**Mme Alvarez** *appears.*
Passemar *is now seated at his desk.*) the former mistress of
Monsieur Ravoire the founder of the company she's the
administrative manager next year she's retiring and who
knows if events don't take another turn with the
Americans arriving it looks as though I'm not in a bad
position to succeed her

Dutôt *appears.*

Mme Alvarez   Yes Dutôt I asked to see you can this
really be true Passemar? I've learned that we're out of
Excelsior stock again

Passemar   We have been yes for three days

Mme Alvarez   Didn't you raise hell with the factory?

Passemar   The factory doesn't follow up

Dutôt   But for God's sake I need the goods my reps are
working themselves to death with this promotion

Passemar   I'm aware of that Monsieur Dutôt the
problem is with production planning they don't react
quickly enough to an excess of sales over forecast I said as
much to Monsieur Grangier

Grangier *appears.*

Mme Alvarez   Yes Grangier I asked to see you

Grangier   Will someone tell me on what basis we're
supposed to plan production if not on your sales forecast?
And what if your forecast's all wrong?

Dutôt   The factory has to provide a safety reserve a bit
of fucking flexibility would help

Grangier   What would really help is a little goodwill on both sides not just ours

Mme Alvarez   A little cooperation yes

Dutôt   Tell me who's not cooperating

Mme Alvarez   Why? Are you taking it personally?

Grangier   Is that all? Can I go?

Mme Alvarez   Yes Grangier thank you (**Grangier**
disappears.) it would obviously be ridiculous to expect any
initiative from the factory what's the matter Passemar are
you dreaming?

Passemar   Given that Excelsior is more expensive isn't
it strange that under the current economic climate it
should be the one with booming sales?

Mme Alvarez   Not only is it more expensive Passemar
but it disintegrates and everything's left in your hands

Passemar   But Excelsior is the one in demand every
product with quilted padding

Dutôt   The product is outstanding so long as you don't
have an elephant's arse

Mme Alvarez   Good paper is like a good sales
department resilient and reliable

Dutôt   A good administrative department keeps up with
trends Madame Alvarez and doesn't interfere

He fades away.

Mme Alvarez   The nerve

Passemar   Benoît hired him against Monsieur Olivier's
advice Monsieur Olivier wanted a seasoned sales manager

Mme Alvarez   It's all very hush-hush Passemar I can't
tell you everything but believe me there's plenty to feel
bitter about give me a cigarette

Passemar   Here Madame Alvarez

Mme Alvarez   Thank you Passemar you see Monsieur Olivier has too many scruples Monsieur Benoît just worms his way in and there you go he's filled the place up with Dutôt and his like. Monsieur Fernand needs to open his eyes I sometimes think about it he was still a student when I joined the company he often came round to have a laugh with me after hours there are still things that only I could say to him but why bother? I'm leaving in November you've still got some way to go before you reach sixty-five Passemar

The nude model has appeared wearing a raincoat, a hat. **Mme Alvarez** *has faded out.*

Passemar   Yes but (*To the model.*) this way I believe (*He escorts her, then leaves her alone.*) when the boss gets home in the evening he likes to paint in a classical style of course he seems to be holding his own

Ausange *and* **Dehaze** *have taken their places, the latter in front of an easel;* **Passemar** *has faded out.*

Dehaze   Lift that shoulder a touch higher darling

Ausange   The young lady has a striking neck

Dehaze   Hard to capture

Ausange   It reminds me of the Velasquez reclining nude

Dehaze   I'm glad you could drop in this evening

Ausange   When I heard your voice on the phone I couldn't wait a moment

Dehaze   How's dear Lucienne?

Ausange   She's fine

Dehaze   It's imperceptible but your left shoulder keeps drooping Miss you know my business mid-sized rolling along nicely immune to economic fluctuations manufacturing a staple product the market leader sales rising five or ten per cent each year all the capital in the family's hands a stable and happy workforce (*A servant has placed a tea service and cakes on a table: during the following sequence, the two men sit on either side of the table, the model dresses and exits.*) at the moment all that's being rather shaken up an American giant has set foot on our turf they're twenty or thirty times our size and with people like that the bigger they are the hungrier they get

Ausange   I'm quite fond of Americans

Dehaze   I don't hate them

The two men laugh long and heartily.

Ausange   They're straightforward

Dehaze   Yes

Ausange   So?

Dehaze   Our sales have been dropping four per cent a month for the last six months so now I'm operating at a loss my choice is to cut expenses or increase them invest in advertising and promotion do I have a choice? Yesterday was the company's annual party a buffet supper dancing the whole team was there they'd have hated it if I'd cancelled money's getting tight

Ausange   What's your next step?

Dehaze   We've never borrowed from banks

Ausange   Banks are made for lending

Dehaze   An old aversion

Ausange   Americans borrow when business is going well to help it go even better

Dehaze   The Americans are hitting hard but we'll hit back harder

Ausange   Excellent

Dehaze   I'm launching a new product superior to theirs and more in keeping with French tastes

Ausange   Good

Dehaze   I'm seizing the initiative Blue White and Red packaging to strike the nationalistic chord it'll be better value and distinctively ours my reps have been hard at work since Monday morning for the first time I've placed three half-page ads in the leading weeklies and to keep up the pressure my friend I need five hundred thousand francs I have to negotiate credit with a bank and there you have it (*He rings, the servant enters, a package in hand.*) yes that's it Yvonne hand it to Monsieur open it look my new baby

Ausange   *undoes the package, pulls out a roll of toilet paper in a Blue White and Red wrapper, holds it with both hands at eye-level, then unfastens the wrapping and begins to unroll it.*

Passemar   That was a fiasco (*Pause.*) appalling if Monsieur Dehaze could have foreseen where it would lead he'd have surely cancelled his little celebration and it would have been a pity because we really enjoyed ourselves this year as we have every year at the traditional annual Ravoire et Dehaze party this is Monsieur Lubin one of the six sales reps Monsieur Lubin's dancing with Joelle the assistant cash clerk Monsieur Lubin seems to be in fine form.

— Where is my drumstick? There was a drumstick on my plate

— I've been feeling low ever since she was born

— It's lovely did it cost much?

— I actually spend more time with you than I do with my husband but I know my husband better than you I don't really know my husband all that well

— Have you really been married for six years?

— I've been in accounting for eight years

— What a beautiful hairstyle

— You're just saying that

— I spend more time with you than with my wife

— Of course it's the same thing

— Monsieur Dutôt is the best dancer look at him going cheek-to-cheek with Bachevski

— Yes it's the same

— Even makes the old girls dance

— He's not choosy

— He's great

— Aren't there any more coffee éclairs?

— Most of the time I spend with my husband is in bed otherwise I do housework and he has his DIY

— On Sundays we my wife and I make a point of going for a walk in the area

— You spend your lives together but you don't or hardly do know each other I don't really know you at all

— Do you want to get to know me?

— Of course

— I'd never have thought it

— I want to get to know who you are

— It gives you a chance to see the people you sit next to in a different light there's no more than six feet between your desk and mine Josette

— You still haven't danced with me

— And your dress is awfully nice

— Monsieur Olivier's above all that

— But not as much as Monsieur Benoît

— When Monsieur Benoît walks past he doesn't even

see you

— Oh Monsieur Olivier is nicer than Monsieur Benoît

— He's a gentleman

— It's a story about three blokes who make a bet to see who'll get into bed first

— Who with?

— When Monsieur Olivier passes you in the hall he never fails to shake your hand

— He's got class

— But Benoît's got more oomph

— He's never shaken your hand?

— The sausages are too salty

— The sausages aren't as good as last year

— Last year we had tuna

— Look at the way Bachevski's dancing

— Last year she got plastered

— Had to carry her home

— Feet first

— Joseph don't dance too closely with young Rose are you deaf Joseph?

— Stay out of my love life

— Doesn't he ever stop how many drumsticks does that make?

— It's your fault if you feel sick

— Why did you come if that's how you feel?

— They throw you a party and won't pay you a living wage

— You didn't have to come

— They're arseholes

— Of course they're exploiting us it's their job what would you do if you were the boss?

— Where's the raise that was supposed to come in February?

— Weren't able to say a thing when we proved that our salaries are the lowest in the business

— They promised to investigate

— Yes, six months ago

— Right now sales aren't moving so well

— Quiet Monsieur Olivier is trying to speak

Olivier   And now a little silence please we're going to proceed with the raffle

— You're tickling me watch it

— She's still on extended sick-leave the antibiotics destroyed her intestinal tract

— Yes-s-s you're tickling me

Olivier   I remind you that the grand prize for our raffle is this beautiful transistor radio right here with both AM and FM facility I'll ask the youngest of the young ladies in the company

— That's you Joelle

— Go on Joelle

— No it's Anne-Marie

Olivier   Come on over here my dear there you're going to randomly pull out a little piece of paper from this hat done? Take the microphone and read the number

Anne-Marie   Eighty-four

Olivier   Eighty-four who's got eighty-four?

— Hey it's Monsieur Lubin

— Is it you Lubin?

— Lucky devil Lubin

Olivier   Come over here Lubin well done many congratulations

— Speech

Olivier   Go on Lubin say something

Lubin   I'd like to thank the company and particularly Monsieur Fernand our president I'm delighted

— Hear hear

Lubin   Particularly since my daughter Jiji is getting married and my wife will be lonely at home all by herself so it couldn't have come at a better time eh?

Olivier   And now I'd like to call on our president to give his traditional annual address

Dehaze   Thank you Olivier ladies and gentlemen dear friends thank you for coming and coming as always in such numbers to our small gathering which I take the liberty of calling a family gathering because those who work together for forty hours a week sharing the same goals form a real community ladies and gentlemen dear friends you work in an enterprise which has the future before it our products are on the brink of a major expansion we're living in a world of great change and to survive and keep ahead we must also change if we bent over for a brief moment it was only so that we could stand up the straighter you know this is a particularly emotional moment for me because we are on the verge of launching our first new product in more than twelve years we shall call it Blue White and Red and in only a few short months this product will become a close companion to millions of Frenchmen and it will provide the utmost satisfaction because its performance is unquestionably superior and thus we shall seize the initiative once and for all

The canteen begins to clear. **Passemar** *remains, a glass in hand. He is swaying slightly.*

Passemar   The subject of the play is simply this the absorption by a powerful American corporation of a mid-size firm in which I myself am a middle manager is it a good thing? Is it a bad thing? I don't know I'd like a clearer view it reminds me of that old story of the Aesir and the Vanir which Monsieur Onde spoke of when I attended his lectures years ago at the Collège de France

M. Onde *is speaking: in the classroom, besides* **Passemar**, *two elderly ladies knitting on a bench at the back, and in the front row a corpulent listener dressed in black taking notes.*

M. Onde   How do we know of this story? Only from four stanzas of a lofty verse Edda called *The Voluspa or The Song of the Sybil* and from the account of a thirteenth-century Icelander by the name of Snorri according to the Scandinavians the world knows of two races of deities the Aesir ruled by Odin and Thor and opposing them the Vanir gods of fertility and voluptuousness

Passemar   A chain of events not governed by fate no not at all things could have turned out differently

M. Onde   The Aesir attack the Vanir and what followed is in the words of the *Voluspa* poet war for the first time in the world Snorri tells how Odin marches with his army against the Vanir but they resist and defend their realm sometimes one camp sometimes the other seems to carry the day each devastates the other's hands and they inflict on each other grievous harm

Passemar   Three hundred and fifty employees a sales revenue of twenty million francs, a family business steeped in tradition which couldn't quite adapt

M. Onde   Suddenly Odin hurls his spear into enemy
ranks victory must surely follow and indeed the Vanir are
seized with terror and take to their heels in a great
commotion and yet the Aesir triumph is not definitive for
we read in the same stanza that against all expectations
the Vanir manage to destroy the Aesir ramparts

Passemar   From Minneapolis they landed and forced
their way into our territory the collapse of the old firm
seemed imminent but there was a *coup d'état* the boss's
illegitimate son took over the firm with a team of young
managers I'm not one of them but that doesn't stop me
being objective they succeeded in turning the tide and
making things pretty tough for the giant from across the
Atlantic

M. Onde   As if they have suddenly tired of this
exhausting alternation of failure and success which seems
to be leading nowhere the Aesir and Vanir broker peace a
peace which none could have expected a peace as
harmonious as the war has been relentless where no
compromise has seemed possible suddenly there grows
understanding and now until the end of time not even the
shadow of a conflict shall ever arise between the Aesir and
the Vanir

Passemar   Today talks have begun on one side there is
financial clout and a formidable machine at the service of
a will for expansion that nothing will stop on the other
side there is dexterity and cunning as well as the
knowledge of one's own terrain at the service of personal
ambition that nothing will stop

M. Onde   *erases the blackboard on which he had written the
names of the principal gods; he shuffles his papers. It's the end of
the lecture. The audience starts to leave.* **M. Onde** *signals that*
Passemar *should come forward.*

M. Onde   I have noticed your presence in my class
several times Monsieur are you a comparative linguist?

Passemar   No not in the least

M. Onde   May I enquire as to your field of research?

Passemar   I'm not exactly researching anything

M. Onde   I'm not used to seeing faces in front of me apart from two or three elderly ladies who come here in winter looking for a little warmth

Passemar   I'm sorry I find it thrilling listening to you

M. Onde   Thrilling? What do you mean? I don't understand what is it that you find so interesting? Forgive me for asking but what is it that you do?

A few minutes earlier the pianist and the three masked **Dancers**, *dressed as Scandinavian gods, began to execute some movements, stopping, starting again, continuing the same series of gestures. The only lines spoken are of the following type: 'Let's start again', 'That's not working', 'There', etc.* **M. Onde** *fades out.*

Passemar   It's an idea that came to me why not spice up these legends a little with mime and dance together with beautiful costumes and avant-garde music? What I'm really after is total theatre where all art forms combine ballet circus cinema opera the problem is that it would be an expensive show to put together aren't I reducing my chances of getting it produced?

The Scandinavian gods take hold of **Passemar**, *knocking him about and carrying him in procession: exodus.*

Second Movement

Blue White and Red

Lépine Bros., **Benoît** *and* **Margery**'s *bedroom, the president's office, two or three other offices,* **M. Dehaze**'s *studio,* **Ausange**'s *office, a hospital room.*

Lubin Something really sensational for you today Madame Lépine

Mme Lépine As always

Lubin Wait and see

Lubin *opens a package, pulls out a roll of toilet paper in a Blue White and Red wrapper, holds it with two hands at eye-level, then rips the wrapper and starts to unroll it.*

Dehaze This will be our record monthly billing since the founding of the company Olivier

Olivier Yes a tidal wave

Dehaze You seem concerned

Olivier As of this morning we have barely two and a half days' worth of goods in the warehouse

Dehaze Do whatever you must my boy but I will not tolerate our running out of stock. Get the factory working in three shifts, sign on temporary staff

Mme Lépine I don't want any I won't take any

Lubin (*continuing to unroll the paper*) As of today Madame Lépine this superb paper in patriotic packaging will find a natural place in all French bathrooms

Mme Lépine I've got everything I need

Lubin Blue White and Red you must admit that the name rings loud and clear in our French ears

Mme Lépine (*examining the paper*) But there's no difference between this and your Perfecto

Lubin I'm pleased to hear you say that which of our brands has always sold best?

Mme Lépine Perfecto since long before I was born

Lubin Exactly our customers have always trusted good old rough stock from Ravoire et Dehaze haven't they?

Benoît (*in bed with* **Margery**) What time is it my little reed?

Margery You're going to be late again

Benoît Never mind who cares after making love

Margery After making love to me?

Benoît To whom else?

Margery And after making love to others?

Benoît What's the difference darling?

Margery Well it makes a difference to me if you're making love to others

Benoît And I love it when you're cross

Margery I'm not cross

Benoît What a pity

Margery You're already late Benoît

Benoît You still can't pronounce Benoît

Margery Benoît

Benoît No Benoît

Margery And your dad will be so upset I adore Daddy I hate it when you upset him

Benoît Why do you adore my dad?

Margery I should have married him not you but I met

you first

Passemar   When all's said and done Monsieur Cohen

Cohen   This American invasion

Passemar   Nothing like it

Cohen   For getting us going

Mme Bachevski   And forging ahead

Passemar   Stops us getting too comfortable

Cohen   Too complacent

Mme Bachevski   Nothing like a strong enemy

Passemar   We're giving them the works

Mme Bachevski   So Monsieur Dutôt was telling me

Passemar   Our reps are carrying the day

Margery   Coochie coochie Benoît you fell asleep again

Benoît   No tickling please

Margery   You look like John F. Kennedy

Benoît   Why do you adore my father?

Margery   Because he's got more sex appeal than you more charm

Benoît   You think I don't have enough sex appeal?

Margery   You don't have as much charm with him it's the whole French culture there's a sort of sadness in his smile and I just melt

Benoît   You should have married my brother Olivier

Margery   Olivier's a clam

Benoît   Clams are your favourite food

Margery   Not for loving

Benoît   It's a pity my father whom you love

Margery   He's great

Benoît   Except that he's no longer in the swing

Margery   You bug the shit out of me with your in the swing and go with the flow

Benoît   A little kiss there

Margery   Benoît listen

Benoît   I do nothing else my little dove

Margery   Everything that you care for is ugly in the swing is ugly and whatever you think about your father

Benoît   Even so you did marry me partly for the money didn't you?

Margery   Yes partly

Benoît   And don't you see that my darling father blind as he is

Margery   It's you who's blind

Benoît   The gold in his hands is turning to sand and the sand is trickling through his fingers and he doesn't even see it

Mme Lépine   Put down a dozen cartons for me that's quite enough

Lubin   Twelve cartons is out of the question Madame Lépine it's been incredibly successful and our stock is limited but because it's you I'll stretch to six and how are the little ones doing?

Mme Lépine   And tell them not to fall asleep on the delivery

Father Motte   Filth and dereliction the pill is the excrement of our civilisation it has caused mankind to regress two or three dozen centuries the most stable institutions are beginning to totter powerful means are needed to dam up the flood waters I'm sure that as a businessman you know what I'm driving at Monsieur Dehaze

Dehaze   Both of us Father Motte in fact I should probably say all three of us including this young lady are in need in that respect she has two small brothers to feed and I'm chasing after money at the moment my dear you've done something to your hair haven't you?

Father Motte   The Pope's encyclical

Dehaze   The head a little lower on the left please Mademoiselle

Father Motte   Is an attempt at stopping this diarrhoea but it's up to us now to follow his lead and work on the masses with every available technique of modern persuasion

Dehaze   More more down a little more

Father Motte   You have a remarkable touch with the brush

Dehaze   It's my way of relaxing I used to ride horses

Father Motte   The Church has never knocked at your door without your answering the call

Dehaze   Nowadays Father I'm knocking on doors myself

Father Motte   Understand that this is not a matter of passing the collection plate I'm mobilising hearts and minds

Dehaze   I suppose you know Ausange from the Bank of Paris and the Netherlands?

Father Motte   He's on my list

Dehaze   During the next few sittings don't change your hairstyle my dear

Father Motte   Could you introduce me to him?

Dehaze   It's not impossible that I'll be able to help you

Father just as you may prove to be of some sort of help to me

Dutôt Hello, the Rueil Company? May I speak to Monsieur Rueil? Dutôt here sales manager at Ravoire et Dehaze no I'll hold (*To* **Benoît**.) same thing at Vacheron and same thing at Simonnot (*On the telephone.*) bonjour Monsieur Rueil this is Dutôt at Ravoire et Dehaze *comment-allez vous?* (*Pause then a long laugh into the telephone;* **Olivier** *has entered.*) Listen Monsieur Rueil we haven't received your restocking order yet for Blue White and Red and since our inventory is pretty low I was wondering if you wanted me to reserve a few extra cartons for you so you won't risk falling short because you know sales are booming yes it's a roaring success (*Pause.*) really I'm surprised (*Pause.*) well did your reps talk it up enough? (*Laugh, then a pause.*) No not at all on the whole it's going well I mean well enough we're banking a lot on this product you know it's destined to become our flagship (*Pause.*) well no well no you'll see and if I may I'll call you back in a week or two

Benoît Dutôt has just called our three principal wholesalers

Olivier He called Vacheron?

Dutôt They still have three-quarters of their first order in stock

Benoît And Simonnot?

Dutôt Simonnot is getting nasty he hasn't even sold twenty-five of his eighty-carton shipment

Lubin How's the little boy doing Madame Lépine and how's business?

Mme Lépine Quiet

Lubin And that good-looking daughter of yours?

Mme Lépine It couldn't be quieter

Lubin   Good what do you say two cartons Madame Lépine to keep you going till Easter

Mme Lépine   Till Judgement Day how many did you put me down for last time?

Lubin   Six cartons

Mme Lépine   I've still got more than four on my hands

Lubin   You must have fallen asleep on them

Mme Lépine   I did my best to force your Blue White and Red on all my customers

Lubin   Just one carton to break some ground for the others?

Mme Lépine   Mushrooms grow on broken ground

Lubin   You'll see when they start selling they'll really sell

Mme Lépine   Like hot-cakes I know how's life been treating you?

Lubin   My daughter Jiji's getting married I won the raffle at the Ravoire et Dehaze annual party a transistor radio which comes in handy now that Jiji's leaving home

Margery   *Bonjour* Daddy you haven't shaved today how awful

Dehaze   How nice of you to come and see me my dear

Margery   Wow shallow perspective *à la* Mantegna in college I wrote a paper comparing Mantegna's perspective to that of Uccello Daddy oh I'd really like to take another look at your snuff boxes again can I open the display case?

Dehaze   Mademoiselle you are intent on making life difficult for me

Margery   What period is this one?

Dehaze   Concentrate

Margery   Louis XVI?

Dehaze   You're becoming quite a connoisseur the enamel is exceptionally pure but unfortunately it's slightly damaged

Margery   Ah yes the little nymph's belly

Dehaze   But I'd rather not restore it actually since old Huterer from Geneva died there are no more restorers

Margery   This one's also from the eighteenth?

Dehaze   Mademoiselle you've shifted position again you know that's a remarkable piece?

Margery   Isn't the shape quite rare? The pearl border's so fine

Dehaze   It's not so much the shape as the subject

Margery   A little dog

Dehaze   It was Madame de Pompadour's lap dog

Margery   The snuff box belonged to her?

Dehaze   My dear if you need to go and stretch your legs a bit please do but come back quickly we must get on

Margery   Tell me about it Daddy

Dehaze   It was made for La Pompadour but she never owned it she fell into disgrace shortly after Louis XV had commissioned it from Ducrollay

Margery   How terrible

Dehaze   The poor bastard never got paid he was left with this priceless piece on his hands it passed down his family from father to son until fifteen years ago when thanks to Toppfer I had the privilege of obtaining it

Margery   How do you know all this?

Dehaze   Toppfer isn't content only to buy and sell he

loves these pieces passionately and researches their history we even know the little dog's name Mimi

Margery   Daddy when you die what's going to happen to all of these marvellous things?

Dehaze   You're a funny little American you don't really want me to disappear too quickly do you?

Margery   Daddy *je suis amoureuse de vous* more than I am with Benoît

Dehaze   And you know you can look at them to your heart's content whenever you come and visit me

Olivier   Your men quite simply haven't done their job Dutôt

Dutôt   They did it as best they could given how little support they had

Olivier   You're the one who's supposed to make sure they're supported

Dutôt   They have to have a product

Olivier   Blue White and Red isn't a product?

Dutôt   I'm not sure that it is

Olivier   It's the same old rough stock we've always sold

Benoît   The product it's not just the product

Dutôt   There's also the image the name

Olivier   You don't like the name? You're looking for excuses because you failed to motivate your men

Dutôt   Whom unfortunately I did not choose

Olivier   Men like Guillaumat and Lubin would give their lives for the firm

Dutôt   They're stuck in their ways, the world has changed

Olivier   It's a manager's job to keep his troops up to date

Dutôt   When there's potential there to start with

Olivier   Before worrying about the potential of those who work for you it's not unwise to look after your own potential

Benoît   My dear Olivier please

Olivier   You haven't even been with us for a year Dutôt you still have things to learn personnel management for a start

Mme Lépine   Ah this time I am happy to see you

Lubin   Is that right Madame Lépine?

Cohen   It's just Monsieur Fernand that for the last two months there's been a considerable outflow and very little coming in

Dehaze   We had to pull out all the stops Cohen

Cohen   Never since I've been here Monsieur Fernand have the company's finances been in such a critical state

Dehaze   These bankers are taking their time I must telephone Ausange (*Lifting the telephone receiver.*) get me the Bank of Paris and the Netherlands

Benoît   We have to start looking at things head on Olivier

Olivier   I agree that we've made a few mistakes

Benoît   These are not simply mistakes it's our whole philosophy it's the boss's whole attitude to problems

Olivier   Perhaps we should talk to Dad

Benoît   That wouldn't change a thing

Olivier   Well then

Benoît   He has to give way

Olivier   Dad has to go?

Benoît   He has to let you take over

Mme Lépine   Going to have to take back these three cartons

Lubin   Don't even think about it Madame Lépine

Mme Lépine   It's dead stock

Lubin   Madame Lépine

Mme Lépine   What?

Lubin   You know full well that Ravoire et Dehaze never take back merchandise

Mme Lépine   Really?

Lubin   It's always been company policy

Mme Lépine   I don't give a damn about your policies you're taking them end of story I'll send them back to you tomorrow and you'll get me a refund

Dehaze   This young little Dutôt that Benoît hired as sales manager is worthless he really botched the promotion

Cohen   He doesn't have Monsieur Levêque's class

Dehaze   Benoît is clearly right to want to shake things up a little but to fill the company with a heap of long-haired youngsters

Cohen   Who think they invented the wheel Monsieur Fernand

Dehaze   Who think that success hinges on turning everything upside down

Cohen   If you'll let me be honest with you they're forming a clique Monsieur Fernand a clique around Monsieur Benoît I wouldn't swear to their loyalty

Dehaze   Loyalty Cohen is a concept which belongs to

our generation yours and mine

Cohen Above all I question Monsieur Benoît's attitude to you Monsieur since the launch of Blue White and Red he hasn't seemed like a man fighting on your side

Mme Lépine Can I help it if this is the one they're all clamouring for? (*She holds up a roll of Softies.*) I unloaded eight cartons in two weeks

Lubin But it costs the housewife twice as much

Mme Lépine And that brings me two and a half times more per roll

Lubin So you're pushing it

Mme Lépine Pushing it? Of course I'm pushing it but pushing alone won't do it there has to be a demand

Lubin The boss didn't believe in quilted padding

Mme Lépine Whatever you say the fact is that yesterday no one had even heard of quilted padding today everyone's rushing into quilted padding

Lubin I can't understand why people go for paper that falls apart in your hands

Mme Lépine It's actually no different from your Excelsior except that

Lubin Excelsior shot off like a rocket

Mme Lépine It's run out of steam

Passemar Exactly what we were afraid of Monsieur Olivier

Mme Alvarez The last straw

Passemar After Rueil Simonnot sent back the goods

Mme Alvarez Rueil was at least polite enough to phone

Olivier What reason did he give?

Passemar   Softies' follow-up promotion

Mme Alvarez   The Americans were just waiting for our reaction

Passemar   As soon as Blue White and Red came out they attacked in force

Mme Alvarez   With exorbitant discounts

Passemar   They launched a contest for their reps first prize two weeks in California all expenses paid

Mme Alvarez   Press conferences at the top of the Eiffel Tower

Passemar   With showers of confetti on the Champ-de-Mars

Mme Alvarez   Endorsements from Johnny Halliday

Dehaze   We do not accept returns Dutôt do you understand?

Dutôt   It's not a matter of accepting or not accepting Monsieur le Président Simonnot sent them back that's all there is to it

Dehaze   Ship them back to him

Dutôt   Rueil called and asked to return his stock very politely

Dehaze   What did you tell him?

Dutôt   I told him fine Monsieur very politely

Dehaze   Phone him back and cancel your agreement

Dutôt   I won't do that Monsieur le Président

Dehaze   Are you refusing?

Dutôt   Enough blunders have been made without losing our biggest client

Dehaze   Those blunders Dutôt have your name on them

Dutôt   I believe Monsieur le Président that the blunders have come from higher up

Dehaze   As of this evening you're no longer a part of this company I'll ask Monsieur Cohen to settle your account

Grangier   Monsieur Olivier here's my resignation

Olivier   Look Grangier this is ridiculous I know you've got problems but

Grangier   I'm paid to have problems I wouldn't complain if I lost the last few hairs on my head trying to find solutions no it's the atmosphere

Margery (*on the phone*)   Hello Daddy hi Daddy it's Margery Daddy I looked in the *Encyclopedia Britannica*

Grangier   There is a complete breakdown in communications sales have been accepting returns right and left without so much as warning my people

Margery   And you know La Pompadour was never rejected Daddy even when she stopped pleasing the king physically

Grangier   And when I grumble because the lorries are rolling in with returned stock and I haven't an inch spare to store it in

Margery   Because she quickly lost her looks but she still kept her intellectual hold over him

Grangier   The whole firm's bailing out there is no more firm Monsieur Olivier there's nothing left but people and people are never very pretty when there's no firm to give them the feeling that they're working for a common cause

Benoît   Dad can I have a word? Watch out for Olivier

Dehaze   What are you saying?

Benoît   I think Olivier may be losing his mind he's convinced that you have to give way

Olivier   I won't let you go Grangier you're one of our most valuable managers

Benoît   I couldn't believe that he'd be disloyal to you so I thought maybe he wanted to test my feelings for you

Olivier   Think it over

Benoît   Or maybe it's the stress

Olivier   I'll have a word with Monsieur Benoît sleep on it and let's thrash it out tomorrow

Benoît   The strain on his nerves with everything that's going on

The phone rings.

Dehaze   Yes I'll take it

Ausange (*on the phone*)   There's a problem I'm afraid you see a loan of this size requires approval from our executive committee I've just been over the file Chasseloup put together

Mme Bachevski   I beseech you the only hope is for you and me to

Mme Alvarez   Me? With you?

Mme Bachevski   Together we could open Monsieur Fernand's eyes

Mme Alvarez   You're the last person he'd listen to

Mme Bachevski   That's what you think

Mme Alvarez   I know it

Mme Bachevski   He's never listened to you

Mme Alvarez   Really? He trusted me more than his own family Madame Bachevski

Mme Bachevski   Fifty years ago

Mme Alvarez   Fifty years ago I was in kindergarten

Mme Bachevski You must have been retarded

Mme Alvarez By then of course your husband had already left you

Mme Bachevski I will not fish around in your troubled waters Madame Alvarez

Mme Alvarez When I see you batting your eyelids at those gentlemen

Mme Bachevski I feel sorry for you

Mme Alvarez You're the one I pity

Ausange (*on the phone*) No there's light and shade in Chasseloup's report you see he concludes that over and above the operational difficulties that you are experiencing there's a let me put it this way there's a fundamental management problem so that extending such a loan would leave the bank with a non-negligible risk

Olivier Well?

Dehaze (*putting the receiver down*) Well

Olivier Dad you look worn out you should unwind for a few days go and spend a long weekend in the country

Dehaze Olivier I'm thinking of unwinding for good

Olivier What do you mean?

Dehaze I'm considering passing the helm to you

Olivier It's a difficult decision a brave one

Dehaze Benoît was right

Olivier Benoît's talked to you?

Dehaze Get out of my sight

Olivier Dad

Dehaze I don't want to see you for the moment

Benoît Dutôt my boy come in my office we have some

urgent decisions to take

Dutôt I'd be glad to but after what's just happened I wonder whether I'd be any use to you

Benoît What's the mystery?

Dutôt The boss fired me

Benoît When?

Dutôt Half an hour ago

Benoît Is that so?

Dutôt Monsieur Cohen is settling my account

Benoît Good take your cheque but don't go too far away my old friend we'll see each other soon

Dehaze You're posing admirably this evening Mademoiselle if you only knew how enjoyable it is to work with you under these conditions ah Monsieur Toppfer

Toppfer Dear Monsieur Dehaze

Dehaze It's kind of you to have come I thought we might discuss this collection of mine I'm just curious to know what it might fetch today

Toppfer Of course

Dehaze There are fifty-two pieces and more than half came from you you should be able to give me a rough estimate they're all in those display cases look them over

Toppfer Ah if you knew what an intense pleasure it is for me to see them again here's the little square Louis XIV such an unusual blend of colours and here's the exquisite box with the lap dog

Dehaze I learned Monsieur Toppfer that Madame de Pompadour never actually fell into disgrace

Toppfer True there were a few squabbles but she

always managed to reel her man in in the end

Dehaze Tell me more of this story Toppfer

Toppfer Absolutely their relationship had its ups and downs you know that when Louis XV began to find her less attractive she was clever enough to go and find girls who would suit his fancy I recently laid my hands on a snuff box that shows a ravishing young lady wearing a locket inspired by Boucher and you know what I discovered? The portrait was of Mademoiselle de Romanet the young prey that La Pompadour had just delivered to her former lover but aren't you feeling well?

Dehaze *has slouched up against the canvas on the easel,* **Toppfer** *goes up to him, lifts his arm which falls back down lifeless.*

Margery (*in bed with* **Benoît**) The American guys I slept with in college I mean they were really friendly

Benoît But?

Margery As soon as they left school they turned into stinky little managers who thought about nothing but making money so I left

Benoît For Paris

Margery And Paris is getting to be almost worse than America except for the students they're still great you know when I joined the barricades I suddenly felt as if not everything had been completely fucked up but as for you you're becoming more like a manager every day

Benoît My little reed it's time to sleep

Margery Eat work sleep

Benoît Make love

Margery Twice a week

Benoît (*answering the phone*) Yes? I'll come right away (*Hanging up, jumping out of bed and dressing.*) Dad's not well

Margery   Is it serious?

Benoît   Seems so

Margery   Oh I'm coming with you

Dr Temple   For the time being no one can say ever since he arrived at the hospital he has shown a flat encephalograph we put him on life support his heart is beating normally for the moment

Olivier   He is breathing?

Dr Temple   He's on artificial respiration

Mme Bachevski   The prognosis is unclear

Mme Alvarez   But science can work miracles hand me that file Passemar

Mme Bachevski   Nine days after the stroke he still hasn't regained consciousness

Mme Alvarez   But all his organs are functioning normally

Passemar   The file's incomplete Monsieur Benoît removed a number of papers

Mme Alvarez   Make sure you get them back

Mme Bachevski   If he recovers will he ever be his old self again?

Mme Alvarez   Now they can retrain the arms the legs the mind

Cohen   There'll never be a man like him

Mme Bachevski   That's for sure

Benoît   Put your scruples in your pocket Cohen when the time comes you'll think of something to tell the bank

Cohen   This is dishonest Monsieur Fernand would never have stood for it and I think Monsieur Olivier

Benoît   I really enjoy chatting with you Cohen but for the moment shut up and do as you're told

Mme Alvarez   Passemar how in God's name has this letter of complaint remained unanswered

Mme Bachevski   When you talk to him

Mme Alvarez   There's no reply

Mme Bachevski   But when you pinch his leg

Cohen   My God

Mme Bachevski   He jerks it back

Third Movement

Seizing Power

M. Rendu's office, **Ausange**'s office, the Ravoire et Dehaze boardroom, **Cohen**'s office, a hospital room, **M. Onde**'s study, **Benoît** and **Margery**'s living room, and 'The Clinic', a jazz club in the Montparnasse district. **Alex** at the piano, sometimes seated facing the keys, sometimes standing while playing chords with his hands or with drumsticks; **Butch**, a black double-bass player; **Art** (also black), a tenor saxophonist. **Art**, in the middle of a piece, goes from saxophone to flute or drums, which include boxes and percussion instruments and various sources of vibration (cymbals, a corrugated metal sheet, a punctured sheet of steel, etc.) set on the ground in different places, suspended from the ceiling, hanging from a heater. Similarly, **Butch** leaves his bass to play percussion or the trumpet. At times, **Alex**'s voice rises above the music. From time to time **Butch** goes out, then comes back. They play. These are pieces of variable length, most of them short, less than a minute: music at the extreme limit of tension, sometimes of audibility. Relaxed behaviour, nonchalant and serious on the part of the three musicians who keep in contact with each other through gestures, looks, sometimes laughter.

Alex   Dribbling butter a dog dies and suddenly in the granite but we're still not there

M. Rendu   In my capacity as director and as legal counsel to your company I am well aware that in a family business procedure tends to be overlooked but even so for practical purposes

Alex   I want it a bit more indescribable

M. Rendu   You would be ill advised to leave the post of president vacant

Olivier   But if my father were to return to health?

M. Rendu   My dear sir your scruples do you credit but

I am sure that if your father had a say in the matter he himself would insist

Olivier   Of course for practical purposes I'm taking over

M. Rendu   Good and your brother?

Olivier   Just between us I have some qualms

M. Rendu   Your brother is not a member of the board

Olivier   My point exactly shouldn't we

M. Rendu   Take care to ensure the support of the other two directors have a word with your uncle and aunt before the meeting

Alex   Hung out to dry splintered sand let's start again needs to be shakier only the skeleton's left pause we're nearly there

Butch   Alex there's a girl she wants to talk to you

Alex   Tell her to fuck off let's start again

Butch   I said fuck off she says the fucking's all been done she says

Alex   Ah

Butch   She says her name is Jiji

Alex   Ah

Butch   You know her?

Alex   No (*Enter* **Jiji**.) you go and sit over there Jiji be quiet

The music starts again. After some time, **Alex** *stands on his heels facing* **Jiji** *who's seated on a stool.*

Alex   No caressing

Jiji   That's for sure

Alex   A dying dog

Jiji I've come to celebrate

Alex You have

Jiji My birthday

Alex Have I seen you before?

Jiji You're not much of a looker

Alex And?

Jiji And we're going to get married everything's arranged

Alex Is it? Are you a good housekeeper can you iron shirts?

Jiji I do what I like I'm organised

Alex You have your father's blessing?

Jiji But no dowry he's a travelling salesman in the toilet paper industry

Alex Mine's dead at the bottom of a cesspit and your mother?

Jiji My mother? The Clinic? The name really suits you and I like this music that chases its tail

Alex We've been working on it for quite a time

Jiji You're no fun

Alex As you say

Ausange Are you sure?

Olivier I'm going to be blunt with you I can't help thinking that a double murder has been committed first the destruction of my character in my father's mind then of my father himself destroyed by the shock of thinking me disloyal so today I feel that my duty is to take command as the only way of ensuring that his life's work will continue as he would want it my goal is to preserve his legacy Benoît clearly wants to blow it to pieces

Ausange   What do you expect of me?

Olivier   I know how close you were to my father sir and I'm hoping that you will extend the loan we need to catch our breath two or three million repayable in two years would be sufficient to pull us through

Mme Bachevski   Barberin won't hear another word he will be paid do you understand?

Cohen   I'm very busy Madame Bachevski

Mme Bachevski   Do you or do you not have my cheque for Barberin?

Cohen   They'll all be paid

Mme Bachevski   Today?

Cohen   It would be reckless of me to promise you that Madame Bachevski

Mme Bachevski   He'll cancel the next shipment are you prepared to let the factory close down?

Cohen   When I was a small child my family often told the story of Rabbi Mendel one day when there wasn't so much as a crumb left in the house the rabbi's son came crying with hunger to his father 'you're not that hungry' replied the father 'otherwise I would have got something to fill your stomach' the child slipped outside without a word but he wasn't fully through the door when the rabbi suddenly saw a silver coin shining on the table he called his son back 'I beg your pardon' he told him 'you really were hungry'

Alex   So you like not doing anything

Jiji   Yes doing isn't really my strong point

Alex   Sleeping?

Jiji   Not really I lie on the ground suck a coke through a straw and sway

Alex   Do you do that often?

Jiji   Sometimes

Alex   What do you sway on?

Jiji   Anything

Alex   That makes it easier

Jiji   I sway on one leg

Alex   You are an organised lady

Passemar   And one day at his invitation I paid Monsieur Onde a visit I still had a thick head of hair I was skinny shy and bold

M. Onde   Come in

Passemar   His desk was quite a sight

M. Onde   You see these growing piles of books? They seem to be governed by an irreversible process of sedimentation

Passemar   Can you find your way?

M. Onde   Sometimes there are landslides deep strata force their way up to the surface

Passemar   In your vast field of research you labour alone?

M. Onde   You know I don't believe in teamwork you don't come across other people when you're a mole excavating your galleries without ever reaching the surface do you know why I approached you one day after my class? You hurt my eyes moles can't bear the sun

Passemar   The way you speak of those deities so many things suddenly make sense connect up and seem to shine

M. Onde   How ironic when I burrow around all I feel is a constant motion through the darkness with perhaps the faintest flicker of a glow that has never been quite extinguished I have never doubted that all mythological systems must in some way help the society that honours them to accept and take pride in their past to feel confidence in their present and future

Olivier   Dear Aunt Yvonne Uncle thanks for coming

Uncle Étienne   My dear boy

Aunt Yvonne   My poor little Olivier

Olivier   Of course you've been asked here not only as family members but as directors of the company

Aunt Yvonne   Is poor Fernand still just as low?

Olivier   Monsieur Rendu insists that while Dad cannot carry out his duties

Aunt Yvonne   He never used to be unwell

Uncle Étienne   There's more and more coronary thrombosis

Aunt Yvonne   Business isn't suffering too much?

Olivier   The board has convened

Aunt Yvonne   Poor Fernand

Olivier   To elect an acting president

Aunt Yvonne   As long as Fernand is out of action who else but you my poor Olivier

Olivier   Only a formality

Uncle Étienne   What must be done must be done

Olivier   After the meeting dinner at Prunier's as usual

Uncle Étienne   The first oysters have arrived

Aunt Yvonne   Fernand loved them so much

Uncle Étienne   Do you believe it would make him happy if old Uncle Étienne looked in at the hospital?

Olivier But my dear Uncle Étienne I've told you that for several weeks now he hasn't recognised anyone

Aunt Yvonne I hope they're spoiling him at this hospital

Olivier They're doing all they can Aunt Yvonne

Aunt Yvonne You think I don't know these hospital nurses Étienne all attentive while you're watching them but as soon as you turn your back they're playing poker on the patient's bed

Jiji You dance?

Alex Let's

Jiji How old were you?

Alex Two and a half and eight when I got out normally children who knew how to walk walked straight to the gas chambers but my mother was an extraordinary pianist she was the greatest living interpreter of Mozart and the kommandant was passionate about Mozart so he found her a place in the brothel my mother was very pretty thin with large dark eyes very long black hair very long slender fingers

Jiji More slender than mine?

Alex Little pointed breasts like yours

Jiji You can't dance

Alex I've never danced

Jiji Didn't your mother dance?

Alex Twice a week he made her leave the brothel for the evening he sat without moving in a red leather armchair smoking a very long cigar while she played sonatas all the sonatas

Jiji And you

Dr Temple And this apparatus controls the artificial

respiration as you see it's absolutely regular

Benoît If you unplugged it?

Dr Temple Instant death

Benoît And what happens when we can't afford this kind of dosh any more?

Dr Temple You must understand that we may be compelled to transfer him out of intensive care and then

Olivier (*appearing*) How is he doing Doctor?

Father Motte The mystery of the nature of life is in constant flux

Olivier He looks more rested today more relaxed are his reflexes as good as ever Doctor?

Father Motte Does the soul still dwell in this shell?

Dr Temple Look I gently pinch his leg he jerks it back

Olivier He does indeed

Dr Temple But there remains no trace of what you might call an operational personality

Olivier Did he sleep well?

Father Motte The soul is like wine in a bottle when you pour the wine

Dr Temple More or less it's still possible to distinguish between states of waking and sleeping at the moment he's presumably awake

Olivier Dad

Dr Temple He's a case we're rather proud of after six weeks in a coma

Olivier Dad it's Olivier

Dr Temple His heart his kidneys his digestive tract are functioning perfectly

Benoît   But what's the point?

Dr Temple   Where there's life

Benoît   We're going in circles Doctor you're saying that life

Olivier   Can't you see he's breathing?

Jiji   Let's keep dancing now you're dancing

Alex   They shot my father with several others while they were shitting in the latrines they reckoned that it was taking too long my father was a distinguished Latin scholar specialising in early Roman history in his youth he was also a famous football player

Jiji   You don't look like an athlete

Alex   My father was an exception Jews tend to look seedy

Jiji   With round shoulders

Alex   And crooked fingers

Jiji   Show me your fingers ouch that hurt

Alex   Jews can hurt

Jiji   How come you're Jewish?

Alex   It's an old story where should I start?

Jiji   Birth

Alex   You're a great midwife

Jiji   I'm the princess of happenings address 8 rue Vaneau

Alex   Phone number?

Jiji   Babylon zero zero forty

Ausange   And you never saw your mother?

Benoît   No I only recently discovered that she was my

grandfather's secretary well-stacked and quite good at her
job no doubt she was brought in to initiate the boss's son
in the mysteries of love it was too bad for her that
contraception was still in its infancy my father married
properly with the family's interests at heart then I upset
everything by being born five months after the wedding
Olivier landed right on time nine months after the same
wedding so my father became a father twice in the space
of four months

Ausange   How is he doing?

Benoît   It should all have been over by now but they're
subjecting his body to some kind of expensive rigmarole
just to keep a few disconnected organs in working order

Ausange   Olivier seems to resent your behaviour

Benoît   Olivier wants to turn Ravoire et Dehaze into a
monument dedicated to his father's memory which means
that in a few short months Ravoire et Dehaze will cease
to exist except in the fond remembrance of a few loyal
old employees who'll be out of a job

Ausange   How old are you?

Benoît   Thirty-one. You commissioned a report on the
company you know what it's worth where it's heading

Ausange   It can only have deteriorated since then

Benoît   It's not too late as long as there's a complete
change of approach we must forget the past and start
from scratch forge ahead in a spirit of adventure the
market potential is enormous there's room more than
enough room for both the Americans and us in fact I'm
confident that we can beat the Americans at their own
game as far as I'm concerned I'd welcome the chance to
have a crack at it and I believe that I can succeed but
only under two conditions first I'm going to need an
immediate injection of cash in the form of a loan not the
five hundred thousand francs on a two-year term which

you refused my father but a loan of six million not repayable for three years my calculations are there for you to look over secondly I need elbow-room that's to say absolute control over all decisions the ball's in your court Ausange

M. Onde The story that will be told in today's class begins with the dreams that came one night to Baldr son of Odin dreams heavy with threats upon his life what do we know about Baldr? Only that he is the wisest of the Aesir gods and the most merciful but his fate is bound by one condition that none of his judgements may ever come to be

Mme Alvarez I want to know how you dared send this letter

Mme Bachevski I want to know how you dare speak to me in that tone of voice

M. Onde Baldr has a brother Hödhr of whom we are told only that he is blind and that he is strong (*The stage is invaded by the pianist and the three* **Dancers**, *dressed as Scandinavian gods, who perform some moves, stop, start again, beginning the same series of moves several times – without interfering with the lecture. The only words spoken are along the lines of: 'Let's start again', 'There', etc.*) when Baldr had recounted his threatening dreams Frigga his mother extracted oaths guaranteeing that fire would do him no harm nor metal nor stone nor earth nor wood nor any living creature when all of that was said and done Baldr and the Aesir amused themselves in the following manner Baldr stood in the middle of the palace courtyard and all the other gods either shot at him or hurled rocks at him yet no matter what they threw at him it did him no harm and it seemed to all a grand privilege

Mme Alvarez That's right wrap yourself up in offended dignity now that suits you very well

Mme Bachevski If you stamp your feet once more the

floor is in danger of giving way beneath your weight

Mme Alvarez   Instead of worrying yourself about the strength of the building tell me how long have you been dealing with customer correspondence?

M. Onde   When Loki beheld this spectacle it displeased him Loki is an intriguing character fond of dreaming up unscrupulous mischievous ideas he enjoys doing for the pleasure it gives him as well as for the pain it causes in womanly disguise Loki went to find Frigga

Mme Bachevski   Don't forget that I was in your shoes a few years ago I know the business inside out

Mme Alvarez   Do you? Monsieur Fernand must have had his reasons if he removed you from trade relations and handed the job to me

Mme Bachevski   Yes he wanted to give me a promotion

Mme Alvarez   Ha ha ha ha ha

Mme Bachevski   Mind your glasses

M. Onde   The two women gossiped and their conversation quite naturally turned to the events in the palace courtyard Loki dressed as he was in womanly disguise asked 'are all beings sworn not to harm Baldr?' Frigga answered 'yes but for one young plant named Mistletoe too young it seemed to me to require of it an oath' no sooner had Loki left her sight than he changed from his womanly disguise and found the mistletoe he pulled it up out of the ground and went to the palace Hödhr was standing outside the circle of revellers on account of the fact that he was blind Loki spoke to him thus 'come do like the others I'll point you toward him throw this mistletoe'

Cohen   Two children you're squabbling like two small children I can't believe it Madame Alvarez and you Madame Bachevski

Mme Alvarez Ask her who authorised her to write to customers

Cohen Good heavens Madame Bachevski

M. Onde Hödhr grasped the mistletoe and guided by Loki threw it at Baldr the shot hit him and Baldr fell down dead on the ground this was the greatest disaster ever to befall gods or men

Mme Alvarez Go ahead ask her

Cohen It seems to me Madame Bachevski that that is more likely to fall within Madame Alvarez's jurisdiction you've chosen to act in the company's best interests no doubt but if we all trespassed on the work of others and no longer respected the allocation of responsibility

M. Onde All of the Aesir fell silent whenever they wished to speak they instead broke out in tears for none could express his pain in words

Mme Bachevski I was minding my own business when Monsieur Benoît stormed into my office infuriated by the inefficiency of sales administration he brandished this letter of complaint from Monsieur Simonnot and ordered me to reply to Monsieur Simonnot myself

M. Onde This tragedy holds within it the very keystone of the history of the world the mediocrity of the present age is now without remedy

Mme Alvarez Ask her who's in charge of this company Monsieur Cohen and how it is she's taking her orders from Monsieur Benoît

Mme Bachevski Who's in charge? Good question

Cohen Monsieur Olivier is the acting president

Mme Bachevski Monsieur Benoît's doing the work

Mme Alvarez And what kind of work is it that Monsieur Benoît is doing? Stirring things up sowing discontent only yesterday he tried to find out through a couple of seemingly routine questions which side my managers were on Passemar what did he ask you?

Passemar Well I don't exactly remember what his actual words were you may be interpreting

Mme Alvarez Oh come on you told me all about it

Passemar Not so that it could be repeated

M. Onde But from the disaster shall come renewal the earth shall emerge from the ocean beautiful and green grain shall grow without being sown and the golden tables of the Aesir shall stand once more on the grass

Passemar When all's said and done wouldn't it be wiser to give up on these Scandinavian gods? The future's not exactly clear at Ravoire et Dehaze and my own career prospects are bleak wouldn't it be a good idea for me to start looking for some kind of emergency exit? Might not playwriting be the solution? But I need to set a limit of three or four characters per play and get rid of all this paraphernalia these dancers musicians

Alex Tear it all up leave nothing behind a little more mystical yes nothing again now bash beautiful nothing doing won't do let's start again who's that?

Butch It's our Jiji

Alex Keep it up let it soak now soft

Jiji Hi it was quite something last night at the Molitor pool

Alex What did you do to your hair?

Jiji They shaved it

Alex Your nose is longer your eyes have grown bigger

Benoît I want you to lay siege to Olivier

Margery You want me to seduce your little brother?

Benoît   He thinks you're my Lady Macbeth

Margery   Bullshit I'm your Pompadour

Benoît   Either way he's afraid of you

Margery   He hates me

Benoît   Because he can't fathom you my little reed

Margery   I'll talk to him about the little doggie

Benoît   About anything you like if it'll help me

Margery   You know I'll write a thesis on this Marquise and present it for my PhD at Berkeley Benoît work it out so that we can hang on to the snuff boxes I'm crazy about them

Jiji   It took place in the pool and around the pool Oldenburg positioned us telling us not to throw things in the pool a boy by the name of Luke fully dressed carries a yellow chair he goes up to the edge and puts the chair on the water several times he tries to sit on it but it sinks he starts again after several attempts he takes off his clothes and carefully ties them to the chair he then lets the whole thing go so that the chair and all his clothes are floating freely and Luke also starts to float we're told to improvise do whatever we want I tie red balloons on strings to all parts of my body while the others do other things Henry arrives with a yellow rubber raft and a rubber oar Barbara gently swims up to Henry's raft

Alex   And your balloons?

Jiji   Two people are holding my head and the third unfolds and sharpens a cutthroat razor he shaves me my hair falls in the pool together with all sorts of other things from the other actions which slowly fill the pool up Oldenburg calls them floats and now it's time

Alex   How could you tell?

Jiji   Oldenburg gives the signal with a spotlight at the beginning and end of each action and now it's time I'm completely covered with balloons I drift into the deep end I'm floating I'm rigid David swims up to me after a moment he bites the balloons which explode bang he bites them one after the other and in the end I sink he moves away

Alex   Was shaving you part of the plan?

Jiji   It was an option Oldenburg hadn't planned anything specific the actors could do whatever they wanted as long as it fitted within the time between the beginning and the end of an action

Alex   When you came in I suddenly saw Mum

Jiji   They shaved off her hair?

Alex   As you were talking I saw I remembered the actions they pronounced it Aktion it's the same word sort of the same thing they were in Lvov in the Ukraine they were also divided into unconnected episodes the difference

Olivier   Oh no Cohen not you

Cohen   Monsieur Olivier when I had double pneumonia last year and the doctors didn't give me any chance

Olivier   You made a fantastic recovery

Cohen   What good did it do? I would have preferred never to have had to live through all this

Olivier   It's only a bad spell

Cohen   Perhaps for you who are still young

Alex   The difference is that the actions you're talking about reach an amazing intensity precisely because they aren't connected to any cause to any past the German actions under the occupation were also incomprehensible why were they doing this and not that? From time to time we Jews were the floats we weren't able to build up any defence because we weren't able to understand because there was nothing to understand but the difference

Olivier   You're regarded as a patriarch you're the rock here it's important for all the people here who respect you to see that you haven't lost confidence Cohen

Cohen   In 1934 you weren't born nor was Monsieur Benoît I was hired by your company as an assistant book-keeper

Olivier   And you climbed the ranks Cohen you're exhausted your nerves are on edge and it's understandable everyone pesters the man who guards the purse-strings

Cohen   For more than a week I've been living by my wits Monsieur Olivier doing anything I can so that no one will say the company had stopped its payments

Olivier   I know nevertheless for the time being I reject your resignation

Alex   The difference is that in hindsight the German actions appear to have had some kind of overall sense

Jiji   What sense?

Alex   The annihilation of the Jews wait we're getting to a very interesting point why did the Germans who had a gift for organisation set about things in such a way that to the people who lived through them these particular events always appeared accidental? No doubt about it this floating of random actions was ingenious

Ausange (*on the phone*)   Oh how stupid of me I'd completely forgotten that you'd invited Father Motte to dinner too no I'm delighted he's a most entertaining fellow so we'll be sixteen at table? But it's not a problem Lucienne I'll send the chauffeur to Fauchon's to get one more lobster now not another word

Jiji   Give me an example

Alex   This takes place in Lvov the Germans search the houses where Jews are registered. They round up the men

separate the young from the old the young men are piled
into a building while the old men are taken into the
courtyard to exercise then the young men are led onto a
hockey field where they are divided into two groups those
in front are set free and go back home those who are in
the rear spend the night on the hockey field in the hands
of the SS who make them run while beating them with
clubs those who fall they trample to death in the morning
they release some who return home the dead are removed
and those who remain are photographed then they ask for
volunteers they take one in five and beat them to death
the other volunteers are loaded into some fifty trucks fifty
men to a truck all thinking that they're going to die but
not at all the trucks drive around the city and then they
are released that was the first Aktion in the city of Lvov
the next Aktion started the same way but from the hockey
field the men were led to an old sweet factory there they
were forced to unload cement bags from a cart and to
load them back onto the same cart then a group were
chosen to throw huge shovelfuls of the cement onto a fire
while being beaten with clubs those who survived picked
up the bodies and were taken to wash themselves in a
shower room where several others died the rest were set
free

Ausange (*on the phone*)   You asked me for two or three
million we feel you need six million besides Olivier we are
not altogether convinced that in the circumstances you
have the right managerial profile I hold you in the highest
personal esteem my dear chap but you are a leader for
times of peace we are therefore making it a condition of
this loan that you hand over control to Benoît who seems
to us to be a nastier individual with him in charge the
bank feels that it could take the risk in addition we
consider it reasonable that the bank be presented with
four seats on your board of directors

*The Clinic begins to fill with people. They are listening to jazz and
drinking, mostly beer and coca-cola: the average age is twenty. But*

*there are also several whisky drinkers, elegant, ten years older and as
noisy as the others are silent. In the meantime, the action continues
in the company's offices, in the boardroom, in a hospital room.*

Mme Alvarez   What? You're back?

Dutôt   Good Lord are you still here?

Dutôt *disappears.*

Mme Alvarez   Benoît's not wasting any time

Cohen   Our time is over

Passemar   How should I reply to this letter Madame
Alvarez?

Mme Alvarez   Ask Madame Bachevski

Cohen   Who's it from?

Passemar   Lépine

Cohen   One of Lubin's clients

Mme Alvarez   Lubin came to the office this morning
he was really upset he'd just found out that his little Jiji's
fiancé is of your religion you can imagine poor Lubin who
has two priests in the family

Aunt Yvonne   Could you close the window Olivier?

M. Rendu (*reading*)   This day September 22nd 1968 the
board is convened to deliberate the following agenda first
provisions to be made as a result of the incapacity of its
president Monsieur Fernand Dehaze

Uncle Étienne   It feels stuffy to me no Olivier leave it
open Benoît my boy haven't you got fatter?

Jiji   I'm going to beat it

Alex   Going out swaying?

Jiji   All these people

Alex   Scare you suddenly?

Dr Temple We're going to have to transfer your father to another floor this evening

Benoît Fair enough

Olivier But why?

Dr Temple This equipment is required for another case which how can I put it seems to us more promising

Olivier Dad

Olivier *cries.*

Benoît I told him yesterday that we couldn't afford the expense any longer

Olivier You didn't

Benoît I did let's say our goodbyes

Mme Bachevski Sunshine after rain Monsieur Cohen

Cohen Sorry?

Mme Bachevski After the skinny cows come the fat cows

Cohen I didn't know you knew the Old Testament Madame Bachevski

Mme Bachevski I don't understand you you cried when the coffers were empty and now that they're full again

Cohen There are a thousand and one ways for coffers to be filled and sometimes it's better to keep schtum one day when Rabbi Zozia was tossing and turning in his bed unable to get to sleep

Mme Bachevski Oh no no thank you

Benoît *and* **Margery** *enter The Clinic.*

Benoît It's a cool little club that's on the up some magazine carried a piece about it last week isn't it fun? Jazz is the latest fashion again

Margery   It makes me blue like everything from the States why do you all have to ape everything that comes from the US?

Benoît   It's all the rage it's wilder than Coltrane's free jazz I think it's a lot of fun don't you? Hi there

A Voice   Hello

Benoît   One of Olivier's friends

Margery   Your brother's a skunk I called him we had a date he stood me up

Benoît   It doesn't matter any more forget about it *c'est vous le patron?*

Alex   *Oui*

Benoît   *C'est amusant chez vous* it's fun

Alex   *On fait ce qu'on peut*

Benoît   No really you've got some great ideas

Fourth Movement

Moss and Heather

*Lépine Bros., the president's and other offices at Ravoire et Dehaze, **M. Dehaze**'s studio, **Benoît** and **Margery**'s bedroom and living room, **M. Toppfer**'s antique shop, a café bench.*

Lubin   It's a sensational offer Madame Lépine we've been thinking of you

Mme Lépine   Sometimes I find myself thinking of you like yesterday evening when I was stocktaking

Lubin   Right the main thing is for the stock to move and to get it moving my company has thought up a great big contest that will sweep every French housewife off her feet

Mme Lépine   United Paper's rep dropped in a couple of weeks ago and they've beaten you to it again you'd better watch out because when those guys start running they really run

Lubin   Their contest is nothing compared to ours Madame Lépine

Mme Lépine   I'm telling you their contest is going to strike gold because the retailers can't get enough of it and you know why? Because Softies brings home the bacon for them

Lubin   We're offering a package holiday to the Balearics

Jenny   Thanks I think I'll sit on the floor

Benoît   Certainly Madame

Jenny   I'm Jenny

Jack   I'm Jack we're going to leave the monsieurs at the coat-check is that okay with you Ben?

Benoît   That's fine with me Jack

Jack   Well then now we've worked out our little diagnosis we've sniffed around the market a bit we've chatted with your people it's a really exciting problem because we'll have to start over from ground zero let me ask you Ben what do you sell?

Benoît   What do I sell?

Jack   Yes

Benoît   Toilet paper

Jack   What's it used for?

Benoît   What's it used for?

Jack   Yes

Benoît   To wipe yourself

Jack   Where?

Benoît   Your posterior

Jack   After having done what?

Benoît   Pardon?

Jack   After having?

Benoît   After having

Jack   It's difficult to get it out huh? But don't you see that is exactly your company's sickness?

Jenny   You're selling a product that's remote abstract

Jack   To win this war you're gonna have to sell some emotion

Jenny   Beginning with the act of shitting

Jack   A fundamentally human act

Lubin   You're joking Madame Lépine

Mme Lépine   Not in the least

Lubin   You can't let me down

Mme Lépine   I got my customers started on the Softies contest and believe me they all want to win the Opel Rekord

Lubin   Get them onto winning the Balearic Islands too

Mme Lépine   Next time

Jack   As a concept food encompasses everything that goes in and everything that comes out the input and the output

Jenny   You're an integral part of the food cycle and you don't know it

Jack   Since prehistoric times the input has been man's main concern

Jenny   But now that needs-based economy is being replaced by one founded on desire huge avenues of marketing potential are springing up and this is one of them

Benoît   Good but I'm a practical man what do you propose as a course of action?

Jack   Action Ben unravels like a ball of string as soon as there's a vision

Jenny   We aren't going to tell you what to do all we can do is force you to open your eyes and see

Jack   But before you can see you'll have to shake up a ton of preconceived ideas and inhibitions all this sterile unproductive silt

Jenny   You'll learn to use Donohue and Frankfurter as a bulldozer guaranteed to remove everything that blocks your view

The three **Dancers***, masked, microphones in hand, have entered the auditorium, and approach members of the audience to ask them questions.* **Passemar** *is alone on the stage, seated in a wicker*

chair.

Market Researchers   Hello Monsieur/Madame I work for a market research company and we're currently doing a study on consumer behaviour and usage in certain domains of everyday life and I'd like to ask you a few questions

First of all could you please tell me if you have lavatory facilities in your home or if you regularly use outdoor lavatory facilities

Do your lavatory facilities include a flushing system. Is it a standard bowl or squat

Have you moved your bowels within the past twenty-four hours

How many times approximately have you moved your bowels over the past seven days

Do you move your bowels irregularly or regularly in the evening in the morning during the day do you tend to have diarrhoea or constipation

When you move your bowels how much time on average do you estimate you spend in the toilet do you read there what do you read there a newspaper a magazine a book an almanac

Does going to the toilet represent a moment of peace or a disagreeable necessity are you more likely to find it pleasurable or unpleasurable or does it leave you indifferent do you notice in these moments an influx of ideas or on the contrary is it relatively empty in terms of mental activity or is it simply normal

Are you indifferent to the odour that your stools emit are you bothered by this odour or on the contrary do you find it to be an attractive aroma are you bothered by the stools of others

In your home what is the term that normally and

typically is used to indicate the lavatory facility and how is the act of passing a motion generally referred to in your home

What do you call toilet paper in your home

Here are samples of different types of toilet paper show me which is closest to the kind you use regularly is this the same as the one which you used most recently

Do you know which brand of toilet paper you use

How long does a roll of toilet paper last in your home before it's replaced

Last time you moved your bowels how many sheets did you use did you double them did you fold them in half

Who bought the roll that you are currently using in what type of shop was it purchased a convenience store grocery chemist supermarket

How would you rate the overall quality of this paper give a score from zero to five

What are its principal advantages wipes well cheap soft the sheets detach easily smells nice pleasing to the eye

What are its principal faults rough slippery not absorbent the sheets detach poorly too expensive not eye-catching doesn't wipe well too thin glossy too thick tears while using not soft enough

What is your profession

What is your age

That concludes our survey I'd like to thank you for the time that you have been willing to spend with me

Passemar No question about it I'm going to cut out these interludes which not only place a strain on production costs but interrupt the flow of the action my problem is that I'm still wavering between two styles of theatre avant-garde or traditional I have to face the fact that the only kind of theatre that's likely to provide me with a viable salary is one that responds to consumer demand you have to offer the public the product they want in other words you have to create the marketing mix which has Ravoire et Dehaze falling over itself it's the word that's been on everyone's lips for weeks I must say it's pretty exciting to be taking part in the upheaval but I'm worried that it may be to the detriment of the older members of staff about whom it's believed a priori that they won't adapt I need to make an appointment to see Monsieur Benoît

Meanwhile, the three **Dancers** *have carried* **Passemar** *on his chair in a procession and have deposited him in* **Madame Alvarez**'s *office where, after having adjusted his clothing, he takes part in a conversation.*

Mme Alvarez   You Passemar you should react

Passemar   But how?

Mme Alvarez   Before things take another turn

Olivier (*entering*)   What sort of turn

Cohen (*entering*)   This invoice Monsieur Olivier I can't believe it

Olivier   What's wrong Cohen? (*Reading.*) Donohue and Frankfurter Marketing Consultants preliminary investigation this has to be a mistake they must have typed an extra zero

Toppfer   You'll please excuse my being unable to control my emotions

Benoît   I've asked you

Toppfer   I was in this very room talking things over with him when suddenly

Benoît   I've asked you to stop in

Toppfer   Do you know what his last words were? He

said 'Tell me more of this story Toppfer' and then he collapsed against the canvas

Benoît I've asked you to stop in because my brother and I plan to sell this collection we need to know its value

Toppfer Each piece has its story

Benoît What's the price for it?

Toppfer Your father was an enthusiastic and knowledgeable customer I believe that he used to honour me with his trust

Benoît How much can we get for it Monsieur Toppfer?

Margery *enters.*

Toppfer If you wish me to make you an offer

Margery But there's no question of selling it

Mme Lépine It's no

Lubin You can't

Mme Lépine That's the way it goes

Lubin Let me at least put you down for a small order of say three little cartons

Mme Lépine I've got plenty thank you

Lubin Just to show that I called

Mme Lépine Goodbye

Lubin You wouldn't let me leave empty-handed

Mme Lépine Well three's out of the question

Lubin All right then two cartons payment on delivery two per cent discount and little Raymond's taking his communion?

Mme Lépine The boy doesn't think about anything but his catechism I hope he doesn't become a priest on me

Lubin   I'm worried about my daughter too

Mme Lépine   She's getting married isn't she?

Lubin   You'd think she'd introduce us to her fiancé she hasn't even told us his name

Mme Lépine   Well have you asked her?

Benoît   You're baring your teeth my little reed

Margery   I have the distinct impression that you've decided to sell these snuff boxes and I have decided they must not go

Benoît   That's quite enough of that won't you come to bed?

Margery   You're going bald

Benoît   There are a few things I need to discuss with you my little flute

Lubin   One day six months ago she told us I'm getting married

Margery   You're going to end up monstrous

Benoît   And rich and famous don't forget you married me for the money

Margery   Not entirely

Lubin   She came to the table her head shaved like an egg this man has forced her to shear herself like a whore at the liberation my wife is on the verge of a nervous breakdown I've got a friend a private detective I asked him to do me a favour

Benoît   In less than five years Margery the good old family business will be worth ten or fifteen times what it's worth today

Lubin   When all's said and done I'd rather not have known about it he's an Israelite who was put through the concentration camps a child of Auschwitz if you like

Mme Lépine   You're joking

Benoît   I'll plough the proceeds from the sale of the snuff boxes directly into Ravoire et Dehaze to raise my stake in the capital

Margery   Money money I'm going to get really sick of your money

Lubin   He runs a jazz club in Montparnasse with a whole crowd of shady characters

Mme Lépine   And your daughter

Lubin   Hangs out there every evening it's a haven for beatniks apparently it's full of Arabs and Blacks

Olivier   Cohen wanted me to look over this invoice for consulting fees

Benoît   They're expensive and quite right to be so

Olivier   How do you mean?

Benoît   Because they find people like me who'll pay

Cohen   I'd like to point out that

Benoît   Of all our investments this will bring the greatest returns

Cohen   Our overhead expenses have risen a hundred and fifteen per cent in the last two months

Mme Alvarez   While our turnover

Saillant   Will continue to tumble for another seven or eight months and during this period our expenses will more than double once again

Benoît   I haven't introduced you to André Saillant our controller on board since last Monday this is Madame Alvarez our administrative manager you'll now report to Monsieur Saillant and this is our chief accountant Monsieur Cohen you too Cohen will report to Monsieur Saillant but I should have begun André by introducing

you to my brother Olivier who from now on will handle
personnel but Cohen you wanted to draw my attention to

Cohen　As I was saying Monsieur Benoît as I was saying

Benoît　Well?

Cohen　Monsieur Benoît since I've been head of
accounts I've always reported directly to the president

Benoît　Yes and now you will report to the controller
but I believe you were talking to me about overhead
expenses

Cohen　You're heading straight for disaster and don't
count on me to be a part of it

Benoît　Calm down let's have a look at this disaster

Cohen　In March our loss rose to a hundred and thirty
thousand

Saillant　In April it will reach a hundred and fifty-five

Benoît　And from May through to December I expect to
lose between two and three hundred thousand a month
you're not telling me anything I didn't know Cohen

Lubin　What's the use?

Mme Lépine　You've got to pull yourself together

Lubin　If business was booming I could be a bit more
philosophical about the state of play on the home front

Mme Lépine　Ask your chemist for some pills

Lubin　If everything was quiet at home I could keep my
spirits up even if I am taking half the orders I had last
year

Mme Lépine　That must put quite a hole in your
budget

Lubin　It's not so much the loss in revenue Madame
Lépine I just rack my brains trying to understand is it my

fault? Good God are you losing it Lubin? I tell you
Madame Lépine at forty-nine I feel in my prime

Mme Bachevski The boss asked for me?

Cohen Monsieur Benoît is holding a meeting of all
senior management

Mme Bachevski What's the fuss?

Mme Alvarez Oh don't you know? He's already let me
in on it

Mme Bachevski Do you imagine he hasn't consulted
me?

Mme Alvarez He who laughs last

Mme Bachevski The first shall be last and the last
shall be first

Cohen Your knowledge of the scriptures never ceases to
amaze me Madame Bachevski

Benoît *has appeared.*

Benoît I'm here to tell you where we are and where
we're going at the moment we're at rock bottom and we'll
stay there for a little while longer bracing ourselves for the
assault and then we're going to leap forward and those of
you who don't rise to the challenge will soon find you
don't belong here any more this isn't a threat it's a
statement of fact I know you can all make it the question
is do you want to? With our new product due for launch
early next year we shall not only recapture all the ground
we have ceded to the enemy but we shall also push back
the very limits of the market if you say to me I'm a
dreamer then I'll answer yes I am a dreamer it has
always been dreamers who have smashed apparently
insuperable obstacles there have been rumblings among
you because I have more than doubled expenditure yes I
have and I did so in order to sharpen our competitive
edge on the other hand there are expenses which you

may think are unavoidable which I shall do away with cutbacks will be drastic in all departments one thing is finished for certain and I'm not asking you this I'm telling you all the squabbling all the bickering in back rooms no longer has any place in the firm for the simple reason that we need all our time and energy to accomplish the task at hand finally I am injecting some new blood into the business together with a few organisational changes Yves Battistini fresh from Proctor and Gamble will start up a department of marketing research Jean-Baptiste Peyre until now product manager at Johnson's Wax will become product group manager Battistini Peyre and Claude Dutôt will form the pillars of our marketing department André Saillant in the newly created position of controller will re-energise our entire financial and administrative structures I have promoted one of you Grangier to the key position of factory manager from now on purchasing shall report to the factory and henceforth Madame Bachevski will be accountable to Grangier one final word in any business what really makes the difference is the people which is why the personnel department is now entrusted to my brother Olivier he will be able to tend to it exclusively now that he is relieved of responsibility for production all that remains is for me to thank you

Everyone disappears except **Passemar**.

Passemar   Now begins the hardest section of the play relating to the birth of the new product a part delicate to realise firstly because it may lead to a series of didactic scenes difficult to dramatise however skilful I am (*The pianist and the three* **Dancers**, *masked and dressed as Scandinavian gods, appear.*) what are you doing here? It's all getting out of control (*The* **Dancers** *have begun their act.*) there's some confusion about the scene order they're all caught up in the stories of the Aesir and Vanir which are rich in choreographic possibilities but they disapprove of the scene in which the lorry drivers unload their box at

Madame Lépine's and find the interlude where I ask them to work as market researchers weak

First Dancer   What do we know about Baldr? Only that he is the wisest of the Aesir gods and the most merciful but his fate is bound by one condition that none of his judgements may ever come to be

Passemar   And then there's the scatological aspect

Second Dancer   Baldr has a brother Hödhr who's blind and strong

Passemar   Anything crude I find personally painful and I don't see

Second Dancer   Baldr recounts his threatening dreams

Third Dancer   Frigga his mother extracts oaths from all creatures and objects

The **Dancers** *have grabbed* **Passemar** *and force him to stand still and upright while they throw all kinds of projectiles at him.*

First Dancer   They enjoy taking shots at Baldr and it does him no harm

Passemar   I don't see how I'm to avoid it

Second Dancer   Loki who enjoys doing harm for the pleasure it gives him is displeased

Passemar   With all the crap to come

Third Dancer   He hands the sprig of mistletoe to Hödhr who is blind

Passemar   Nauseating

First Dancer   Hödhr clutches the sprig of mistletoe in his hand

Passemar   I'll be accused of giving in to fashion

One **Dancer** *gestures for the mistletoe to be thrown at Baldr;* **Passemar** *falls stiffly; the ballet continues.*

Second Dancer   This was the greatest disaster ever to befall gods or men

Third Dancer   This tragedy holds within it the very keystone of the history of the world the mediocrity of the present age is now without remedy

First Dancer   But from the disaster shall come renewal

Third Dancer   The golden tables of the Aesir shall stand once more on the grass

Jenny   Okay Jack and I have gotten the scoop on your business

Jack   We were saying to each other Jenny and I that now that we're all together we should chuck a few balls about

Jenny   Perhaps all you really need to do is loosen a bit you're all always so serious

Jack   The key to the Donohue-Frankfurter method is what we like to call guided spontaneity

Jenny   First you're going to suffer okay?

Jack   Claude what's an arse?

Dutôt   It's the it's

Jack   Jean-Baptiste?

Peyre   It's a person's posterior

Dutôt   It's the backside

Jenny   Yves?

Battistini   It's the backside

Jack   Right you see you're all so uptight

Jenny   Conventional

Jack   Ben what's an arse?

Battistini   An exit

Benoît   An entrance

Jack   Ah shall we take a look inside?

Jenny   Jean?

Passemar   A cavern

Battistini   A backwards mouth

Peyre   A crack in the body

Benoît   A fissure

Dutôt   A soft and shadowy thing

Passemar   A valley in the shadow of two sunny hills

Benoît   A mine

Jack   From which we extract what?

Benoît   Coal

Dutôt   Squishy coal

Peyre   Stinking turf

Battistini   Diamonds

Jenny   You hear that? Who'll advance me on diamonds?

Passemar   Black gold

Jack   A mine that is all yours

Jenny   An ore from which you'll extract enormous wealth

Jack   If you resolutely penetrate therein

Jenny   It's up to you to exploit its resources

Jack   It'll take your breath away

Jenny   But you're sat in front of the gate

Jack   For more than seventy years you've been sitting on a treasure if you'd only once stood up and looked between your legs

Jenny Why haven't you ever looked between your legs?

Jack Listen up this is Jenny's deepest intuition

Jenny Well then say why? Why don't you look between your legs?

Dutôt Because it's not very pretty

Jenny Revealing answer who can do better?

Peyre a) It's pretty awkward and b) I'm sorry but to watch yourself dropping a turd in the bowl isn't exactly a transcendental moment

Jenny Are you sure? That's not what you thought a while back

Peyre Excuse me?

Jenny When you were one or two don't you remember how interested you were in looking at this and touching that when Mum left you sitting all alone on your potty?

Peyre I'm sorry but other interests replaced that one pretty fast

Jenny Yes replaced that interest which we held closest to our heart

Peyre Well you'll have to pardon my saying so but there is a certain development that every human goes through from the most basic interests such as crying to get some sweets to mathematics poetry

Jenny You've used three different phrases to ask me three different times to excuse you

Peyre What?

Jenny You said 'excuse me' 'I'm sorry' and 'you'll have to pardon my saying so' as if I'd caught you in the act and you felt guilty

Jack Guilty of what?

Jenny Of having fiddled around with your shit with no end of pleasure. You didn't like me reminding you of that

Peyre This is all so stupid I've had it up to here you're really getting up my nose

Jenny Look how angry he is

Jack And look at the imagery he uses

Jenny He wants to throw his chair at me he'd do it if his boss weren't here

Peyre Have you finished?

Jenny Did you hear that? 'Have you finished?' Those are the words his mother used when he wouldn't get off the potty

Peyre *springs up from his seat and leaves, slamming he door.*

Benoît I don't really see where all this is taking us time's marching on

Jenny And you have letters to sign

Benoît A phone call to make

Jack You've basically had enough

Jenny You all want this over with

Jack And that's the moment to go on

Benoît I don't see any deep intuition in all this crap

Jack Did you say crap?

Dutôt So what do we do now?

Jenny We could maybe ask why we're all so uncomfortable

Battistini What makes me uncomfortable is that we're all busy people with a lot on our plate plans for the launch of a new product for one thing

Dutôt If you add up the paid hours we're spending

here

Jenny   Forget how uncomfortable you're feeling and ask yourselves

Jack   What causes the discomfort?

Jenny   When I'm surprised in the middle of doing something bad I get uncomfortable right?

Jack   Which means?

Battistini   It means you're embarrassed

Dutôt   You're ashamed

Jenny   Yes I'm ashamed

Jack   And what is being ashamed?

Benoît   We're going round in circles

Jack   No we're in a spiral

Jenny   That rises and carries you up until you discover a view you never expected

Passemar   Being ashamed is the feeling you get when someone discovers you

Jack   Doing what?

Passemar   Something forbidden

Jenny   And why do you do it?

Dutôt   Because you want to

Jenny   You want to what?

Dutôt   Do anything

Passemar   To

Benoît   To give yourself pleasure

Jenny   The feeling you get when you take a shit Ben if you'd make the effort and concentrate on the feeling of the stuff passing through the anus ultimately becoming detached

Jack   Doesn't that give you a certain physical pleasure?

Jenny   Even if you're not really paying attention?

Battistini   Yes

Dutôt   Yes

Passemar   Yes

Jenny   Too bad Jean-Baptiste isn't here call him back in

Passemar *goes out, returns with* **Peyre.**

Jack   I simply want to reach a point where we can investigate the premise

Jenny   That's my intuition kids

Jack   That shitting is a pleasure

Jenny   And for many reasons a forbidden pleasure

Jack   And if that's so

Jenny   You begin to see exactly what our mine contains

Jack   Wouldn't it be possible to go from there and create a product and release it with a force that's truly explosive?

Jenny   Never mind that toilet paper is no more than an aid to the act of shitting

Jack   It's our job to infuse this aid with all the symbols of a pleasure made even more desirable by being forbidden

Jenny   Now we can tell you

Jack   Yeah Jenny said to me these guys think they're in love with their product but in fact they can't get it up

Jenny   The product has to burrow into our deepest self

Jack   There is in each of us a great erotic reservoir

which can tune in to the reservoir within every consumer
and form an oilfield richer than those of Texas and
Alaska

Jenny   There's no reason why a French enterprise with a
bit of savvy shouldn't do a lot better than the generally
pretty stupid subsidiary of a giant American conglomerate

Jack   So long as it throws itself into marketing

Jenny   And I ask you what is marketing?

Peyre   Marketing ahem means bringing the consumer to
the product rather than pushing the product at the
consumer

Battistini   It means taking account of the buyer's
concerns

Dutôt   It means recognising that the world changes

Benoît   And causing that change

Passemar   Marketing is everything that strives to make
a difference

Dutôt   Marketing is the synthesis of the spirit of
enterprise with the creative imagination

Peyre   It's a vision of the world

Benoît   And yet a frame of mind

Peyre   Action in the offing

Passemar   Innovation galore

Battistini   For me marketing

Peyre   For me

Jack   Well shit guys I think that's excellent how about
you Jenny?

Jenny   Excellent Jack

Jack   If you ask the French a question as long as it

doesn't embarrass them

Jenny   You see fireworks

Jack   It's almost as if you'd all taken an exam

Jenny   In the end marketing is everything

Jack   Which means nothing shit you kids have a hard time shaking up the bugs in your brains unleashing yourselves now stand by here come the Tablets of the Law according to Donohue and Frankfurter there are seven laws just as there are seven branches on the candlestick of Moses they're written down on the sheets which Jenny is handing out now listen

(*Reading.*) Law the first the number of man's needs is limited but his desires and his fears know no number through marketing may they grow
Law the second the man of marketing and the consumer form a couple the man of marketing is the male the consumer is the female
Law the third the man of marketing is subject to call when he draws his bow the finger which grasps the arrow is soft as a newborn child's
Law the fourth the man of marketing is in a state of constant amazement he marvels at the most commonplace of things he climbs to the river's source
Law the fifth the man of marketing is a thief and a voyeur he gleans and pilfers all that shines
Law the sixth the man of marketing is his product's lover he takes it even to bed with him
Law the seventh the man of marketing is a priest and a soldier a man of faith and of steel doubting nothing and defying all created of both fire and ice

All vanish, except **Passemar**.

Passemar   The fact I was present at and even took some small part in this working session is entirely and unexpectedly due to the interview I sought with Monsieur Benoît he was most kind actually I quite like the boy

Benoît   So what can I do for you?

Passemar   To start with Monsieur if I may I'd like to tell you that since you took over as president

Benoît   How does it feel?

Passemar   You've opened the window and let in fresh air

Benoît   It's only the start

Passemar   Whenever big changes take place people begin to wonder and I'm wondering too

Benoît   Where does Passemar fit in?

Passemar   Exactly Monsieur

Benoît   You've operated as sales administration manager now for about ten years you have a satisfactory record

Passemar   It's gratifying to hear you say so

Benoît   If things had stayed as they were you'd probably have found yourself sliding into Madame Alvarez's seat but how ambitious are you really?

Passemar   Monsieur I have to admit that an urge to reach the top at all costs isn't really part of my character at my age and with my responsibilities to my family

Benoît   You make it sound rather static Passemar in a dynamic outfit if you stop climbing you tumble down

Passemar   But climb where Monsieur?

Benoît   I'm making you an assistant product manager this will test your potential and if when all's said and done you've broken the mould a brand new career is open to you if you don't do so well

Passemar   You'll show me the door

Benoît   No you're a valuable player and not everyone has the nerve for marketing if you fail I'll return you to your current position whatever the outcome it can only be to your benefit

Passemar I'll do my best thank you so much (**Benoît** *disappears*.) I regretted this last phrase which sounded old-fashioned and not at all like marketing 'I'll do my best thank you so much' a man of marketing would have said 'great I'm rarin' to go'

Toppfer How wonderful Madame to find in you such a passion

Margery These things have a soul of their own it makes me shiver just to touch them

Toppfer They send us such intimate messages from beyond the dust of centuries don't they

Margery They tremble in your hands

Toppfer Take this tiny marvel between your fingers open it

Margery Oh my

Toppfer Yes the lords and ladies of that century often entertained themselves with licentious scenes

Margery But what are they doing?

Toppfer Making love Madame

Margery But backwards?

*In **Benoît**'s office, entirely renovated, very sparse, white lacquered furniture: seated or lying on the carpet are **Peyre**, **Dutôt**, **Battistini**, and **Passemar**. A bottle of whisky and glasses.*

Toppfer Here's another it arouses me just to look at it

Margery Oh let me see

Toppfer It's a unique piece

Jenny Hello boys what are we going to call it? Let me remind you there's nothing so crucial to the destiny of a new product as its name

Jack   Let me just remind you of the rules each person says what comes into his head no censorship no irony okay? Ready? Shoot

Toppfer   It depicts Madame de Romanet the young prey whom Madame de Pompadour provided to gratify the desires of her former lover

Margery   Oh I'll talk to Benoît he has to buy it

Toppfer   It's a highly priced piece at the moment it's set aside for a South American client

Margery   But I want it

Toppfer   I have the impression Madame although I could be mistaken that your husband is rather less a buyer than a seller

Margery   Sure he wants to get rid of the lot including the one I'm crazy about with the portrait of Mimi

Margery and **Toppfer** *have disappeared.*

— Soffipap

— Pappisoft

— Pappydream

— Softresist

— Adam and Eve

— Paul et Virginie

— Blooming Garden

— Virgin Snow

— Snow White

— Angel's Breath

— Chrysalis

— Sigh

— Soft Kiss

— Hot Kiss

— Hot Crystal

— Silky Web

— Cozy Quilt

— Duvet

— Moss

— Tuft of Grass

— Algae and Seaweed

— Cowlick

— Moss and Lichen

— Moss and Seaweed

— Muslin Dream

— Oak and Fern

— Moss and Heather

— Cascade

— Oasis

— Lagoon

— Capri

— Cytherea

— Venice

— Maidenhead

— White Flower

— White Nettle

— Ermine

— Ecstasy

— Hosannah

— Amen

— Heaven and Earth

— Morning Dew

— Angelus

— Morning Glory

— Virgin Vine

— Gentle Breeze

— Fresh Air

— Milky Way

— Cherubim

— Desdemona

— Ophelia

— Ariadne

— Wonder

— Longing

— Softness

— Caress

— Kitten

— Pussycat

— Dragonfly

— Green Pasture

— Laughing Dell

— Dolcissimo

— Pianissimo

— Dream

— Diana

— Water Lily

— Forget-me-not

— Intimacy

— Confidence

— Happy Worker

— Neverland

— Honeymoon

— Eden

— Fairy Tale

— Noa-Noa

— Savannah

— Prairie

— Cloudburst

Lubin You see the point is my wife's at the end of her tether

Cohen Yes

Lubin I'm afraid she's going round the bend which makes it hard for me to keep a level head

Cohen Yes

Lubin Mind you I am holding my course

Cohen Yes

Lubin And as far as work's concerned everything's fine you do know it's not my fault if sales are falling

Cohen No

Lubin But when evening comes

Cohen Yes

Lubin I mean there aren't many Jews left in France why did she have to fly the nest with one? It's not easy for Marguerite she has a brother and an uncle who are both priests it's not so much his race that bothers me you know

Cohen Yes

Lubin It's his nature a drifter I know two or three Israelites whom I consider men you for example

Cohen Yes

Lubin You're a friend I'm telling it to you straight

Cohen Yes you know there isn't a Jewish race at most you can speak of a community and every community has its lost sheep

Lubin It's precisely because you people stick together so closely that I decided to come and see you I thought to myself maybe Monsieur Cohen will agree out of friendship for Lubin to do a little research into this fellow

Benoît How was your brainstorming?

Battistini An avalanche

Jack Do you know the real strength of this method Ben? A brainstorm

Jenny Cannot fail

Jack Man needs objects in which he can project his desires in ancient times he related to the moon water fire serpent or rock

Jenny Or he made fetishes like in Crete in black Africa they're great I have quite a collection

Jack Then came Jehovah Mohammed Christ

Jenny But now that's all out of date

Jack   With the advent of mass consumption

Jenny   Man finds solace in companions of another kind

Jack   More useful because they can also wash your clothes your face your dishes go pretty fast on the highways

Jenny   Or wipe your bottom

Jack   Soon enough

Jenny   Religion literature art will fade into the past

Jack   Man's creativity will find refuge in marketing

With two pints of beer, on a café bench.

Alex   What is it you want from me?

Cohen   To read you

Alex   Which page shall I open the book at?

Cohen   Your mother was the great Rosa Klein

Alex   Seems so

Cohen   Once I heard her give a recital of Mozart sonatas at the Conservatoire

Alex   Very touching I trust there was a full house

Cohen   So frail yet when she started to play she became a giant I gather she died at Buchenwald

Alex   At Auschwitz

Cohen   Was Dr Klein professor of Roman history at Warsaw University your father? Is he dead?

Alex   At Auschwitz

Cohen   Were you at Auschwitz yourself?

Alex   It was my childhood playground

Cohen   How did you escape death?

Alex With style

Cohen Do you know this? (*Takes a booklet from his pocket and reads.*) 'Contribution to a new approach to complex multiple variables by Alex Klein delivered before the Academy of Science'

Alex Now empty your pockets let's see if we can find another touching relic

Cohen Of the whole family there's no one left but you?

Alex Isn't that enough?

Cohen I feel a great trampled suffering in your answers

Alex Is this the Last Judgement?

Cohen I'm trying to read

Alex Who are you the messenger of God?

Cohen My name is Cohen I'm the chief accountant for a company one of whose salesmen is a man I've known for a long time he came to find me because he's worried about the impending marriage of his only daughter Genevieve whom they call Jiji

Alex Ah Jiji?

Cohen So I've come to ask you how you know her

Alex She came to hear me play a few times. I didn't take much notice

Cohen And then

Alex One day she introduced herself she said we were going to get married

Cohen She's always loved her joke that one

Alex I talked to her

Cohen What about?

Alex About me about Auschwitz and Lvov she listened

closely she didn't ask a lot of questions

Cohen   What are you going to do?

Alex   I just let things happen don't you think that's better? Shouldn't you be getting back now?

Benoît   Bruno de Panafieu welcome at Ravoire et Dehaze Bruno is our advertising agency's account executive who will be in charge of the campaign working alongside Hughes Jaloux welcome Hughes one of the agency's star copywriters it seemed important for both of them to sit in at this meeting in which Monsieur Reszanyi whom I've retained as a consultant will report on the results of the motivational study he has conducted

Reszanyi   At an early age children pass through a phase in which the libido is concentrated in the anal region the child experiences poo-poo as its own child or creation which he will play with to gain a narcissistic pleasure or claim as his property to affirm his independence or brandish as a weapon to fight with it is apparent that the most important categories of social behaviour play gift-exchange ownership fighting all originate in the anal phase of an individual's development and money is nothing but fecal matter expressed in a form which need not be repressed because it has been deodorised dehydrated and polished to a shine

Margery, *answering the doorbell, has opened the door to her flat for* **Olivier**, *who stops in his tracks:* **Margery** *is dressed as an eighteenth-century courtier.*

Margery   So come in you'll catch cold

Olivier   How are you my little Margery?

Margery   As you can see I'm celebrating my thirty-fourth birthday today

Olivier   *Ta robe est ravissante*

Margery   I knew Benoît wouldn't remember and the

idea of staying home alone was so depressing that I said to myself I'll phone Olivier whom I haven't seen in centuries

Olivier   That's true

Margery   My brother-in-law whom I like more than he likes me

Olivier   The very idea

Margery   I'm an American upstart who wormed her way into the Dehaze family to get her hands on it through the bastard wing but here take off your raincoat

Olivier   Watch out it's drenched

Reszanyi   If we examine the material gleaned from the forty in-depth interviews two distinct groups of individuals emerge on the one hand those for whom the act of excremental evacuation is a punishment we'll call them the oppressed on the other hand those for whom it constitutes a relief we'll call them the liberated

Margery   I've buried myself in history look at all these books I've been boning up on eighteenth-century Versailles are you cold?

Olivier   My feet are soaked damned rain

Margery   Get changed you'll find everything you need behind the folding screen I'm throwing a costume ball

Olivier (*behind screen*)   Are you expecting many people tonight?

Margery   Everyone's arrived

Reszanyi   Another polarisation should be noted between those who essentially experience the act as an expulsion and those who experience it as an accumulation

Olivier   You want me to put on all this?

Margery   Of course

Reszanyi   But most significant is the breakdown of our subjects between those who tend to reduce the act to a physiological function let's call them the one-dimensional type and those in whom we observe outbursts of spiritual meanings and symbols we'll call them the multi-dimensional type

Olivier   But this is frighteningly complicated I don't even know how to get into these breeches

Margery   You should have seen the bitch of a time I had myself

Reszanyi   The lexical distribution of names attributed to the place of evacuation is striking the loo the lavatory the john the smallest room the toilet the w.c. the little boys' room where can I wash my hands

Olivier   *appears in courtier's garb.*

Margery   You were a skunk Olivier

Olivier   What do you mean?

Margery   Why did you stand me up?

Olivier   But I phoned

Margery   I think I'm open with you you should be open too

Olivier   Okay I didn't want to come

Margery   Why?

Reszanyi   There must be some reason why people wish to wipe themselves with paper the same colour as their excrement as if one needed to mistake the matter for its support and hush the whole thing up

Margery   Do you like caviare? That's all there is for dinner but I bought a five-hundred gram container that cost me almost as much as a snuff box and look here's the vodka

Olivier　*C'est parfaitement délicieux*

Margery　You didn't want to come because I horrify you

Reszanyi　Themes of tense versus loose hard versus soft emerge frequently

Olivier　What are you saying?

Margery　Benoît horrifies you and I horrify you even more

Olivier　Listen Margery I've been going through a bad spell but things are beginning to heal now

Margery　Do they have to heal?

Olivier　What else can they do?

Margery　You know one night Benoît and I were in bed talking about you he said he couldn't understand why I had a crush on him and not on you and I said to him it's true you're more my type but that you're somehow a bit of a clam

Olivier　I don't understand

Margery　A clam you know a mollusc

Reszanyi　These in-depth interviews can be illuminating listen to the end of this one with a multi-dimensional type as an example of the wealth of material made available to your advertising agency's copy-writers

He turns on the tape recorder; **Benoît**, **Peyre**, **Battistini** *and* **Passemar** *gather round. A young voice and that of* **Reszanyi**.

—　The soil bordering the path was wet a rabbit was passing by

—　A tuft of dandelions in my hand oh stop it you're torturing me

Sound of a slap; **Reszanyi** *mimes being slapped.*

— Ouch Mademoiselle you still had your eye on the rabbit when

— I hadn't quite finished

— Knees bent thighs apart bust forward the rabbit had melted into the undergrowth the thing wasn't completely detached were you pushing?

— I was longing ah don't torture me any more

Sound of a slap; **Reszanyi** *mimes being slapped.*

— Ouch we're getting there longing for what?

— Softness

— Go on

— Then I melted away myself

— Like the rabbit excellent then you yanked up the second clump of dandelions

— I wanted to kill wanted to cry

Olivier I do open and close in a way that's true

Margery And you bravely stay stuck to your rock come what may

Olivier It's better to stick to something than to rape and pillage like you two

Margery Ah I like seeing you get angry Monsieur le duc de Haze

Olivier I'm not getting angry

Margery You're furious with me and not a moment too soon

Olivier What game are we playing Margery?

Margery A man who lets himself be flung to the ground makes me sick

Olivier I know about you and Ausange

Margery   Oh?

Olivier   I know that you curled up in his bed so that the bank would choose Benoît as Dad's successor

Margery   I went to bed with Ausange of the Bank of Paris and the Netherlands?

Olivier   That's what they say

Margery   And what else do they say?

Olivier   It's thanks to you that I was passed over

Margery   If that's true what am I doing here with you?

Olivier   Oh there are still a couple of things for you to squeeze out of me

Margery   Such as?

Olivier   I don't know such as the half of the business that still belongs to me

Margery   That's true

Olivier   I have reasons to suspect that Benoît went to Dad and told him I was plotting to get him out of the way and take over

Margery   I don't suspect it at all I'm sure he did

Olivier   Of course you're sure you were the one behind the whole hideous lie

Margery   No Olivier I was shocked by Benoît's total lack of feeling for Daddy and I told him that Daddy was the man I respected and cherished most in the world

Olivier   How can I believe what you're saying?

Margery   How can I make you believe it?

Olivier   You once told me you married Benoît for his money

Margery   Yes it was partly for the money but I also

loved him you know I love life more than anything I'm a simple girl

Olivier I don't know what to think

Margery For example I've got a terrible urge to sleep with you and I don't think it's the vodka

Olivier You say you want to sleep with me

Margery Yup

Olivier Yes I know I've been drinking too but that could fit my theory

Margery Let's drop the theories

Olivier It makes me dizzy

Margery You're not impotent Olivier?

Olivier No

Margery I have been told I'm just warning you that I can sometimes be frigid it starts off well but then

Olivier You were told this?

Margery I've been told a lot of stuff okay? You think I want to go to bed with you so I can manipulate you like a spy in a detective novel?

Olivier I didn't say a word

Margery I want you that's all and not only for tonight but so what everything I say is turned against me

Olivier Margery

Lubin Madame Lépine something sensational for you real news

Mme Lépine Do tell

Lubin Christmas is coming the season of giving so we've decided to offer our faithful customers a very special present

Mme Lépine   Let's have a look

Margery   You been to America?

Olivier   Why do you ask?

Margery   I'm going back to Berkeley to present my thesis on the political role of snuff boxes as gifts in the power games at court between 1740 and 1769 Toppfer has been very useful by the way he showed me the snuff box he was describing to Daddy when Daddy collapsed oh Olivier we have to acquire it in memory of Daddy I talked to Benoît about it but Benoît

Lubin   As well you know after Christmas housewives feel the need to concentrate on the essentials January is always a month of increased consumer demand for toilet paper so to encourage you to stock up we've put together this unprecedented special offer with a gift for you

Mme Lépine   So you don't get the gift unless you buy? Great gift

Margery   All I'm asking is that when I divorce Benoît and marry you you'll buy me a little dog and we'll call her Mimi

Olivier   Mimi?

Margery   She'll have chestnut eyes and white fur with little brown tufts and Olivier we'll undress each other

Olivier   What breed?

They undress each other.

Margery   A poodle I am terribly drunk but it doesn't matter we're going to sleep with each other if we don't make love it doesn't matter right? Oh be careful with the lace or the place I rented it from will make me pay for the repairs we'll move to San Francisco and we'll open a French beauty parlour you're so French it'll cause a sensation we'll call it Madame de Pompadour the doggie will play in the reception hall and the snuff box will be in

a display case with an official certificate signed by
Monsieur Toppfer

Battistini   Now then we sifted through the two hundred
and seventy-four names produced by the brainstorming
session and came up with six finalists which we put to a
panel of representative consumers

Lubin   Madame Lépine all you have to do is place an
order doubling your average over the last six months and
you'll receive with the compliments of Ravoire et Dehaze
this magnificent lamp which will take pride of place in
your living room

Mme Lépine   Stick it

Lubin   You're not serious

Mme Lépine   Do you think I'm daft?

Lubin   Not at all you're a very reasonable person and
that's exactly why

Battistini   The test gave us some pretty remarkable
results White Flower scored poorly so did Angel's Breath
Water Lily tended to suggest a paper what would
disintegrate Algae and Seaweed split the group for some it
conveyed the purity and savage grandeur of the ocean
while others were repelled as if from something dark and
gooey that smelled bad Ariadne came out positively
combining impressions both of desert dryness and
harmonious softness as a paper it would be clean and
gentle and yet resilient in short Ariadne rated pretty
highly but the name which came out ahead by a long
way was Moss and Heather with an overall score of
thirty-eight per cent which is exceptionally high given the
choice of six let me list for you the principal images
triggered by Moss and Heather the beauty of unspoilt
woodland wide open spaces solitude intimacy the
awakening of love toilet paper sold under this name would
be worthy of trust offering at once the required strength
the desired softness an attractive appearance and

favourable scent particularly in urban middle-class areas
where some seventy-eight per cent of our short-term
priority targets are concentrated

Mme Lépine   Why should I stock up on a product
whose demand is plummeting every day when I can move
this one which sells like hotcakes and brings in four or
five times as much? You realise that their contest did
better than they had ever expected? If things carry on as
they are I bet that in six months no one will so much as
mention Ravoire et Dehaze ever again

Lubin   All right then Madame Lépine let me tell you in
strictest confidence that we're about to turn the corner
we've got a pack of young wolves on board who are
preparing us for a major strike

Mme Lépine   Really? And has your daughter's hair
grown back?

Benoît   We want a stunning headline

Panafieu   That will trigger the purchasing reflex

Benoît   Get the brand name across loud and clear

Panafieu   With a resounding consumer plus

Benoît   That will single out our product

Panafieu   And tilt the balance

Lubin   Mind you he's a handsome man tall and well-
built you'd never know he was a Jew

Mme Lépine   Well that's not so bad is it?

Lubin   No but the thought of shaving his fiancée's head

Mme Lépine   That's a worry

Lubin   My wife's checking into a clinic the doctor wants
to try sleep therapy

Battistini   If you consider that last year's consumption
of toilet paper per capita was point seven kilos in France

compared with five point five kilos in the United States

Lubin I love my job Madame Lépine selling's in my blood that's why when the competition gets the upper hand I take it personally

Battistini That in 1967 out of the forty million kilograms of toilet paper consumed in France thirty-eight million were rough stock and only two million had quilted padding

Mme Lépine But you say your people are preparing to react

Lubin Yes but I only hope

Mme Lépine You should always hope

Battistini The market is doubly underdeveloped both in terms of the low overall volume of consumption and the dismally small proportion of superior grade paper

Lubin I do hope you know the firm is advertising to hire new reps

Mme Lépine That's a good sign

Battistini Hence the fantastic opportunity

Lubin We in the old guard hope it isn't with a view to giving us the sack

Mme Lépine Yes indeed

Lubin I hope that when Ravoire et Dehaze launch . their all-out offensive you'll find me fighting in the front line of the shock platoon

Mme Lépine As always

Peyre On the media front our primary objective is to penetrate urban housewives between the ages of twenty-five and forty in the higher and middle income group who are the most permeable to the message that Moss and Heather is the one and only product on the market bringing an exclusive consumer plus on the creative front our primary objective will be to get this message across coating it in an air of modernity of youth living life to the full of primal desires while ensuring we don't upset the values prevailing in the middle-aged middle-class sectors of the population that form our priority target

Benoît   Jack do you have anything to add?

Jack   No I think that's fantastic I'm impressed by the ability you French have to put things in clear and simple terms the only thing that worries me is that you're going about this so well that it's all in danger of becoming a bit tame the consumer is basically a great mouth and a great arse stuff has to go in and it's got to come out and where it comes out is what interests us Saint Augustine said '*inter urinas et faeces nascimur*' we are born between urine and faeces everything is concentrated in a couple of square inches suffering love ecstasy and filth we come out from there and it comes out of us and then we wipe man is an animal that wipes after shitting you find me one other animal that wipes Nietzsche said man is an animal that makes promises it all fits together what is promising? It's being constipated by the past in learning to promise man has bound the future to the past I owe you and you owe me as he seeks to escape the eternity of the moment man flees from the present because he's ashamed so he suffers guilt and why? Because of the repression which began when he was born now then this has to be handled carefully but what we have to do is open a doorway into one of life's great forbidden pleasures our axiom could be that it's enjoyable to shit and we at Ravoire et Dehaze can make it even more enjoyable it's all pretty rough but can't you imagine how it would sound set to some really fine music?

Fifth Movement

The Triumph

The classroom at the Collège de France, the president's and other offices at Raviore et Dehaze, The Clinic, the English Bar at the Plaza-Athénée Hotel, Lépine Bros., **Benoît** *and* **Margery**'s *bedroom,* **Ausange**'s *office.*

Cohen But honestly Madame Bachevski you do have to concede that for several days now Madame Alvarez has been nodding and saying hello to you

Mme Bachevski Yes she flicks her head at me dry as a dead branch

In the first row of listeners the corpulent man in black; in the back row the two old women are knitting; in the second row the three **Dancers** *and the pianist.*

M. Onde When the wolf-cub Fenrir was born the gods knew he must devour them so what do they do? They have a collar made with a magical thread so thin it's invisible and yet unbreakable Fenrir is invited to put his head through it just for fun to test his strength the wolf-cub accepts but only on condition that one of the gods puts a hand in his mouth during the game as a token of good faith

Mme Bachevski She goes around poisoning the atmosphere in the office with her insinuations about Monsieur Benoît's private life and all because she's lost the privilege of answering directly to the president

Cohen So have I but I'm happier now the work is so much more stimulating

M. Onde Tyr stretched out his arm thus and plunged his right hand into the mouth of the wolf

Cohen Monsieur Saillant is au fait with the latest most

sophisticated management tools next to him I'm just a
child

M. Onde   The wolf could not break free the more he
struggled the tighter grew the cord

Cohen   A child marvels and learns

M. Onde   And so he shall remain until the end of time

Cohen   Last week we implemented a system of standard
costs with automatic variance analysis

M. Onde   The Aesir laughed all except Tyr whose hand
was gone

Cohen   Who would have imagined it?

Passemar *has appeared in the classroom; he remains standing,
facing the* **Dancers** *rather than* **M. Onde.**

Passemar   They've got it into their heads that they've
stumbled on a theme for a cosmogonic ballet which will
rocket them to fame they're looking for a financial backer
all they'd need then is to get on television

The pianist has sat down at his piano and the three **Dancers**
*continue their choreographic investigation of the wolf-cub Fenrir; from
time to time they say, 'Let's start again', 'That's not working', etc.*

Mme Alvarex *has appeared.*

M. Onde   What is the significance of this episode? That
fraud has become the very underpinning of law

Mme Bachevski *vanishes.*

Cohen   I've noticed Madame Alvarez that Madame
Bachevski has spoken to you briefly on several occasions

Mme Alvarez   By choosing to say hello I systematically
force her to reply

Cohen   Life is a series of small advances that little by
little add up

Mme Alvarez   It sickens me to see her licking the boots of every bright young thing we take on board

M. Onde   Thus what the divine society had gained in efficiency they lost in moral and mystical strength they are now nothing more than an exact representation of those terrestrial gangs or states whose only aim is to win and conquer

Cohen   You take a rather bleak view of things

Mme Alvarez   I may be the only one who hasn't let myself be fooled by Benoît's shenanigans even you Monsieur Cohen

M. Onde   This lowering of the ceiling of sovereign power condemns the whole world gods and men to be no more than what they are since mediocrity no longer results from accidental imperfections but rather from essential limits

Passemar   The mole continues to excavate his galleries keep digging Monsieur Onde one day our houses will crack and the ground will give way beneath our footsteps

M. Onde *steps forward to the area where the three* **Dancers** *are working.*

M. Onde   Monsieur

First Dancer   Me?

M. Onde   Several times now I've noted your presence and that of these good people in my class tell me are you engaged in some form of comparative research?

First Dancer   We're working on a ballet

M. Onde   May I ask what is it that inspires you in this dreary classroom? It is surely in no way conducive to summoning up the spirit of the dance

The three **Dancers** *surround* **M. Onde**, *enveloping him in their movements.*

The Three Dancers YOU are the spirit of the dance

Peyre, **Battistini**, **Panafieu** *and* **Jaloux** *have appeared,*
Passemar *is there, and from time to time* **Benoît** *takes part in
the advertising agency's presentation.*

Panafieu We worked from the basic assumption that
for the time being those who use newsprint are to be
abandoned to their fate and set as our primary target
those who currently use toilet paper per se

Alex *and* **Jiji** *are sitting cross-legged next to each other on the floor
surrounded by musical instruments, swaying, almost humming.*

Jiji Art and Butch have gone

Alex Art went and then Butch

Panafieu This consumer has a problem to which we
provide a solution

Jiji Art and Butch have fucked off

Alex Without leaving an address

Jiji Where did they go?

Panafieu What is his problem? It is that the toilet
paper he uses is an odourless colourless tasteless product
which is also rough and therefore at best uncomfortable
unless it is smooth in which case it neither absorbs nor
wipes well

Alex *jumps to his feet and goes to the piano, he improvises.*

Jiji Why did they go?

Alex We became too close maybe so close

Jiji That they left

Alex Of course there's always a reason

Jiji To do what you do

Panafieu The solution to his problem is a paper
pleasant to look at to smell to touch it absorbs without

scratching and strokes without tearing

Jiji   I want to cry

Alex   Why?

Jiji   I liked Butch

Panafieu   We segmented the target population according to their awareness of the problem which led us to identify five consumer types ranging from total unawareness to total awareness passing through innocent awareness guilty awareness and partial awareness

Alex   Me too

Jiji   I slept with Butch

Alex   Me too

Jiji   He's always so quiet never smiles

Alex   His whole body is a smile

Panafieu   By far the broadest segment is the totally unaware because they don't know that they have a problem they have no interest in the product and therefore our creative concept

Benoît (*on the phone in his office*)   Get me Ausange at the bank then Ralph Young at United Paper Europe

Panafieu   Is to manufacture the problem by convincing the consumer that he's unhappy and explaining to him why

Benoît   I'm calling you as promised Ausange you know things aren't going at all badly everything's rolling along according to plan one thing I probably underestimated is our working capital requirement assuming we want to keep the pressure on

Jiji   What are we going to do now?

Alex   Luckily we don't care

Jiji　There are other musicians in Paris

Alex　Paris is full of musicians we keep the disco going I
serve the drinks you keep performing your little
happenings they love that and we don't care

Jiji　The jazz

Alex　Is over

Benoît　Well then we could have a drink together
Monsieur Young would that suit you? But I'm pretty tied
up for the next two weeks Friday the sixteenth? Great
how about seven o'clock the English Bar at the Plaza-
Athénée

Jiji　No caressing

Alex　A dying dog

Panafieu　So from there the next step was for us to
determine which creative concepts would crystallise over to
you Bernard

Jaloux　Thank you Robert these are only rough sketches
we're still very much at the exploratory stage to start with
we did the rounds of the competition to see what they're
saying (*Turns page on flipchart.*) velvety discreet resistant
different

Lubin　Madame Lépine this time you're going to see
what you're going to see

Jaloux　Incomparably soft

Mme Lépine　Couldn't you come back in the
afternoon?

Lubin　Brace yourself for something really sensational

Jaloux　Absorbant crumples without a sound as you can
see their emphasis is always placed firmly on a product
plus and nowhere on the benefit to the consumer well
right from the word go we decided to angle ourselves
towards consumer benefits so what should our message

be? To the totally unaware we must say you're unhappy and this is why to the guiltily aware we must say nothing could be more natural than taking pleasure in natural functions so we let the cauldron bubble and came up with this (*Displaying a mock-up.*) the visual shows a generic suburban interior and what does the headlines say? 'BRING SOME LIFE TO YOUR HOME! In ours we have Moss and Heather!'

Lubin Okay Madame Lépine you can be frank with me what do you say?

Mme Lépine Are you really going to plough three million francs into advertising?

Lubin That's right

Jaloux A couple are happily standing in a corner of the flat surrounded by what looks like a wild little garden

Margery (*in bed with* **Olivier**) Olivier my little Lolo

Olivier My little Yankeebird

Margery I'm crazy about your name Olivier

Lubin And of course it's not plastic or vinyl but genuine leather from the Vosges

Jaloux We're telling the consumer who's totally unaware that he's made unhappy by this lifeless décor and we're guiding him to the solution by emphasising the incredible difference made by a little patch of happiness at his fingertips

Lubin Our market research has shown that nothing would please retailers more than a large format family photo

Margery Have you called Toppfer my Lolo?

Olivier I've told you I can't afford it right now

Lubin Especially if it's taken by the best photographer in town and presented in a luxury frame like this one

Jaloux   A disadvantage to this creative approach is that it is somewhat oblique we're asking the consumer to interpret

Lubin   And offered by you Madame Lépine not by Ravoire et Dehaze but by the wholesaler to her client

Margery   But my Lolo the option I took out expires tomorrow Toppfer's going to sell it

Lubin   Eh? Wouldn't you be happy to present each of your retailers with a lavish gift safe in the knowledge that we're the ones paying?

Margery   Won't you just call and ask him to hold on to it for one more week?

Jaloux (*displaying a mock-up*)   So here's what we came up with next now our two characters seem almost drunk with pleasure between the trees in the ferns among mossy rocks and our headlines says 'HAVE YOU FELT THE JOY OF FROLICKING AT THE HEART OF THE FOREST?' subtitle 'Recapture it day after day using Moss and Heather'

Peyre   That's good

Benoît   That's great

Battistini   And it speaks to the guiltily aware as well as to the totally unaware

Jaloux   But we can't run the risk of a credibility gap affecting our claim so we've been looking for a less lyrical version of that same message (*Displaying a mock-up.*) in this visual the young lady of the house is shown twice

Lubin   You don't seem enthusiastic

Mme Lépine   Should I be leaping in the air?

Jaloux   On the left we see her frolicking in the forest on the right jumping for joy in her apartment and the headline says 'FREE AND EASY WITH MOSS AND HEATHER'

Lubin   But honestly what do you think of it?

Mme Lépine   You've certainly made an effort this time

Lubin   Coming from you Madame Lépine that's praise indeed

Mme Lépine   Will you be finished soon?

Lubin   As soon as I've got your order

Mme Lépine   Make it twenty-four cartons

Lubin   Did you really say twenty-four?

Jaloux   But the bra business has been beating the 'Free and Easy' drum so loudly in recent years that we found ourselves drawn irresistibly back to the suburban flat which after all does allow for strong identification and we've ended up with the following campaign which will be the agency's recommendation (*Displaying a mock-up.*) this time the whole family is gathered in the wild little garden which forms an oasis in the flat and what do we say? 'NOW AT HOME WE ALSO HAVE MOSS AND HEATHER' the first thing you'll notice is the extraordinary simplicity with which several highly complex themes are fused together

Margery   Olivier dear we're going to swap with Benoît

Jaloux   The phrase 'at home' immediately establishes a place of sanctuary the hearth intimacy the word 'now' serves to suggest a transformation from unhappiness to delight 'now at home' carries an amazing charge

Peyre   Now at home

Benoît   Now at home

Jaloux   'We also have Moss and Heather' there's nothing more positive nothing more affirming than this 'we also have'

Peyre   We also have

Benoît   Now at home we also have Moss and Heather

Peyre   Now at home we also have Moss and Heather

Margery   What's Ravoire et Dehaze worth?

Olivier   I haven't the least idea

Margery   Say two million bucks suppose you swapped part of your half of Ravoire et Dehaze stock with Benoît's half of the snuff box collection

Olivier   That's great my sweet little Yankeebird now that everything's settled can we get some sleep?

Margery   We quit the business and take two suitcases the collection in one if it's worth five hundred thousand today it'll be worth two or three times that in a few years nothing increases in value as quickly as snuff boxes in the other we pack two hundred and fifty thousand cash which is enough

Olivier   Enough to?

Margery   Have you forgotten my dear Olivier? In the fine city of San Francisco

Olivier   Ah yes San Francisco

Margery   In the heart of the most elegant part of town

Olivier   Yes yes

Margery   Ladies and gentlemen the marquise

Olivier   Welcome

Grangier   The inventory is the crux let's size up the situation shall we?

Mme Alvarez   Do you remember the disaster when Excelsior was launched?

Grangier   Who doesn't? But there won't be any disaster this time get me the latest figures

Mme Bachevski   Coming up

Grangier   Cumulative orders as of this morning?

Dutôt   I scarcely dare tell you we're about three

hundred per cent above target

Grangier   And I thought I was playing safe planning production at twice your shipping estimates

Dutôt   You're positive you won't run out of stock?

Grangier   The factory's working three shifts I've stopped all Perfecto production

Mme Bachevski   This time I can feel it

Mme Alvarez   What?

Mme Bachevski   Triumph

Mme Alvarez   Which is what you felt when Excelsior was launched right?

Mme Bachevski   And you when we launched Blue White and Red

The three **Dancers** *and the pianist have appeared with* **M. Onde** *in holiday wear: white trousers, orange polo shirt and straw hat; he is sitting in a wicker chair, an open book on his knees. The* **Dancers** *use their cosmogonic dance exercises to warm up.*

Cohen   We've just reeled off the first set of variance analysis schedules

Saillant   You didn't spend your weekend on it did you Cohen?

Cohen   It's dazzling I can't get over it as if the whole business were stretched out in front of me like an open book

Passemar *appears.*

Passemar   So this is where you've been all this time you're dead wrong if you think you can always do as you please come on let's get going

The three **Dancers***, under* **Passemar***'s watchful gaze, interrupt their dance in disgust and change into pale green and mauve mini-dresses.* **Benoît**, **Saillant**, **Grangier**, **Peyre**, **Battistini**, *and* **Dutôt** *sit at a conference table.*

Benoît   Complacency can be fatal I've called this meeting because I have a nagging feeling that we're resting on our laurels the launch is proceeding at full speed

Passemar   Okay you can go

The three **Dancers** *each take the end of a rope of about fifteen metres in length onto which clusters of gift-wrapped packages are attached, and perform a farandole which brings them into the middle of the audience, the chains of packages dragging behind them. With a pair of scissors attached to their dresses they detach the packages and distribute them to audience members.*

Benoît   But now is the time we should be stepping up the current

First Dancer   Are you Monsieur Guillebaud?

Second Dancer   Are you Madame Bosselat?

Third Dancer   Forgive me for asking

First Dancer   But I have a mission to deliver this package

Second Dancer   To Monsieur Guillebaud

Third Dancer   To Madame Bosselat

First Dancer   In person

Second Dancer   Hello Madame Bosselat

Third Dancer   Hello Monsieur Guillebaud

First Dancer   Ravoire et Dehaze

Second Dancer   Have instructed me

Third Dancer   To come and greet you in person

First Dancer   And to bring you

Second Dancer   This modest little gift

Third Dancer   You can open it without fear

First Dancer   But do open it come on

Second Dancer   No danger

Third Dancer   It doesn't contain anything explosive

First Dancer   Or rather it does

Second Dancer   Its contents are most explosive

Third Dancer   Because Ravoire et Dehaze

First Dancer   Are launching a bomb

Second Dancer   Onto the toilet-paper market

Third Dancer   So go ahead and open it Monsieur Guillebaud

First Dancer   So go ahead and open it Madame Bosselat

Second Dancer   There was a time

Third Dancer   When toilet paper

First Dancer   Was a purely functional item

Second Dancer   Now the time has come

Third Dancer   For Moss and Heather

The audience members open up their packages, finding in them, amongst real moss and heather, a roll of toilet paper that is coloured mauve and pale green in patches, packaged in the same colour wrapping with a picture of a forgotten corner in a wild forest.

First Dancer   Are you Monsieur Béranger?

Second Dancer   Are you Madame Vignon?

Third Dancer   Forgive me for asking

And the text repeats.

First Dancer   Are you Mademoiselle Naville?

Second Dancer Are you Monsieur Desjardin?

Third Dancer Forgive me for asking

And the text repeats.

First Dancer Are you Madame Borde?

Second Dancer Are you Monsieur Gauthier?

Third Dancer Forgive me for asking?

And the text repeats.

Benoît Now is the time for us to address the question where do we go from here? Yes Grangier

Grangier Develop a quilted product that's untearable we'd call it reinforced

Peyre Announce it as third-generation toilet paper

Benoît Even if it's not on tap by tomorrow

Saillant 2000 is on the horizon

Benoît · The year 2000 is tomorrow

Peyre This morning as I was shaving I thought about the tens of millions of square metres of paper which pass through the hands of consumers all that good space going to waste

Benoît What would you use it for?

Peyre Print facts on it all sorts of facts today everyone's looking for more facts this is the age of non-stop information

Battistini Or pictures we could print pictures which show up on several different rolls and get consumers who find identical ones

Dutôt To send them in to us and win a small gift

Peyre As a way of encouraging brand loyalty and think about the market segments we haven't even touched barracks hospitals schools

Dutôt Prisons

Battistini Religious communities

Peyre Where we've never had so much as a foot in the door

Saillant Soon our battery of management control tools will no longer be keyed to past performance but to projections of future performance so what if sales are ten per cent above last year's if they're five per cent below budget? This philosophy will gradually transform every aspect of the business leading to a new objective-driven approach and I must say that although at first I found old Cohen to be an apprehensive opponent to change in no time at all he's turned into an inspired and zealous disciple I've just told him to go and take an introductory course at IBM since we're about to take the big step of installing a computer

Benoît Good and how about personnel?

Saillant That's your brother Olivier's territory

Benoît Why didn't he come to this meeting?

Silence.

Saillant We're moving towards a more motivating salary scale although of course our people don't work for money alone they regard their jobs as a way to participate in collective success which we're encouraging by creating cultural and sporting groups

Benoît Thank you I think enough has been said for each of you to realise that there's unlimited scope for the company to expand and endless opportunities to further your personal careers as long as you keep going full steam ahead

Passemar My three dancers are furious they've vowed never to set foot on stage again they told me that they found the gift-giving interlude not only degrading but also repetitive as far as I'm concerned I relish repetition with a slight variation each time

Lubin   Good to see you Madame Lépine

Mme Lépine   Ah you've finally showed up

Lubin   Were you hoping to see me for a change?

Mme Lépine   There's my telephone ring your firm and tell them to ship me at least twelve cartons straight away. I absolutely must have an emergency delivery at once do you hear me?

Passemar   It would certainly brighten my prospects if this play met with commercial success because at Ravoire et Dehaze there are clouds on the horizon not just for me I'm thinking of poor Madame Bachevski it's as if the ground's just opened beneath her feet

Mme Bachevski   You asked to see me Monsieur Benoît?

Benoît   Have a seat I thought we might have a little chat about your future how long have you been with the company now? Thirty-nine years? That's wonderful we've talked this over Grangier and I and we've decided to offer you the rest and relaxation you've unquestionably earned without your having to wait another four years until your sixty-fifth birthday

Mme Bachevski   But Monsieur Benoît I feel in great shape

Benoît   People say that and suddenly fall apart

Grangier   Especially bubbling dynamic personalities like you Madame Bachevski

Mme Bachevski   Does my work no longer please you?

Grangier   You've been doing splendidly

Benoît   But you're stuck on certain methods and old-fashioned attitudes

Saillant   And there comes an age when it's difficult

Grangier   If not impossible

Saillant   To recycle yourself this is not a criticism

Benoît   You've served the company earnestly and loyally

Saillant   And in recognition of this we've worked out a plan

Benoît   To ensure a gradual transition from your present income to that of your elderly years you'll hardly notice the change

Mme Bachevski   When must I leave?

Grangier   Today's Friday?

Benoît   This evening Madame Bachevski

Passemar   What dumbfounded her above all was to have been disposed of while her old adversary Madame Alvarez three years her senior had never lost an opportunity to sneer at Monsieur Benoît openly

Benoît   Send Passemar to me will you and ask Peyre to come in too

Grangier *and* **Saillant** *disappear;* **Passemar** *heads for* **Benôit**'s *office.*

Passemar   They say the mortality rate climbs with dizzying speed as soon as people are pensioned off

Benoît   You've nearly completed your six-month trial in marketing Passemar

Passemar   Yes sir

Benoît   It's time to take stock

Passemar   As far as I can see it hasn't really been conclusive

Peyre   In what way?

Passemar   I've shown enthusiasm I believe I've made some contributions brought in some ideas

Peyre   Certainly you have

Passemar   But I haven't how shall I put it? Really thrown myself into it

Benoît   How do you mean?

Peyre   Your abilities to analyse a problem have really been appreciated you've got a good brain

Passemar   Yes but there's something withdrawn in my character I can do nothing about

Benoît   Then you'll return to your old position on Monday morning

Benoît *and* **Peyre** *fade out.*

Passemar   I don't know what can have possessed me to indict myself like that perhaps if I'd said nothing they wouldn't have been so harsh perhaps they'd even have let me continue?

Mme Lépine   I'm counting on you you know?

Lubin   Have I ever let you down?

Passemar   A setback can never be wiped from your record it leaves a mark I can't really expect to last another how long? Twenty-three years?

Mme Lépine   Delivery tomorrow evening? Guaranteed?

Passemar   Twenty-three years in the same hole not on your life I suppose I just didn't want to hear them say what I was afraid they were going to say

Passemar *fades out.*

Lubin   How many of your clients are going for the family photo Madame Lépine?

Mme Lépine   All of them you know when I decide to push a promotion

Lubin   Nothing can hold you back

Mme Lépine   After that it's easy they love your product it's a winner

Benoît   I'm here to meet Monsieur Young

Young   Are you Monsieur Benoît Dehaze?

Benoît   Monsieur Young?

Young   Pleased to meet you Monsieur Dehaze it's kind of you to put youself out

Benoît   Delighted a scotch

Young   Two scotches I really admired your launch

Benoît   Coming from you that's a real compliment

Young   You've done a real professional job you're bound to succeed

Lubin   And how's Softies doing Madame Lépine?

Mme Lépine   I still sell a few from time to time

Young   Let's have a little talk about the future because as far as our worldwide expansion projects go we don't have any preconceived ideas when the time seems right we set up a subsidiary like in France whenever we sense a good opportunity we take over a company as in Italy in some countries we do both

Benoît   My company is not for sale

Young   Of course but I thought it might be useful for you to keep in the back of your mind that we have the means at our disposal to help a French company develop especially if it's ambitious and is having difficulties finding the necessary resources locally

Benoît   For the time being Monsieur

Young   Call me Ralph

Benoît   Ralph

Young   Can I call you Ben?

Benoît   Of course for the time being we're simply looking to hurt you as much we possibly can

Young   Well damn it Ben you're making a good job of it

Lubin   Yes this time it seems that they're going ahead and getting married

Mme Lépine   Good

Lubin   I've seen him he's a nice boy

Mme Lépine   Good so much the better

Lubin   Doesn't look at all Jewish you know?

Mme Lépine   That's good and when will it be?

Lubin   In less than a month I hope my wife will be out of the hospital

Mme Lépine   Very good

Lubin   Because every night she talked about suicide you know

Mme Lépine   She did?

Lubin   But seeing that her little girl's getting settled

Benoît (*in bed with* **Jenny**)   Why won't you marry me?

Jenny   I can't take the time off

Benoît   We'll find a moment

Jenny   I can't even afford a couple of hours to go to the hairdresser so I decided to cut it all off

Benoît   Makes you look like a page boy

Jenny   When I feel like being a lady I go through my

collection of wigs didn't I tell you about my new hobby? I already have a hundred and sixty-one

Benoît   We'll move into my father's apartment it's full of display cabinets we can use to exhibit your African fetishes and wigs

Jenny   No kidding Benoît there's a fantastic marketing opportunity there

Benoît   Why won't you marry me?

Jenny   If I had two or three lives maybe

Benoît   You marry me and I'll get Olivier to sell me his share of the business then when it's worth five or six times what it's worth now we'll go full tilt into this fantastic new marketing opportunity

Jenny   What will you do with your wife?

Benoît   We're getting divorced

Jenny   You're not taking me seriously wigs could really be a hit

Benoît   Do I look as though I'm laughing?

Jenny   Giving every woman the chance to multiply herself endlessly

Lubin   Well then I'll say goodbye take care of yourself Madame Lépine

Mme Lépine   Goodbye until next time Monsieur I'm sorry I can never remember your name

Lubin   Lubin that's all right you have to deal with so many of us

Mme Lépine   I suppose so yes so see you next time

Lubin   There won't be a next time I'm leaving the company

Mme Lépine   You don't mean it

Lubin   I'm afraid I do it's been a bit of a shock but what do you expect? If Monsieur Lévêque was still around to see how they're sending all his old reps to the block but when they heard my reply

Mme Lépine   What did they offer you?

Lubin   A place in the factory warehouse

Mme Lépine   And you turned it down?

Mme Lépine   I'm a born salesman Madame Lépine can you see me filling out receipts and issue vouchers from dawn to dusk?

Mme Lépine   But with your wife's condition what's going to happen to you?

Dutôt   Same thing same story (*Phone rings.*) hello? The Rueil company?

Benoît   Same at Vacheron? Same at Simonnot?

Dutôt   Pick up the other line (*On telephone.*) hello Monsieur Rueil what's that? Running low already? A tidal wave no rest assured we'll get it to you the lorry will leave tomorrow evening (*Hanging up.*) reorders are up one and a half times on the launch

Benoît   Are you keeping pace Grangier?

Grangier   I am

Benoît   Great hat Jack where's it from?

Jack   Moscow a pan-European vodka crab and caviare promotion

Benoît   Nice of you to stop in

Jack   I came to get news about the baby

Benoît   Doing pretty well at the rate we're going there'll soon be no room for anyone else

Jack   United Paper?

Benoît   Feeling the squeeze

Jack   Don't count your chickens Ben

Benoît   They just keep fucking up

Jiji   You freeze come here

*On the stage at The Clinic all musical instruments have been
replaced by assorted objects: pillow, hatchet, scyth, clothing,
vegetables, buckets of milk, pig tied to a stake, open sunglasses, bidet,
old books, television, bathtub, sausages, vat of manure above which,
suspended, seated on a swing,* **Jiji** *points at one or other of the
customers with the assistance of a water-pistol.* **Alex** *serves drinks.
Canned jazz comes through speakers.*

Father Motte   Who me? Oh I couldn't

Jiji   Yes you (**Father Motte** *is pushed on stage by the
crowd.*) and you come here and you too and you (*A man
and two women join* **Father Motte**.) you're crawlers, you
don't yet know how to walk, you haven't been born yet
(*The four chosen people lie on their stomachs among the objects.*)
birth is bad birth is nasty you're going to do everything
you can not to be born go on all of you you have two
minutes by my stop-watch to do the whole lot (*Still on the
ground, they perform various actions using the objects.*) you enter
the bathtub which is your mother (*They tumble into the
bathtub.*) it feels good here you don't want to leave you
build a barricade in your mother's vagina the mother of
the blessed and the damned Trotsky Guevara Ford
Rockefeller and you cry out you cry but the world doesn't
hear you

Climbing off her swing, **Jiji** *throws objects and liquids at random
into the bathtub as the four scream.*

Young   Oh that depends we use one year's turnover or
twenty times net profit as a yardstick

Benoît   Out of the question

Young   Sure but just in case let me add that a lot

hinges on our feelings about the business's growth potential

Benoît   Our growth potential? Practically unlimited

Young   And we attach a fundamental importance to the quality of executive personnel

Benoît   You'd keep on the executive team?

Young   We'd be fools not to

Benoît   Let's suppose it were to happen

Young   Yes?

Benoît   You'd fold your French subsidiary?

Young   Probably not

Benoît   You'd merge them?

Young   Why? We enjoy competing with ourselves

Benoît   As far as operations are concerned Ravoire et Dehaze would maintain its autonomy?

Young   Just like today the only difference being that we would plough in all the capital you need

Benoît   Which we could easily obtain elsewhere

Young   Good luck

Dr Temple   I'm sure we've already met (*The stage has emptied,* **Alex** *is tidying up, wiping, sweeping, while* **Jiji** *is back on the swing.*) I'm Dr Temple

Father Motte   I don't remember

Dr Temple   Didn't you assist one of my patients in his final moments? An interesting case of terminal brain damage

Father Motte   Indeed indeed

Dr Temple   Father Motte if I'm not mistaken

Father Motte Yes indeed this is a fascinating phenomenon

Dr Temple What is?

Father Motte This vogue for short improvised theatrical games their obscenity reflects the state of extreme distress into which our youth have plunged

Dr Temple Really? I find it rather entertaining I was watching you in the bathtub you seemed to be having the time of your life

Father Motte My life is devoted to helping the suffering

Benoît Things are going well I'd even say very well Ausange

Ausange My congratulations I've been reading your interviews in the financial press you've become a bit of a hero

Benoît Thanks to your support we were able to prove that initiative and success can thrive in this country

Alex Jiji

Jiji Alex

Alex Do you know what we're going to do because it's gone on long enough look at these people I mean look at them

Jiji These people are people

Alex Precisely

Jiji What are we going to do Alex?

Benoît To maintain momentum we need a two-fold increase in working capital

Ausange Your capital will increase fast as you reinvest profits

Benoît Not fast enough

Ausange Don't be in such a hurry

Benoît If we slow down the Americans will have time to catch their breath and crush us

Alex We're going to get up this basement as a gas chamber it's not much of a job all we need is a few pipes

Ausange We've already taken a huge risk with you

Benoît Can you or can't you Ausange?

Ausange To the extent that you've suggested? No bank could throw in that amount it's financially unthinkable

Alex Shower heads here and here in rows at the corner of the walls and ceiling and then one evening just like any other

Jiji With you and me inside?

Alex You and me and all these people

Benoît, **Jenny**, **Saillant**, **Peyre**, **Battistini**, **Dutôt**, **Grangier** *appear*.

Benoît I reserved a table for seven

Alex *seats them*.

Grangier This is great

Benoît Good Lord it's Father Motte isn't it?

Father Motte You come here too?

Benoît What are you doing here?

Father Motte A priest has to try and understand the world

Benoît You're not leaving?

Father Motte I've stayed far too long I'll come and see you soon I used to visit your father from time to time he was never deaf to my calls

He disappears.

Alex What'll you have Monsieur Dehaze?

Benoît We've known each other long enough why don't you call me Ben? I'm in such a good mood tonight what should I call you?

Alex Alex

Benoît Sit with us for a moment Alex I have to tell you Jenny Alex is a terrific guy he started this club from scratch look at what it's become

Peyre It's quite something

Benoît Alex is an intriguing fellow on the surface he always seems not to give a fuck but in point of fact he has to be a great marketing man

Jenny Indifference can be one hell of an image-builder

Benoît You sensed that free jazz was going to come back and you were the first to offer it on a regular basis

Alex Ah yes yes

Benoît It really took off then it went out of fashion and then came the stroke of genius the happenings

Alex The genius is my sweetheart Jiji

Peyre The girl on the swing?

Benoît In any case you know which way the wind's blowing my friend and that's what we're looking for right? You can search hard for people with flair

Saillant So if at any time you feel that

Benoît You've had enough of this life which I'm sure must be pretty hard-going

Peyre Like motor racing you shouldn't push it too long

Benoît Okay Alex? Whenever you're ready

Sixth Movement

The Wedding Banquet

On all sides buffet tables bearing mountains of food, barrels of Beaujolais and Black and White on tap. Everyone is there, eating, drinking, dancing, talking; two carpenters are building a small stage which an eletrician is equipping with spotlights, microphones and speakers; the stream of music is a mixture of pop, free jazz, Mozart piano sonatas; there are flowers everywhere; the managers, including **Benoît**, *are handing out plates, filling glasses and removing dirty crockery when they are not dancing. The talk is jumbled with occasional moments of clarity.*

— When?

— This time I've had it

— No why?

— Watch it

— Aren't you eating at all Joelle? Grab that nice little sausage

— I couldn't

— Why?

— Poor Bachevski

— It was kind of them to invite her all the same

— Don't tempt me I'm watching my figure

— I don't feel so sorry for her

— But your bottom's disappeared Joelle

— He wants me to stay under forty-five kilos

— Because he earns even less than me

— Shut up he's telling a story

— But the filling's good

— Who? Lubin?

— Not any more

— He resigned

— Happens every year

— I love the sun we went to Portugal

— How long had he been with us?

— But it rained for three weeks without stopping

— Last year he won the transistor radio

— That's the trouble with our kids they don't know how to have fun any more

— Two months later she got hemiplegia she'd been perfectly healthy until then

— My husband and I bought a new sofa

— As I was saying she'd only retired a couple of months earlier

— It pulls out into a bed

— She hasn't got over it has she?

— It comes with a lifetime guarantee

— That's what's breaking Joseph's heart

— Nice and comfy in front of the telly

— How fast can it go?

— The second or third already

— If you're tired it's a mistake to think that what you need is a rest

— But bringing home two salaries

— They were riding their brand new Italian motorcycles

— And some people want to abolish the death penalty

— But we live better than our parents did don't we?

— Don't touch me

— I just wanted to say something to you

— We've moved into two rooms couldn't be better

— By slamming her head against the table until she was dead

— How many times?

— Now the kiddies sleep in one and we've got our own

— You know she's not wearing a bra?

— Ask Monsieur Cohen he should know he lived through all that

— Under her blouse when she stands under the light

— On the motorway the other day

— The news came by telegram

— One of the three was an Arab

— Are you surprised?

— And another was Armenian

— Imagine Portugal and it rained all the time

— She said she'd take up upholstery

— That won't fill her days

— Yes in the shower

— Opposite the Town Hall

— With no hooks buttons or zips

— That's handy

— It holds up all by itself

— Mother would never let me

— You won't tell him?

— Three days without sobering up

— Tell me why do we work?

— My husband would love to get to know you

— Better this way

— Why's that?

— Of course I told him about you

— And what do you think the swelling was?

— Never in a good mood but he's nice

— That's the main thing

— I love seeing you like that

— Like what?

— I don't know

— What are you thinking about?

— We could see each other

— It's finished now

— Never say that

Benoît *has climbed onto the stage, he takes the microphone.*

Benoît   First and foremost we're gathered here today to hail and honour our friend Lubin come here Lubin come on up here next to me Lubin (**Lubin** *climbs onto the stage.*) has decided to part with us to start a new life this is an occasion for me to say loud and clear that Lubin has been and will always be remembered as a great salesman and a great member of the team so we all say good luck to you Lubin (*Shakes his hand.*)

— Hail Lubin speech Lubin speech

Lubin Monsieur le Président dear friends I think this is
really something this whole feast really is something
sensational it's hard for me hard to put into words but

— It's all too clear

— Don't pinch me

— It wasn't me

Lubin I do appreciate everything that you've done for
me I know you've done it out of the goodness of your
hearts

— In this kind of case you should lodge a complaint

— What could she have said? She doesn't know who it
was

Lubin It's such a wonderful day and my wife who can't
be here with me to see it

— But they don't have the right to

— Go and tell them at the police station

Lubin The doctors won't yet say what effect the shock
therapy will have but Jiji you'll tell her all about this
you'll be kind to her Jiji my Jiji's going to be happy and
I'd like to thank the company for the magnificent wedding
present which Jiji has been given come up here Jiji (**Jiji**
climbs onto the stage.) and show them the present a
Moulinex Universal food processor there's nothing it can't
do

Benoît You're not leaving us entirely Lubin because
your son-in-law here is going to join our team I'd like to
introduce Alex Klein to all of you come on up Alex

Alex *climbs onto the stage followed by* **Mme Lépine** *who grabs
the microphone.*

Mme Lépine Listen on behalf of all Monsieur Lubin's
customers I'd like to say that he's always been an honest
man who did his job properly we'd become quite used to

him

Benoît He carried the banner of the firm year in year out

Mme Lépine I used to let him count my stock he'd say Madame Lépine you need so many fine I'd say to him put me down for so many if he said you need six cartons I told him put me down for six cartons he knew my turnover you could really trust Monsieur Lubin and I say he served his company well

Mme Lépine *climbs off the stage in tears.*

— An unpredictable bloke

— He does things to you

— I love it

— Shut up if only you knew

Benoît Lubin will linger on in our thoughts but he's not leaving us entirely since his son-in-law is jumping on board to start a new department the merchandising department where all his talents will be put to good use

— Did you see it?

— I missed it

— It'll be on again

— I cried and cried

Benoît And may this friendly little gathering serve as a wedding banquet for him and this radiant young lady here who is as bright as she is sweet and I see in the forthcoming marriage of this charming and ambitious couple an omen predicting an era of unrivalled prosperity for our company

— Bravo

— Long live the bride and groom

—   Speech

Alex   My father died falling backwards into a pool of shit pushed by an SS officer and now I'm

—   Louder

Alex   I'm entering I'm falling headlong

—   We can't hear you

Alex   I said I'm falling headlong

—   Volume

Alex   But not a free fall no that would be monotonous I'm bouncing from side to side I'm entering normal life

—   No more worries

Alex   Normality until now forbidden me is bliss too great a temptation what a view tongue hanging out eyes wide open

—   If you can

—   Don't give up

Alex   Nostrils flaring if you only knew

—   You're all dolled up today Mademoiselle Louise

Alex   What's been let loose but the die is cast Ariadne my sister who's accommodating whom? Who's screwing whom? When you're screwing you're being screwed farewell light come Jiji let's take the first step together hold my hand it's slippery

Jiji, **Alex**, *and* **Lubin** *get down off the stage while* **Father Motte** *climbs up.*

Benoît   And we wish you every happiness and now here's Father Motte over to you Father

Father Motte   We all know instinctively that a celebration such as this is an infinitely precious source of hope of more than hope of the desire that we share that one day everything shall be as one one in all and all in one that which unites us outstrips that which divides us reconciliation must surely follow discord when brother confronts brother each rediscovers the path which leads to the other's heart this morning while giving my blessing to the young couple before the altar

Benoît   And now I must announce to you that my brother

Father Motte *leaves the stage.*

—   I said I was sorry

—   But it was too late

Benoît   Is leaving us he has decided to sail away

Olivier *climbs onto the stage.*

—   Did he recognise you?

Benoît   Am I right Olivier? So as to invest all of his energy

Olivier·   Yes concentrate all my efforts

Benoît   On a new enterprise which he plans to found beyond the seas

Olivier   On the other side of the ocean

Benoît   It is grievous of course to see him sever his ties with a company which he has served so well and lo and behond although we thought him a confirmed bachelor

Olivier   Yes I'm getting married

Margery *climbs onto the stage.*

Margery   My friends at dawn tomorrow Olivier and I will set sail in *Le France* for the United States I'm leaving a large piece of my heart behind me because I love your culture so much my Olivier and I are bound for San Francisco waving the flag of La Pompadour a beauty parlour which we'll open as a French challenge to all those heartless salons where beauty is sold off at the assembly line and if any of you ever happens to find yourself passing through

Toppfer *leaps onto the stage and grabs the microphone.*

Toppfer   Words fail the seasoned antique dealer who stands beside you my dear sweet Madame to tell you of his joy tinged with sadness

Margery   Same for me joy and sadness all at once

Toppfer   Following so many other treasures of the old world they too are off to America those snuff boxes so lovingly collected through the years by your zealous president

— We know you know and I know

— You don't have to tell me

Toppfer   But thanks to your overriding passion they shall be spared the unfeeling hammer of the auctioneer

— You understand

— Like hell I do

Toppfer *leaves the stage.*

Benoît   Three men who have proven their worth in the heat of action

— I thought it was

— I took some

Benoît   Now see their merits recognised with a promotion (**Saillant** *gets up on stage.*) André Saillant succeeds my brother as assistant general manager Claude Dutôt who wrought havoc among enemy ranks (**Dutôt** *gets up on stage.*) becomes director of sales

Dutôt   What is a captain without his troops? My thanks to the whole sales force

Benoît And Jean-Baptise Peyre (**Peyre** *gets up on stage.*) is promoted to director of marketing even though the success of Moss and Heather lay in our combined creative effort

— A stupid accident

— At a crossroads

Benoît The product needed a mastermind

Peyre All I did was tap your brains only a few short months ago do you remember? We had to birth it feed it protect it and now that it's up and running there's no stopping it

Saillant, **Peyre**, **Dutôt** *leave the stage.*

Benoît And now a case of recycling that should be an inspiration to all of us come on up Cohen where is Cohen?

— Here he is

— He's coming

Benoît Head of accounts for twenty-two years thirty-six years with the company and younger at heart than any of us

— Bravo

Benoît Now he's promoted to information systems manager hardware software programming in bas cobol or fortran are no longer mysteries to Cohen he's mastered all the latest techniques

Cohen, *who seems to have hurt his leg, is cheered onto the stage.*

Cohen Yes yes I'm reminded of a story my grandfather used to tell on Shabbas when I was a little boy I used to hide under the table to put off the moment when I had to start my lessons but the rabbi said to me look at what the flowers on the hillside are doing they are singing and the birds smell wonderful and there isn't anything that isn't

springing up again it's true that suffering exists who better
than me to bear witness to that? But suffering is the
singing flower on the hillside for which we must thank our
management and above all Monsieur Benoît

Benoît   And she tells me that she has never in her life
been so busy nevertheless she agreed to interrupt all of
her activities come up here dear Madame Bachevski
(**Mme Bachevski** *gets up on stage while Cohen is helped off.*)
in order to join us today and see all her friends again

Mme Bachevski   Besieged with things to do can't cope
with it all my little garden you should see the lovely beans
shooting up my upholstery when they rip you open and
pull out your bowels they stitch you up again but there's
a hollowness inside that keeps you awake I've never made
a secret of what I think never had any hidden thoughts
I've always given more than I've received and I gave my
whole self to the company I thank Monsieur Benoît for
inviting me thank you thank you for everything that
you've done thank you all of you thank you for everything

Mme Alvarez *climbs on stage and takes the microphone.*

Mme Alvarez   Everything she's said is true we rose
through the company together she and I watching her go
was like watching a chunk of me being torn off she was
always dedicated to her job and I wish for her in her
remaining years

Mme Alvarez *and* **Mme Bachevski** *weep, hug each other,
and leave the stage.*

Benoît   Come on up Ausange remember the day I
spoke to you

Ausange   Indeed between money and poetry

Benoît   And you believed me

Ausange   Both instruments of exchange between men

Benoît   This act of faith was the origin

Ausange   The difference

Benoît   Of the great boom

Ausange   Is more apparent than real

Benoît   Which has carried us

Ausange   The poet and the banker

Benoît   Soaring high

Ausange   Have one and the same duty

Benoît   Against all the odds

Ausange   To quench the thirst of whoever is in need

Jack *and* **Jenny** *appear.*

Jack   Hi there

Benoît   Here are the craftsmen

Jenny   Hello boys

Benoît   The alchemists

Jack   Shut up Ben

Benoît   The engineers

Jack   You French

Benoît   Of our comeback

Jack   You're robbers

Benoît   As a token of my gratitude

Jack   You're tearing her away from me Ben you've got your paws on her and what am I supposed to do? Ah who cares big kiss Jenny

Jenny   God bless you Jacky boy

Jack   So long sweetheart

Jenny   Be good now

Benoît   We've decided Jenny and me

Jenny   We're going to start a company

Benoît   Metahair

Jenny   Limited and then married we shall be

Jack   To wigs and your health

Jenny   To opportunity

Benoît   Cheers

Jack *leaves the stage,* **Benoît** *and* **Jenny** *embrace.*

Jenny   Our confident philosophy

Benoît   Our aggressivity

Jenny   Our carnivorous savagery

Benoît   Enemy joined with enemy

Jenny   To forge a new identity

Benoît   Endowed with each fine quality

Jenny   Tried and tested *aujourd'hui*

Benoît   This *rapprochement* or unity

Jenny   Affords us unrivalled glee

Benoît   We're forming an alliance with the most powerful company in our field anywhere in the world

Jenny   Just believe in what you see

Benoît   Here's Ralph Young

Young *has climbed onto the stage.*

Jenny   We're personally quite proud of this

Benoît   Senior vice-president United Paper Company of Minneapolis

Jenny   Exceptionally soft

Benoît   Velvety

Young   My friends *c'est avec beaucoup d'émotion*

Jenny   Gentle wipeability

Benoît   Durability

Young   *C'est un réel privilège*

Jenny   Easy to maintain

Benoît   And finished to the nth degree

Young   You're joining a great family United Paper Company has taken root in sixty-one countries and every one of our plants displays the same family spirit the U-P-Co spirit we like to call it *l'esprit U-P-Co* you can tell a U-P-Co man wherever he is at the airport on a beach he's got an open face a confident walk you've shown you've got the nerve all you need are the lungs to breathe better and that's all we're giving you a really great lungful of air it's up to you to run with the ball of course we'll be around to guide you with our know-how in the areas of research and development financial planning and marketing we'll work out the really big decisions together but otherwise you're on your own the company that we're buying isn't just the machines or the buildings or the products it's the people *c'est les gens* it's all of you that we want it's you that we have it's you you you U-P-Co U-P-Co ra ra U-P-Co U-P-Co ra ra

The festivities continue.

—   The poor thing was so bloated I hardly recognised her

—   A few palm trees the sea

—   I'm going

—   Where to?

—   To gobble you up

— Sand in your eyes

— My heart doesn't react any more

— I'm afraid are you?

— We don't have time

— The kids won't have any of it

— I've put mirrors everywhere

— Keep the change I told him

— And I'm hardly overplaying it

— But is it real?

— How many times?

— You give him

— Everything you've got and the rest

— She takes it from you

— I don't know if it was Marion

— Or Helen

— Who's that dancing with her?

— And what does that do?

— Especially the blood test

— I never wear gloves even in winter

— The contact with the steering wheel

— There's no test for it but I'm sure there's a virus going round

— It lays you out

— Alone on the ground floor

— It's a great occasion

— The police didn't hang around

— He was afraid someone would give him an injection
— There was a time when children
— In the morning when I get up
— They had to
— My head falls back down
— He said he and his friends needed a drink
— Yes but things are different now
— Don't you think she's attractive?
— Skinny
— For crying out loud
— She doesn't suspect a thing
— She took out a jug and glasses
— What do you expect?
— And then
— No the head
— Against the wall?
— No against the table
— Run-of-the-mill stuff
— When I'm behind the wheel it's different
— It's because the war's over
— Kids
— We could never find them before
— Wall-to-wall carpeting whatever colour you like
— It's the freedom
— And when there's no sun?
— Yes it's practical

— Me too

— But not as much?

— It's different

— On the terrace

— I can't

— We put in some bonsai trees from Japan

— A man that I didn't recognise

— I think I'm going to be sick

— And that'll be an end to it

— We don't any more

— We buy when we want to

— The good life

— Leave it

— I can't

— Soon

— Do tell

Passemar   Keep a cool head don't let yourself get off track bite the bullet (*Reading from a handwritten sheet, pen in hand.*) are you looking for a dynamic experienced sales administration manager (*The festivities continue, but the sound is cut.*) with a taste for innovation and responsibility? Sounds better than the first which said up-and-coming young graduate able and confident should I include my age? Most ads in the Wanted columns say you're an aggressive executive twenty-five to thirty-five which makes me a good ten years older than what they're looking for but there's bound to be a firm at least one that'll find what I have to offer attractive anyhow I'm coming to the end of my play I think I may have put too much in it I'm not opposed to a bit of pruning what I hope to preserve is the structure

which I don't mind admitting I borrowed from
Aristophanes all of his plays finish with a sacrifice as well
as a marriage at the end there's a feast and a
procession which is how the actors leave the stage what
with this classified ad and the play you could say I'm
throwing two bottles in the sea at once who knows? They
might keep me on till retirement twenty-three years from
now but I'm a little sceptical when I hear this man from
United say nothing will change of course everything will
change soon enough for better or worse who knows? In
any case I've struck a deal with my dancers they'll play
the scene where they unload the lorry which they think is
trivial and they'll even do the market research interviews
which they loathe as long as I let them put on a little
dance at the end they've worked hard at it and they
promise that it'll be over in no time

The three **Dancers** *come forward with the pianist and* **M.
Onde** *who, dressed in sportswear and seated on a wicker armchair,
takes his place on stage in front of the microphone.*

M. Onde   And yet the Aesir triumph is not definitive for
against all expectations the Vanir manage to destroy the
Aesir ramparts and as if they have suddenly tired of this
exhausting alternation of failure and success which seems
to be leading nowhere the Aesir and Vanir broker peace a
peace which none could have expected a peace as
harmonious as the war has been relentless where no
compromise has seemed possible suddenly there grows
understanding (*The three* **Dancers**, *really enjoying themselves,
grab hold of* **Passemar**, *lift him and carry him in a procession
and, joined by all the revellers, dance the farandole.*) and now
until the end of time not even the shadow of a conflict
shall ever arise between the Aesir and the Vanir

Passemar   So that the end meets with the beginning

Situation Vacant

La Demande d'emploi

a play in thirty pieces

translated by JOHN BURGESS

Characters

Fage, *forty-three years old*
Louise, *his wife*
Nathalie, *their daughter*
Wallace, *director of Executive Recruitment, CALI*

They are on stage throughout.

Author's Note

The play was written in 1970, i.e.

– two years after the student uprising of May 1968 and the ensuing political events which nearly toppled the French Fifth Republic; radical action persisted through the following few years, particularly in schools and universities;

– two years after abortion was made legal in the United Kingdom, and five years *before* a law to that effect was voted in France.

The play takes place in Paris at the time it was written.

12 April 1989

Situation Vacant was first performed in the UK on 16 March 1989 at the Orange Tree Theatre, Richmond, with the following cast:

Fage   Paul Moriarty
Louise   Auriol Smith
Nathalie   Emma D'Inverno
Wallace   Gareth Armstrong

Directed by Sam Walters

One

Wallace   Born June 14th 1927 in Madagascar

Louise   Darling

Fage   Physically I'm

Wallace   Obviously

Louise   What time is it?

Nathalie   You can't do this to me Daddy

Fage   It's a shared ideal I mean one's not just in it for the money

Louise   Why didn't you wake me?

Fage   I was going to but you were fast asleep

Wallace   What were your parents doing in Madagascar in 1927?

Fage   You had your arm bent you looked lovely

Nathalie   Look if you force me

Louise   I didn't do your shoes

Fage   My father was a doctor in the army serving overseas

Louise   They were all muddy

Nathalie   Daddy answer me

Fage   Stationed at Tananarive

Wallace   In our firm

Fage   Of course I can't remember that far back

Wallace   What we're interested in is people

Louise   And I was going to give your trousers a press as well

Fage   That's one of the reasons why I answered your

advertisement why your firm appeals to me

Wallace   You weigh

Fage   Sixty-seven kilos

Wallace   And are how tall

Fage   One metre seventy-one married with one child a girl sixteen soon be seventeen we had a son as well but he was killed in a car crash   .

Two

Fage   Physically? Completely fit

Wallace   Yes I can see that strong constitution

Fage   It's all arranged I've got your two tickets to London

Wallace   How about your nerves?

Louise   Except she says she won't go

Fage   I'll put her on the plane by the scruff of her neck

Louise   But darling

Wallace   How about your nerves?

Louise   They won't let you through passport control

Fage   Give her some pills or something

Louise   What sort of pills for heaven's sake?

Fage   My nerves? Pretty steady they need to be

Nathalie   Daddy there's something I want to tell you

Fage   Well?

Nathalie   I'm going to have a baby

Fage   By whom?

Nathalie   Somebody called Mulawa

Wallace   So you decided to hand in your resignation

Louise   It's the little things that make the difference at a first meeting shoes nicely polished clean nails

Fage   I know tie straight

Louise   Clean shirt

Wallace   Go on

Nathalie   You've met him I brought him home a couple of times

Fage   Trousers pressed

Wallace   The person we're looking for won't be dictated to by circumstance

Fage   Won't let himself be fobbed off

Wallace   He'll get a grip on things

Fage   There's a whole stream of them passing through how do you expect me to remember

Nathalie   Of course you remember him he's black

Louise   The post darling Renault we regret to inform you that the vacancy has already been filled Dim Stockings thank you for your letter unfortunately Philips thank you for letting us see your curriculum vitae but Givenchy in reply to your letter asking if we had any vacancies Pingouin thank you very much for your

Fage   What do you mean black?

Nathalie   Pitch black

Louise   They might at least try to make their circumstances a bit less anonymous ah but there's a genuine letter it's from Colgate Palmolive looks like they've actually answered

Wallace   What was it made you resign exactly?

Fage   Black are you serious? Well I must say have you told your mother?

Louise   They want to see you as soon as possible darling it's quite encouragingly written

Nathalie   I thought I'd leave that to you

Louise   Two o'clock Tuesday at Courbevoie

Fage   I'll go along and see good solid firm I must say I never thought they would ask to see me

Wallace   You resigned because

Nathalie   Aren't you going to say anything?

Louise   Why not?

Wallace   I see what you mean you're not cut out for sheer repetitive drudgery

Fage   Those big multinationals won't even consider you once you're over thirty-five

Three

Wallace   Do you smoke?

Fage   Thanks I don't

Wallace   You don't either

Fage   You've given it up as well have you?

Wallace   About three years ago

Fage   Me too about two and a half years ago something like that

Wallace   Your fingers are still a bit yellow

Fage   No

Wallace   A bit

Fage This letter's dated the 3rd of February today's the 16th when did it arrive?

Wallace Would you say you were a straightforward sort of person?

Louise I don't know I'm sure I've never seen this envelope before instead of shouting at me why don't you go and ask Nathalie she's usually the one who goes to get the post

Fage Perrier they're keen to see me but it's too late

Nathalie You haven't seen my maths book have you Daddy?

Wallace What we're looking for is someone with drive well not only drive

Fage The appointment was for yesterday

Louise Why don't you phone them and explain?

Nathalie What envelope? How should I know?

Fage Nathalie listen to me will you I'm trying to get a job just one that's all and every letter that comes could be that one job

Nathalie I want to have it and keep it

Fage Just one miserable little job that's all

Louise Darling when did she tell you? Are you sure it's not some kind of joke?

Fage Nathalie you're still at school

Nathalie I don't want to keep it for ever just a couple of years or so until it learns to talk

Wallace A combination of drive and a deeply creative personality

Fage You don't want a me-too kind of person you want someone who will generate new ideas which is exactly what I'm good at

Wallace   Well it's not just a question of having good ideas

Fage   You've got to carry them out

Wallace   Not only that Monsieur Fage you must have a very special feel so that each and every one of your ideas will tie in with company philosophy

Fage   Look Nathalie it's not asking much

Wallace   Blend

Fage   Just see if you can't think about other people for a change when you go and get the post all you're interested in are your own letters otherwise you just put them down wherever you happen to be and leave other people to find them again two or three weeks later if they're lucky do you know how many offers like this I've received since I started? Do you?

Wallace   Maybe now you'd like to tell me what makes you think you'd be successful if you got the job

Louise   Why don't you give Perrier a ring?

Fage   I don't think that'd make a very good impression

Louise   Perhaps it got stuck in the post darling down at the bottom of one of the bags

Fage   She just couldn't care less

Louise   Oh no that's terrible

Wallace   Yes tell me what it is you want out of life

Fage   Professionally or life in general?

Louise   She lives in a world of her own

Wallace   What's your goal? Where do you want to get to?

Louise   She wants to see it walk and then give it away?

Nathalie   You're not going to make me go to London

Louise   Oh intellectually she's mature enough dealing with abstractions but as far as real intelligence goes in real life

Nathalie   My maths book Mummy

Louise   Wasn't it lying about last night in the kitchen somewhere?

Wallace   Not any higher? Why not? What I'm trying to do is get a feel of what your limits are

Louise   She wants to see it start to talk and then kiss it goodbye as if she didn't know the first thing they always say is Mama

Fage   Why don't you have a talk with her?

Louise   You know perfectly well she refuses to have anything to do with me

Four

Fage   The job fits me and I would fit the job you could almost call it a perfect fit

Nathalie   Careful Daddy you'll have to watch that turn it's a sheer drop on the other side

Wallace   Well yes human contacts being of paramount importance and that's what you're particularly good at establishing aren't you?

Nathalie   Don't drift mind the curve of the slope

Fage   It's breathtaking

Louise   The only way to get her to London is for you to take her she won't go with me

Nathalie   Beyond those pines it drops about forty metres it's narrow so you'll have to *schuss*

Fage   Given the circumstances I'd have thought it was more the mother's job

Louise   Yes but she's got a thing about me my fault of course I've always been firm with her but you

Fage   I'm much stricter with her than you my love

Louise   Strict all you do is crawl

Fage   With you it just develops into a shouting match I can't understand it you're normally so even-tempered

Nathalie   After that it's plain sailing

Louise   I can feel her shutting this door in my face

Nathalie   Ready?

Fage   No go on you lead the way

Nathalie   That was fantastic Daddy

Five

Nathalie   Oh go to London with you? We could go to Carnaby Street and down King's Road do the shops go to a disco

Fage   Sugar Bun we're not going to London just for the fun of it

Wallace   Have you got something in your mouth? You look as if you're chewing something

Fage   It came as a real relief to me

Wallace   In seven years you'd tripled the turnover reorganised the sales force built up custom introduced modern merchandising techniques

Fage   When this pathetic creature Bergognan ushered me into his office with a mournful smile

Wallace   Didn't you say that you resigned?

Fage   They made it look like that but in fact they just threw me out overnight like an errand boy they typed out a letter of resignation for me to sign standing in the corridor

Louise   Kiss me

Nathalie   Griffith who takes us for Complementary Studies is really super this morning

Louise   Hold me tight

Fage   By that time Bergognan was no more than a puppet

Louise   Tell me it's going to be all right

Nathalie   This morning he had us all sitting on the floor in a circle introduction to Buddhist meditation you know there are special techniques for meditating but girls are so silly

Louise   Yes I am a bit frightened

Nathalie   Some of them got the giggles

Fage   It's been twenty-three years but you want to know something that'll surprise you I'm glad

Louise   No it's not that I don't think you'll find another job I know it'll all work out you'll find exactly what you're looking for

Nathalie   Boys aren't that self-conscious they thought it was super

Louise   I'm frightened of losing you

Fage   Particularly when one's at the height of one's powers and is determined to bounce back

Nathalie   One of them actually managed to take off

Louise   I want you to tell me

Fage   It comes as a bit of a shock sets you back a bit

but once you manage to pick yourself up off the floor

Louise   Darling a woman needs

Fage   Bang marvellous I think it's the best thing that could have happened to me especially when it hits you like that out of a clear sky it really shakes you up

Wallace   So you say a thankful prayer for Monsieur Bergognan

Fage   A poor fish if ever there was one

Wallace   For having taught you that hard rock certitudes can just go up in smoke?

Nathalie   We were all of us sitting in a circle it was unbelievable Griffith was really nervous

Louise   Where did you get this spot on your coat from darling?

Fage   Of the two of us my love

Louise   What?

Fage   You're the stronger

Nathalie   We waited for him to surface

Fage   The more courageous

Nathalie   It was so intense

Fage   Nothing's changed no of course not

Louise   I don't seem to be able to

Fage   Don't worry

Louise   It isn't grease

Fage   That's the real acid test

Louise   I've tried everything

Fage   Better days ahead

Louise   Tired?

Fage Anything in the post?

Louise Come to bed

Six

Wallace For this job? We must have had between one hundred and fifty and two hundred applicants

Louise What with the airplane tickets the clinic the hotel and all the extras

Fage I don't see what else we can do

Nathalie Daddy's pulling the most awful face I know where he's been

Wallace This first screening allows us to sort out thirty or so likely candidates who then get a preliminary interview from my subordinates

Louise I'm just thinking about the money

Nathalie He's been to get his weekly allowance

Louise You mustn't talk about your father like that Nathalie

Nathalie He always has this awful face when he gets back

Fage Very well done too your people are real pros I've done enough interviewing myself to appreciate

Louise It's not very nice for him he has to spend hours standing in a queue they're all mixed in together office workers labourers executives

Wallace In this particular case we selected six for interview in depth

Louise Dinner's ready

Nathalie It's like a fairy story

Louise   What's that face supposed to mean?

Nathalie   Veal stew ugh

Wallace   Which I conduct myself

Nathalie   Once upon a time in this little cottage

Louise   It was today's special offer

Fage   Delicious

Nathalie   The Redundancies an everyday story of life on the dole once upon a time in this little cottage there lived Father Redundancy and Mother Redundancy and their little daughter Baby Redundancy it was a very cosy little cottage every day Mother Redundancy would come back from the shops where she'd bought all the special offers Father Redundancy would bury his nose in the paper

Fage   I think you're laying too much stress on the psychological side of it

Louise   No she's really very sensitive

Wallace   Of these six I try to eliminate four leaving me with two whom I can put forward to the head of the department for a final interview but it sometimes happens I put forward three or only one or even none at all and then we just have to start again

Louise   It's just that she bottles it all up inside

Nathalie   Little Miss Redundancy was listening to the radio lying on her stomach with her feet in the air when suddenly

Fage   So it's not you

Wallace   No it's always the head of department who makes the decision occasionally if it's a position of particular importance the managing director himself may decide to attend the final interview

Louise   It's bound to be traumatic for her

Fage   They put them to sleep they don't feel a thing it's like posting a letter

Louise   It's not as simple as that

Wallace   It's the one area where you simply can't afford to make a mistake yet it's also the area in which mistakes are the most difficult to avoid

Louise   Psychologically and physiologically any woman would find it a shock

Wallace   There are so many imponderables

Louise   And she's still so young

Wallace   It's a real bogey subjective factors count for so much of course it'd be a mistake to try and eliminate them what should happen between the company and the new recruit is something in the nature of a love match

Fage   I'll take her off skiing for a week that'll cheer her up

Nathalie   What do you do while you're waiting? Tell each other dirty stories?

Louise   Nathalie

Nathalie   What's wrong with imagining things?

Louise   A week at Courchevel? What are you going to use for money?

Wallace   We like to look on each applicant

Louise   London and then Courchevel? Sounds more like a honeymoon to me

Wallace   You for instance

Fage   Me?

Wallace   As being potentially the next chief executive

Fage   Why me?

Wallace   I look at every applicant in that light

Fage   Don't worry darling

Louise   I'm not worrying I'm just counting how much we've got left in the bank

Fage   Everything'll work out for the best

Louise   This little jaunt of yours

Fage   I think I can see a gleam of light at the end of the tunnel

Louise   What it's going to cost

Fage   Sssssh

Seven

Wallace   Considering CALI's profile as a company young modern dynamic

Fage   Where does the name CALI come from?

Wallace   Guess

Fage   Well there's a Hindu god

Wallace   Yes more and more nowadays the West is turning to the East for the spiritual resources it needs to stand up to the chilly antiseptic atmosphere of a technocratic society I'll give you a clue something something Leisure Industries

Fage   Something activities

Wallace   Not activities no

Fage   Community something Community Adventure

Louise   Time we were going

Fage   Come on Nathalie

Nathalie I'm not going near that clinic

Fage We'll talk about that on the way

Nathalie Man takes daughter to London to kill her baby I can see it in the Sunday papers

Fage Something something Leisure Industries

Wallace Creative Alternative Leisure Industries there's hardly a month or a week even goes by without some offshoot from the original stem which first came into existence five years ago the idea was for it to be the same sort of thing as the Club Méditerranée but with the accent more on the search for peace getting together people from a wide range of countries and backgrounds you see CALI came into being as the result of a meeting between two conscientious objectors a Frenchman and an American

Fage I'm forty-three years old I was born in Madagascar

Louise Where have you been it's very late

Fage They kept me hanging about for no reason at all it was most humiliating

Louise You look worn out

Fage They were incredibly rude

Louise You weren't what they were looking for?

Nathalie We had Greek unseens today

Fage It wasn't that so much it was just a Christ-awful job

Nathalie A rude bit of Thucydides

Fage And the pay was ludicrous

Nathalie I had a couple of slips fair enough but a bit of it was so rude she thought I'd got it wrong the truth is she couldn't understand it

Louise   Just for once in a while you won't come top

Nathalie   It's so boring seeing the two of you every day

Fage   They had the nerve to call it a senior sales executive position what they wanted was a graphic artist someone to design handouts

Wallace   Apart from skiing and tennis what other sports do you play?

Fage   For a new brand of cheeses

Louise   Look after yourself

Fage   Yes

Louise   And God bless

Eight

Fage   When I took over the sales force the first thing I did was I got rid of all the dead wood and replaced it with younger men all raring to go

Nathalie   I met him at the university bookshop in the mythology section

Fage   Within a couple of years I'd completely turned the situation round you see Bergognan

Nathalie   He thought I was one of the shop assistants

Louise   Darling I find you a bit frightening at the moment

Fage   Artistically there's no question about his talent he designs all the new models himself but talk to him about management about methods

Nathalie   He asked me if I'd got *The Raw and the Cooked* by Lévi-Strauss

Wallace   Would you say you were temperamental?

Louise   I know it's been four months now but we can hold on for six months or more

Wallace   Easily hurt?

Nathalie   I told him I was just passing through

Fage   Call it luck the three men directly under him proved to be on top of their job a trio who believed in what they were doing

Wallace   Persevering?

Fage   Who could see the potential that was in there an advertising man an accountant and we got stuck in with a vengeance

Nathalie   He said he was sorry

Louise   Provided you don't lose heart my darling I know how talented you are

Nathalie   I laughed

Fage   Because you see when Bergognan put me in charge of sales

Louise   You know I've always been proud of you yes I really admire you

Fage   There was no policy no strategy no nothing

Nathalie   I helped him look for his book we went through the shelves together

Louise   Even more now than when I first met you

Fage   You ask me if I'm go-ahead it's not just a question of getting things moving

Louise   It's just that if sales are your speciality you ought to try and sell yourself a bit more

Nathalie   He told me he was descended from cannibals and his grandfather was a chief

Louise   You ought to try and push yourself a bit more

Fage   It's a question of faith it's incredible the amount of energy that was needed because it was Monsieur Bergognan's attitude to oppose initiative always

Louise   You've had some splendid successes

Nathalie   He asked me to have a fruit juice with him

Fage   I mean you've only got to look at the size of it now

Wallace   Are you easily put out?

Nathalie   I asked him what he did

Wallace   Do you ever get carried away? Say things that you later regret?

Fage   Last year when we launched our new He Man range we took second place in the market behind Petit Bateau Bergognan started panicking it made him feel dizzy

Nathalie   He said he was a student and doing a bit of pushing on the side

Louise   You've got to be patient keep calm till the time comes you'll be able to bounce back higher than you were before you see

Wallace   Are you ever dissatisfied with decisions you've taken? Are you a perfectionist?

Fage   People were telling him he couldn't hope to hold his own he ought to get out while the going was good there were these sharks who'd had their eye on him for some time a German an Italian and two American firms

Wallace   What about your wife? As a woman

Fage   My wife it's funny she's not the kind of woman who

Wallace   Do you usually plan things out thoroughly in advance?

Louise   You've got no authority over her

Fage   We're happy

Louise   Blind

Fage   A happy family

Wallace   Have you a head for figures?

Fage   Oh but she's an accomplished skier she's fast and absolutely fearless sometimes

Louise   I think you're looking at her through rose-tinted spectacles

Wallace   Are you a fast worker?

Fage   She takes me to such places no one would dare

Wallace   Once you've started so you see things through?

Fage   Oh yes always

Wallace   Punctual?

Fage   That's right no slacking

Wallace   Easy to get on with?

Fage   I should say so

Wallace   Approachable?

Fage   Very

Wallace   Able to take unpopular decisions?

Fage   Taught myself to be

Wallace   Tough?

Fage   How do you mean?

Wallace   With your subordinates

Fage   When I have to be but not cold

Wallace   Fair?

Fage   Yes

Wallace   Cautious?

Nine

Wallace   What about your daughter?

Nathalie   Can't you understand how fantastic it is having a baby?

Fage   It's a serious business you know not something to be taken lightly

Wallace   How old is she?

Fage   Quite a big girl now nearly finished at the lycée she's very bright no problem there I'm taking her to Courchevel for a week to recover

Wallace   Has she been ill?

Fage   A little accident

Wallace   I'm very fond of Courchevel myself

Fage   What is it you want?

Nathalie   I want to know what it's like giving birth breast-feeding it teaching it to walk then I'll pass it on there's any number of people wanting to adopt

Fage   Oh yes Les Trois Vallées for skiing there's nowhere else like it in Europe

Wallace   We've got a development underway there ourselves two and a half million

Fage   I just don't understand you at all

Nathalie   That's because you're only seeing me on one level but I exist on lots of levels

Fage   Where did you get that belt?

Nathalie   I bought it

Fage   With whose money?

Nathalie   I took it from Mama's handbag

Fage   You know how much we're trying to economise your mother and I

Nathalie   I wish we really were penniless I'd like to be either very rich or very poor (*Cutting up the belt with a penknife.*) money doesn't mean a thing money's just what you get for working

Wallace   As an organisation what makes CALI unique is that it's a beast with two heads one in New York the other in Paris. You speak fluent English of course

Fage   I can get by

Wallace   The post we're trying to fill has come up as a result of the need to find a new formula for the vast number of American tourists who are left with the choice of either planning their own trip and making a mess of it or else going on a package tour where they're herded together like cattle in the same way this new department will be two-headed with someone at the New York end to look after sales and get the groups on their way and someone at the European end who'll look after the itineraries and generally see to their welfare it's important that he should be a salesman too because it's the success of the trips he organises that will turn each of his clients into a walking advertisement for CALI Mrs Jones in Brooklyn telling her neighbours about her night in the Ankara Hilton the spit-roasted lamb and so on will be drumming up custom for the following year this is why your being primarily sales oriented

Fage   You mentioned the Hilton will we really be putting people up in the Hilton?

Wallace   Why not? The purchasing power you'll have at your disposal will enable you to book entire Hiltons in the

off-season for the price of a third-class hotel which means
that you'll be able to offer people holidays beyond their
wildest dreams

Fage   My head's buzzing with ideas I'd book my
reservations one year even two years in advance even the
most palatial establishments would be tempted by a
guarantee like that

Wallace   You'd have to arrange trips to the largest
possible number of cities in the shortest possible time
you've got to give them the impression they're seeing
something that no one else has ever seen

Fage   I'd show them the Coliseum Notre Dame Big Ben
of course they wouldn't want to miss all that but I'd also
take them to the old quarter tucked away the women
doing their washing the men playing cards in the sun

Ten

Fage   But you're not a fool Nathalie you're a sensible
girl I don't see how it could have happened

Nathalie   The past doesn't exist

Fage   All the same it happened

Nathalie   Oh look is that a dress?

Fage   Looks more like a nightshirt

Nathalie   With fur cuffs

Fage   It's completely

Nathalie   Transparent yes

Louise   Well

Nathalie   It didn't happen to me

Louise   And what did you get up to in London the pair
of you?

Fage   Well who to then?

Nathalie   Someone else a different me

Fage   So you're not in love with this boy?

Louise   You were there three days

Fage   I tried

Louise   How?

Fage   I did all I could

Nathalie   I'd like to lose my memory

Louise   What did you do?

Fage   Walked about

Wallace   How old?

Fage   I had a feeling you were going to bring that up but age is something quite relative some people are old at twenty-five I've always taken care to do my exercises for half an hour every morning

Wallace   Your age isn't necessarily a handicap

Fage   Sport plenty of sport go to bed early get enough sleep

Nathalie   What I'd really like is I want to live my life as a series of moments to give myself completely to one thing then to another and not try and join them up

Wallace   Sleep yes you want to sleep so you sleep it's a question of will-power you keep on the go lead with your chin

Louise   And you bought her this dress

Fage   You're running away from your responsibilities

Nathalie   Responsibility is obscene

Fage   It was a bargain

Louise What?

Fage We got it in the sale

Wallace You build your life

Fage Down King's Road

Nathalie Responsibility that's why everything's so gutless why parents are like they are

Fage Nathalie has it ever occurred to you if your parents weren't responsible people what

Nathalie Don't start on that

Fage What will happen to the baby listen to me

Nathalie Look isn't that pretty

Wallace You're a deeply satisfied person

Fage No not at all I think one can always do better

Louise If you stood up to Bergognan the way you stood up to her no wonder he managed to get rid of you so easily

Wallace You like yourself and you do whatever's necessary to go on liking yourself a bit more every day

Fage Do you want that dress?

Nathalie Daddy are you out of your mind?

Louise Bergognan can't have had to lift a finger you just took it all lying down why didn't you stick up for your rights why didn't you tell him the firm was as much yours as his you hadn't spent twenty-three years of your life building it up for nothing didn't you want to grab him by the shoulders and shake him till he

Fage Till he

Wallace There are other less egocentric ways of staying

young like simply not thinking about it not being so
concerned about oneself

Nathalie   Why are you laughing?

Fage   What are we going to say to your mother?

Eleven

Nathalie   Daddy's being really hellish

Louise   Can't you think of something to cheer him up?

Nathalie   He looks so miserable I think I'll buy him a
revolver

Wallace   Excellent excellent

Fage   That's not all turn each batch of tourists into a
self-governing body

Louise   What do you expect? He's not used to being at
home all day

Fage   True but what I have in mind goes a lot farther

Nathalie   Perhaps I should teach him to meditate

Fage   No listen introduce a random element

Louise   Darling instead of prowling round like a cross
old bear why don't you sort out your magazines?

Fage   Start each trip off with a brainstorm the first
evening when they arrive the guide outlines the various
different choices which can go to make up the tour
Ancient Rome the Norwegian Fjords Soho by Night the
Berlin Wall an unlimited number of combinations which
people can adjust to suit themselves

Nathalie   Look Daddy you sit down like this with your
legs crossed

Fage   Each trip will be unique an expression of the group personality

Nathalie   But first I'd better teach you about breathing

Fage   Shaping one's own trip a unique selling proposition a complete break from the formula used by all other tour operators

Wallace   Though aren't you forgetting the small matter of reservations?

Louise   You can't go like that darling not in muddy slip-ons

Fage   I had no idea she was interested in boys

Wallace   Born in Madagascar no wonder

Louise   It's not a question of elegance you just want to look nicely turned out that's all

Fage   Quite the opposite in fact

Wallace   Almost predestined one might say

Fage   Quite I don't like standing still

Louise   Those shoes look much better

Nathalie   Poclain Hachette Prenatal

Fage   Travel's in the blood

Louise   Hachette have already found someone Prenatal acknowledge receipt they'll be in touch again later it's a circular it's not signed

Fage   My father was chief medical officer of that regiment of colonial infantry

Louise   Is that a letter from Mulawa?

Nathalie   Mulawa doesn't write letters

Louise   Where is he?

Nathalie I don't know

Louise Poclain have thought it over carefully but they're looking for someone less highly qualified at least they've had the decency to write

Fage They got me to dig my own grave so that when the time came all it needed was a little push

Louise It's a good letter

Fage They only had to breathe on me and I went down

Wallace How was that?

Fage Two and a half months after the take-over they sent in one of their young lions John a very nice young man just to get the feel of the market ten days later he'd got it all sewn up started giving me advice I had to close down two-thirds of the wholesale outlets slash retail profit margins increase them for the supermarket chains I tried to explain to him why the small wholesaler and the corner shop are still indispensable on this side of the ocean a fortnight later John was made senior sales director over my head I was just plain sales director I asked them to clarify our two functions they told me everything was to go on as before it was just that John would have a general overview it got to the stage where I was having to look for things to do to fill up the day it had all been taken out of my hands in the distribution list of internal memos my name was being omitted I had to stand by while they demolished everything it had taken me years of work to build up

Louise Darling you look so absorbed

Fage I'm busy

Louise Sorry to disturb you but you'll have to clear away those papers and what have you got all your pipes out for? I want to lay the table what are you doing?

Fage   Cataloguing my collection

Twelve

Wallace   Of course you no more thought of killing Bergognan than you would your wife

Fage   Kill my wife?

Wallace   The two of them seem very closely associated in your mind

Fage   We're very happy together there's not many couples you can say that about after twenty years of marriage

Wallace   Why be so defensive?

Fage   There doesn't really seem very much point discussing Bergognan a complete nonentity worth no more than an old rag that's been thrown in the dustbin

Wallace   You gave yourself away there

Fage   What?

Wallace   That's what I'm after

Fage   The manner in which I gave myself away?

Wallace   No I'm trying to get you to give yourself away as often and as much as possible that's the whole point of the interview I'm not interested in the facts so much

Fage   Nor in what I think?

Wallace   Not really but do go on you were saying you like to collect things

Fage   I collect pipes from all over the world

Wallace   How did you get on to that?

Fage   What I was talking about earlier the urge to get away each pipe evokes its country of origin

Wallace But you don't smoke a pipe yourself?

Fage My father did

Wallace Ah your father did?

Fage Why?

Wallace That's interesting

Fage Yes he started the collection oh he only had a few he'd picked up here and there in the course of his travels with the regiment either as souvenirs or for his own use there are one or two odd ones he broke in himself

Wallace From the way you talk about him I can see your father still means a lot to you you never smoked a pipe yourself?

Fage No just cigarettes and I don't any more

Wallace Yes you gave them up two and a half years ago

Fage Well I had a little relapse

Wallace A long one?

Fage I don't want your bloody birthday cake

Louise Well I've bought it now so you'll have to

Fage Oh yes?

He throws the plate with the cake on it to the ground.

Louise Sorry darling I just wasn't thinking

Fage What about for Christ's sake?

Louise Contraception there was no reason for me to suppose it was something urgent though I did think I'd better not leave it too long otherwise it might be too late she refused to discuss it I was greeted with one of those awful silences you know

Thirteen

Wallace   At the outset the interviewee is like a field of virgin snow on which I leave my imprint a blank canvas

Louise   You understand darling? Everything we've made together

Fage   Well?

Louise   I don't want to lose it

Wallace   The painter at his easel with his brush he starts to fill in the white that's what it is little by little covering over all that white

Louise   I don't give a damn about our lifestyle or what the neighbours think I'm ready to start again from scratch if we have to you know I'm even less tied to material things than you are just so long as we've got something to eat and somewhere to sleep somewhere warm you know I feel the cold somewhere properly heated that's all I ask well I don't even mind it being a bit chilly

Wallace   Get to the core of the individual

Louise   We'll snuggle up together and keep each other warm

Wallace   Tests no we don't believe in them

Louise   Say you love me

Wallace   They are the lazy way you think you're getting some sort of objective truth when all you're doing is projecting your prejudices on to these gadgets which tell you what you knew already

Louise   Suppose we let her have the baby

Wallace   But interviewing can be a creative process

Louise   Of course there'll be gossip it won't be very nice but I suppose we'll get over that as well

Wallace   It's no good looking at the candidate from the outside

Louise   People are bound to chatter but they'll soon get tired of it suppose they cut us dead well good luck to them if that's what they want it's not that which frightens me what frightens me is that I feel it all as some kind of threat

Wallace   You've got to engage his sympathy put your own personality on one side get inside the other person's skin

Louise   To me to you all three of us

Wallace   Probe his depths get to the core

Louise   I don't want to let it all fall apart

Fage   No Nathalie

Nathalie   If that's your last word

Fage   Yes absolutely my last word

Nathalie   I'll go elsewhere

Fage   I'd be interested to know where I always thought money was something you earned

Nathalie   Not necessarily

Louise   I'm not worried about that I'm sure you'll find the job you deserve I'm more confident than you more patient too

Wallace   I'd never employ someone who didn't lie it'd be a sign of abnormality a failure to defend oneself

Louise   Because I believe in you

Wallace   The candidate presents an image therefore he is lying if he's doing his job properly he should say things which put him in a favourable light and conceal anything which might be to his disadvantage

Louise   It's Nathalie that frightens me and you not wanting to face it

Wallace   An interview if properly conducted is always an act of aggression but it can also produce great gentleness and intimacy

Louise   Taking pride in her doing well at school there's no doubt intellectually

Fage   She wanted a hundred francs for Red Solidarity

Wallace   One candidate whom we finally turned down wrote to me afterwards and thanked me I don't know I suppose the interview helped him get at his real self behind the multiple disguises

Louise   Oh I know you can't blame her really she's just copying the others they're all doing it nowadays parents don't get much of a look in

Fage   But who is he?

Nathalie   A boy from school

Fage   What was he doing?

Nathalie   Painting on walls

Fage   What?

Nathalie   Words

Wallace   It meant a good deal more to me than just professional satisfaction

Louise   But when she comes in and says I want to go ahead with this baby that's what she said wasn't it? Go ahead? Go ahead with it in the holidays keep it for a year and then pass it on

Nathalie   The rest of us managed to get away

Louise   I know you said it was out of the question

Nathalie   They nicked him

Louise Just what exactly did happen in London?

Fourteen

Fage You've completely the wrong end of the stick

Nathalie Has your dole money come yet?

Fage No no

Nathalie I need some money today

Fage If you think that then I can't have put it right I must have expressed myself badly

Nathalie We're taking a collection

Louise I phoned Germaine who knows a doctor who would do it

Fage Quite the contrary

Wallace Yes four hundred and fifty metres above Courchevel

Fage Fundamentally I'm an optimist it's part of my basic make-up

Nathalie I said I'd put in a hundred francs

Fage Always starting from the premise that I'm going to make it

Wallace At the foot of the glacier an Olympic swimming pool

Louise She said I wasn't to tell anyone his name even you

Nathalie It's for the defence fund

Wallace You can ski right down to the water's edge

Fage Extraordinary

Nathalie   I've got to have it

Wallace   People have got their swimsuits on underneath

Fage   They take their trousers off and in they go

Louise   No nothing sordid he's an idealist Germaine says he does it because of his convictions and only when he feels it's really justified

Fage   No my handicap would be that I come from an entirely different sector

Louise   He's taken quite a considerable risk

Nathalie   Well Daddy?

Fage   I'll have everything to learn

Wallace   A few weeks time and you'll be on top of it

Nathalie   Daddy's spent the whole morning slumped in that armchair

Louise   What's all this about Red Solidarity?

Nathalie   A guy from school that's been put in prison

Louise   I don't think it's funny at all

Wallace   Selling is the same whatever one sells

Louise   Your father's most upset by it

Wallace   No that doesn't worry me at all what does worry me though

Louise   Asking him for money at a time like this

Nathalie   What?

Louise   It's childish and inconsiderate

Nathalie   We're not animals are we?

Wallace   Twenty-three years

Fage   Yes

Wallace   That's a lot of loyalty a bit too much perhaps

Fage   When you've built up a team and you're doing a job you believe in a job that's never finished perhaps I've got a slightly old-fashioned belief in human dignity but I don't regard myself as a piece of merchandise

Wallace   After the take-over by this American firm

Fage   We were in the middle of a very important campaign I couldn't just walk out

Louise   Why didn't you wake me?

Fage   You were fast asleep

Wallace   All the same you knew what was coming

Fage   I was still hoping deep down

Wallace   Meaning?

Fage   I told you I was an optimist

Louise   It was raining yesterday

Fage   My love

Louise   Your shoes are all muddy

Fage   You forgot to do my shoes

Louise   What's the weather like today?

Fage   They're disgusting

Nathalie   Daddy I'm trying to do my maths

Fage   So what?

Nathalie   Can't you keep your voice down?

Fage   I hoped they'd see the light

Wallace   You thought it'd all blow over

Fage   Dig in sit tight hold on

Wallace   Deep down you were afraid

Fage   They were the ones who were worried about their future not me

Wallace   Afraid of cutting loose you'd grown too attached to the firm

Fage   I had to protect my people

Wallace   Generous as well as optimistic

Fage   Besides loyalty isn't something to be derided

Wallace   Of course not it's all too rare

Fage   My father made it as a doctor even though his own father could hardly write his own name

Louise   Darling have you finished cataloguing your collection?

Fage   He was appalled when I went to Bergognan to sell underwear

Louise   If you're not going to get rid of all these old magazines why don't you go through them and sort them all out?

Wallace   He didn't understand?

Fage   He thought it was an awful come-down and yet

Louise   Find something to take your mind off things

Fage   Years later I got him to admit that sales are no worse than soldiering although he only went into the army because his parents couldn't afford to set him up in a practice nowadays he'd be in the public sector he wasn't in any way competitive

Wallace   What did he want you to do?

Fage   Study go to university whereas the real world was what interested me I couldn't wait to get stuck in

Fifteen

Wallace   Does your wife go with you?

Fage   Not usually she's all right on skis but not much
more

Wallace   I don't do much downhill stuff myself I prefer
to wander off cross-country

Fage   That's something we do too go off on long treks
spend the night in a small hut whole days in virgin snow
why don't you come with us one day I'd take you to
some places which other people haven't got on to yet

Wallace   Last year I chanced upon a couple of spots
myself yes why not one day but with you it's obviously a
real passion

Fage   When you lead the sort of life I do

Wallace   Hectic I know

Fage   Skiing is a complete break from everything
confused and devious it's like being weightless you just
drift off taking off into the unknown you're using every
muscle in your body it's as if there's a sort of harmony
between the wide open spaces all round you and your
inmost self my daughter and I we're a well-matched
couple well-known at Courchevel in fact people point us
out there's the Fage girl and her father

Wallace   What time do you get up in the morning?

Fage   Early I'm usually on my feet between five and six

Wallace   What do you do between getting up and
leaving for the office?

Fage   I beg your pardon I don't quite understand

Wallace   No I'm sorry perhaps the question wasn't clear
enough

Fage   I have a shower

Wallace   Nice and hot?

Fage   Lukewarm while I'm in there I go over in my mind everything I've got to do that day

Wallace   Do you spend a long time in the shower?

Fage   I forgot to mention that before showering

Wallace   Ah

Fage   I do my exercises starting with the salute to the sun it's a yoga movement very simple which helps you gather your forces for the day ahead

Wallace   Is this before you shave?

Fage   I can't shave until I've had a cup of coffee

Wallace   Do you do a lot of yoga?

Fage   I cribbed the movement from a telly programme it looked rather interesting so I thought I'd have a bash myself

Wallace   To get back to the shower

Fage   Sorry while I'm in the shower I often manage to solve problems that have been bothering me the decisions just seem to take themselves I sometimes lose all sense of time till a knock on the door reminds me that my daughter Nathalie wants to use the bathroom before she goes to school

Wallace   Supposing this Mulawa character wanted to marry your daughter

Fage   She's only sixteen she's not interested in getting married yet or in having an abortion

Wallace   How would you feel about it?

Fage   Do you have any children of your own?

Wallace   Supposing the father had been white?

Fage   Are you suggesting I'm a racist?

Wallace   It's very interesting this passivity of yours in the same way you let Bergognan walk all over you

Fage   I beg your pardon?

Wallace   They asked you to drop your trousers and walk about with your bum in the air and you did

Fage   What did you say?

Wallace   No I'm sorry it's not so much congenital cowardice you're naturally rather courageous it's this need to be protected there's something rather childlike about you

Fage   I can tell you now I was really relieved when it was all over

Wallace   Exactly you let them do what you knew you ought to be doing yourself but didn't dare and then you say you were relieved

Fage   Those young men I'd taken on and trained I had a responsibility

Wallace   Then you appeal to your sense of duty to provide you with an alibi for your refusal to face up to things which makes you even more reluctant to act than you were before

Fage   Excuse me I've just remembered I've got another appointment

Wallace   Sit down

Fage   Take back what you just said

Wallace   That's enough now quiet

Fage   Just you shut up

Wallace   Good I note your different reactions ability to take punishment self-control outburst of affronted dignity

Sixteen

Nathalie   What's that tower over there?

Fage   That's Big Ben

Nathalie   And that great big building?

Fage   That's the Houses of Parliament

Nathalie   Daddy I keep on throwing up you know in the morning

Fage   That's Westminster over on the right

Nathalie   Daddy why are people happy?

Wallace   If you succeed

Louise   It's in the bag

Wallace   We've got projects under way in all sorts of places

Nathalie   Oh but Daddy I am happy really happy

Louise   I start on Monday

Nathalie   The whole city no it's not the city it's the whole world put your hand here so you can feel my heart beating

Wallace   Once you've demonstrated your ability once you've pulled through this little Americans Overseas operation

Louise   Of course I was a bit frightened but everything passed off wonderfully

Nathalie   Now put your hand here no lower down there's another small heart beating there you can't hear it but I can feel it

Louise   And the money's good as well I'm absolutely over the moon

Wallace   If you have what we call the CC the CALI

calibre you won't be left there long we'll be moving you on to start on something bigger perhaps in the field of mass archaeology still virtually untouched or setting up a network of pilgrimages or of holiday camps for delinquent and handicapped children

Louise   And you won't have to sell your collection after all at least not for the time being

Nathalie   Daddy I'm going to have to sit down a minute

Fage   What's the matter don't you feel well?

Nathalie   No I'm fine it's just I'm a bit overwhelmed

Louise   Just the thought of it made me feel quite sick

Fage   But I don't want you to go out to work

Louise   It's all done now darling I've signed the bit of paper besides it'll be very good for me

Nathalie   It was like a sudden warm glow everything lit up

Wallace   There's a great surge of interest in potholing at the moment as recently as a year ago it would have seemed inconceivable but we were ready for it and sailing and parachute jumping no there'll be no question of letting you rest on your laurels before you've so much as got your breath back you'll be pushed on further to even dizzier heights

Fage   I like that

Nathalie   Daddy do you know what they call the oceanic feeling?

Fage   I want to sell them anyway

Louise   Why?

Wallace   There is this gaping hole people have more and more leisure but are less and less able to cope with it which is where we come in

Fage   I got bored with them

Wallace   To fill the hole

Louise   Darling where have you been?

Fage   To see the doctor

Louise   Not about Nathalie?

Wallace   All these complicated hungers that are still unsatisfied

Louise   Who then?

Fage   Doctor Wolf

Louise   Who's he?

Wallace   The chairman was saying only the other day at a management meeting gentlemen you must never forget that we're selling in a real sense of the word nourishment we're in the food business

Fage   Come on Nathalie we'll be late

Nathalie   Where are we going?

Fage   Just for a little check-up he's a cardiologist

Louise   Is anything the matter?

Wallace   It's nothing less than paving the way for a new humanism

Fage   No no on the contrary couldn't be better

Louise   Well then

Fage   When we get to the clinic look listen

Nathalie   Not again

Fage   I kept getting this tingling feeling in the fingers of my left hand Wolf said it was nothing to worry about I'm perfectly all right has there been any post today?

Louise   Look here's your coat back from the dry
cleaners looks as good as new mother phoned she said
she'd thought of something that might help what's so
funny darling?

Fage   Nothing it's just that I was thinking how lucky I
am to have a little wife like you life may have its ups and
downs but I wouldn't miss it for anything

Seventeen

Fage   We got to the clinic at half past six

Louise   Did you go in?

Fage   No

Wallace   What about politics?

Fage   Not really my line

Wallace   And sexual freedom?

Louise   Why not? How long did you wait?

Fage   Not that I'm narrow-minded but take my daughter
she is at the age of sixteen already worn out with doing
what she wants all the time she just drifts with whatever
current's in vogue at the time when I say she does what
she wants she doesn't actually want anything she just has
a succession of whims the trouble is these little whims just
grind you down family life becomes a joke there's no
community of interests we simply can't keep up my wife's
past being shocked she's just worn out and her being
exhausted wears me out too it's a vicious circle I think the
pendulum's bound to swing the other way there's only so
many new ideas to go round and after that they'll just
have to start going into reverse revolution huh you know
what that means don't you something that goes right
round till it ends up where it started

Nathalie   It was like music

Louise So you turned round and came away?

Wallace Which of the following two things do you identify with more readily arm leg?

Fage Leg

Wallace Head heart

Fage Heart

Wallace Leopard bee

Fage Not immediately

Louise Well I think I have a right to know

Fage Leopard

Wallace Vase carpet

Fage Vase carpet?

Wallace Vase carpet

Fage Carpet

Wallace Crowd desert

Fage I've already told you

Louise Was it you who changed your mind? Or was it her?

Fage Crowd

Louise And you who

Wallace Clothed naked

Fage Naked

Wallace Cheat bully

Fage Cheat

Wallace Weep shout

Fage Shout

Louise   Dinner's ready

Fage   I strolled down to Place Saint-Sulpice it was very pleasant

Nathalie   Lovely Mummy I will say this for you you make the most fantastic chips

Fage   Now darling what's your mother dreamed up now? I'm in cracking form I just got back from Colgate Palmolive

Nathalie   It was between three and four a.m.

Fage   Top-flight people

Nathalie   We'd been working quietly for quarter of an hour twenty minutes I was keeping a look-out on the corner

Fage   They really know what they're doing

Louise   Are they interested?

Fage   Very we talk the same lanuage though there are several other likely candidates

Nathalie   The patrol car came from the other side

Louise   Aren't you hungry darling? Nathalie

Nathalie   They had their truncheons out in a flash

Louise   You're spoiling his appetite darling you know how highly mother thinks of you she thinks all it needs is for one or two firms to know you're on the market the problem is how to let them know she says you could write to *Le Monde* about the difficulties of an executive still in the prime of life the casual rejections the sapping of morale the increasing stress and so on they'd quite likely to publish it you could mention your professional experience your capabilities your successes

Fage   Then the accident and then nothing

Louise   Not complaining of course just pointing out the inequities of the system

Fage   I don't understand what your mother's talking about I don't see that it's any of her business

Louise   It's just what's needed

Fage   Disposable people that's what's needed why shouldn't they be disposable? Twenty-three years to become disposable

Nathalie   I've never run so fast in my life you couldn't see me for dust

Fage   What a performance

Nathalie   Only Roland stumbled

Louise   Who's Roland?

Nathalie   And they got him

Fage   Twenty-three years they should have a clear out every two years it's ages since I've breathed so freely you know I can still do four point eighty-five metres on the long jump Nathalie you've never worn that dress we bought in London

Wallace   Steel wool

Fage   I'd like to see you in it

Wallace   Sun moon

Fage   Sun

Wallace   Sperm snot

Fage   Sperm

Wallace   Arrival departure

Fage   Departure

Wallace   Rat hyena

Fage   Rat

Wallace Belly back

Fage Does all this go into my file?

Wallace I fill in your answers on this grid it gives me a profile which enables me to cut a few corners belly back

Fage I refuse to go on

Wallace It's up to you

Fage Belly

Wallace Perversity mediocrity

Fage Whichever one I say it puts me in an unfavourable light I won't go on

Wallace Relax perversity

Fage Mediocrity

Wallace Proximity distance

Fage Proximity distance proximity

Wallace Oil petrol

Eighteen

Wallace Forty-three years old born Madagascar father a doctor in the army mother didn't work parents both dead married one child last employment sales director for Bergognan no university qualifications

Fage No I came up the hard way any qualifications have been won in the field

Louise Where does this come from?

Nathalie I don't know

Fage My qualifications are a turnover which doubled every three years profit multiplied by fifteen over the last ten years while our main competitors were marking time

Louise   What is it?

Nathalie   A bow

Louise   So I can see

Fage   The organisation I left behind no weak links ready for anything the climate I created

Louise   And you've no idea?

Fage   A climate of friendly rivalry every one of my people put the firm's interest first I'd only got to say let's go and they'd go or that's the way it's got to be and they'd fall in line immediately

Wallace   How much did you earn?

Fage   With everything thrown in it came to ninety-one thousand

Nathalie   I can't see any arrows

Wallace   And what do you expect to get?

Fage   As far as I'm concerned it's not money that's the important thing what I'm looking for above all is

Louise   One of your boy friends?

Nathalie   It must be Daddy

Wallace   All the same when they get to your age people don't just resign because they feel like it without making some provision for the future

Fage   There's such a thing as being too careful you lose your self-esteem

Nathalie   You're always telling him to find something to do

Wallace   Perhaps you'd like to explain

Nathalie   It's brand new

Louise   But

Nathalie   And here was me wanting to buy him a revolver

Louise   That's not funny

Nathalie   I like it

Fage   Oh the usual story firm taken over because it was doing too well Americans who hadn't the faintest idea I'd have had to stand by while they destroyed everything I'd built up

Wallace   Your resignation was really more in the nature of a statement

Fage   Tell me Nathalie why do people work? To earn a living? But what do you mean live? I know I ought to occupy myself I'm going to occupy myself following this speck of dust

Nineteen

Nathalie   Do I love him? Really Mummy

Wallace   There's this image

Louise   The least you could do is bring him home

Wallace   Some images are so strong you simply can't shake them off the more they upset you the more stubbornly they persist naturally enough you react very strongly against the idea of your sixteen-year-old daughter in bed with a negro just down from the trees and that this should happen not only without violence but without passion without emotion without even bothering to take precautions

Fage   It isn't his colour

Wallace   But isn't that an important part of the picture? Together with the associated image of a little boy with thick lips and crinkly hair and the sound of his voice calling you grandpa

Louise   Seems to me it would only be natural Nathalie

Fage   Yes why don't you invite him to lunch?

Louise   Or dinner one evening that'd be more relaxed we could have a nice little chat

Fage   How do you know it's going to be a boy?

Wallace   You've never got over the death of your son

Nathalie   I will if you like

Wallace   You've never forgiven yourself for your carelessness in trying to overtake that sports car on the hill coming out of Lyon

Fage   Normally I'd have been able to get past him

Nathalie   Only I can't imagine what you'll find to talk about

Fage   If that Peugeot behind me hadn't pulled out at the same time Nathalie doesn't want to keep it more than a year or two she wants to trade it in as if it was a car then when she wants one to keep she'll have another by someone else maybe that one'll call me grandpa but

Nathalie   He's not exactly talkative

Fage   I can't say I'm in any great hurry

Louise   Does he have any interests?

Wallace   One's got to get a sense of the man as a whole one's not drawing up a balance sheet with strong points on one side and weak points on the other what's important is the totality single and indivisible

Nathalie   He's got this thing about water

Wallace   Very difficult to get hold of

Nathalie   If you want to track him down he's likely to be at the swimming-pool that's where he meets his regular clients

Louise   I suppose he's some kind of socialist

Fage   Is he the one that's been putting all these ideas into your head about being an urban guerrilla?

Nathalie   He's completely uninvolved politically he's only interested in Marxism from the semantic point of view he couldn't care less about the struggles against colonialism and imperialism I tried to explain it to him but he just yawned in my face

Louise   I can see we're in for a charming evening

Nathalie   He's very interested in anything to do with food

Fage   You'll have to do something impressive darling

Louise   Will he eat anything?

Fage   What does he like?

Nathalie   His favourite is kidneys flambé

Fage   What does he do? Does he do anything?

Nathalie   He collects jokes he's writing a doctoral dissertation on the structure of jokes he's really great he just doesn't talk that's all

Wallace   It's unfortunate but understandable

Fage   I must admit

Wallace   After being inactive for so long

Fage   Jokes what do you mean jokes?

Nathalie   Stories that people tell to make each other laugh

Fage   If you're trying to make me contradict myself

Wallace   I thought you said you disapproved of politics

Fage   What I said was

Wallace   Aren't you interested in what's going on in the world what's happening in this country?

Nathalie   More than half of them are about bottoms

Wallace   The controversial issues housing education the bomb

Fage   What I meant was

Nathalie   Then there are the ones about clergymen ghosts jews lunatics

Wallace   You don't want to get involved yourself politics is something that's best left to other people is that what you mean?

Nathalie   Soldiers doctors and patients corpses and undertakers

Wallace   Isn't that what you mean Monsieur Fage?

Nathalie   He analyses variations between all existing versions of one and the same joke until he's able to isolate the non-varying core the nucleus

Louise   What's the matter darling?

Fage   Oh nothing

Louise   You know she's got a very lively imagination and I sometimes wonder

Fage   Bergognan never really understood what was meant by team spirit

Wallace   The boot up the backside

Louise   I sometimes wonder but no she couldn't

Fage   Mulawa Mulawa

Louise   But I wonder

Nathalie   Mummy why is Daddy laughing all by himself like that

Fage   Finished in the shower Mulawa?

Louise   You know how much she enjoys making us look ridiculous

Fage   The patience this girl had at the agency she tried I don't know how many hotels there wasn't a room to be had for love or money

Louise   I wonder if it's not all some gigantic hoax

Fage   London is completely booked out

Louise   Right from the word go

Fage   In the end I managed to get just the one room with only one bed no bathroom

Louise   Running into him like that in the bookshop the baby I wonder if she hasn't just made it all up if so we'd better go and have her examined

Fage   Apparently it's a double bed

Louise   Well that's all we need darling especially if they admit her the same day have you got the tickets? Will you run us to the airport?

Twenty

Wallace   About your private life

Louise   Throw them away

Fage   Burn them

Wallace   I want to make it quite clear it's no concern of ours

Louise   All right suppose we threw them away

Wallace   Except in so far as it might affect your professional activities

Nathalie   Wanted sales manager exceptional calibre wanted

Fage   Not in the dustbin someone might come along and pull them out

Wallace   Are there any upsets in the candidate's home life? Or is everything running smoothly? Of course there's some relevance in our knowing something about that

Louise   Burn them? How? We haven't got a fireplace

Fage   You couldn't burn them in a fireplace

Nathalie   Have you answered this advert in *Le Monde* Daddy? You ought to wanted and this one wanted wanted they all want you

Wallace   That's not to imply there's any definite rules about it I'm not saying we should disqualify anyone just because he's a Don Juan because he's fond of a little bit on the side as they say

Nathalie   I want you you want me

Wallace   Or because he was impotent or for instance only last month I appointed this homosexual

Nathalie   Here I am take me let me gobble you up

Louise   You could take the car and dump them in the rubbish tip

Wallace   It was a highly confidential position but his confessed homosexuality was part of a dynamic structure in which the tensions balanced each other out in a harmonious way conversely I often find myself mistrusting someone who's completely normal

Fage   Go out into the country and bury them

Louise   It'd be easier to go down to the river and throw them in

Fage   That's not a bad idea yes

Wallace   The normal individual is quite often rather repressed his energies are bound up in a series of conflicts played out at a subconcious level

Nathalie   Daddy about that one hundred francs

Louise   But there'd be bound to be somebody watching

Nathalie   I'll give it you back

Wallace   Quite often the most unbridled terrors are lurking just beneath the surface

Nathalie   We have to raise fifteen hundred by tonight to pay the printer

Wallace   But a neurotic by which I don't mean a psychopath

Fage   You have extensive sales management experience a self-starter an entrepreneur a challenging job which will suit a person of considerable ambition able to put the pressure on where needed

Wallace   You for example

Nathalie   Daddy will you please let me have that hundred?

Wallace   Would you say you were a normal person?

Twenty-One

Wallace   What do you normally do in the evening?

Louise   I do wish you'd sort out all those old magazines

Wallace   Do you have a lot of friends?

Nathalie   What's that you're hiding?

Louise   Ssssh it's a little surprise for your father

Fage   I usually take one or two files home to work on my wife's always on at me to take an evening off now and again in front of the telly

Louise   A surprise for you

Wallace   You'll report on a monthly basis sales profit contribution expenses net profit competitive developments

Louise   Aren't you going to open it?

Fage (*opens the packet*)   Well

Wallace   Customers' reactions and complaints

Louise   Do you like it? It belonged to a Captain Bodington who commanded a frigate under Nelson it's never been smoked since the day he was drowned

Fage   Who?

Louise   Captain Bodington of course

Fage   Ah

Louise   It's still got the original dottle

Wallace   Relations with the hotel chains with the airlines

Fage   I don't like you getting mixed up in this sort of thing Nathalie

Nathalie   But Daddy it's such fun pigs in plain clothes wandering about the school

Fage   You'd do better

Nathalie   They're so stupid

Wallace   Run down on the socio-economic trends including a comment on the political climate

Louise   I bought it for you out of my first pay packet

Wallace   Take this little compartment here

Louise   It dates from the time of the French Revolution

Fage   Sits nicely in the hand

Wallace   In this little compartment you jot down all the things wrong with the organisation anything which clogs things up anything which causes delays paralyses the decision-making process

Louise What have you done with it?

Fage What?

Louise Your collection

Fage Got rid of it

Louise You've not gone and sold it have you?

Fage No no

Louise Ah

Nathalie Daddy's gone down the street you know what he did?

Wallace That's how the firm stays young fights off hardening of the arteries constant reappraisal

Nathalie He stopped at Place Saint-Sulpice stood outside the Bonaparte cinema and gave his pipes away to the audience as they went in and out

Fage I want to go back to Madagascar

Louise But you've never been there darling except when you were born

Fage Set up as a mechanic

Louise But you know how hopeless you are at repairing things it's always me that has to do it

Fage Yes you always do

Nathalie The funny thing was people didn't have the nerve

Louise To do what?

Nathalie Take them put out their hands they thought there might be something underneath a booby trap and then there's the police station just around the corner

Fage   Go hunting for snails in Madagascar

Nathalie   There was this guy with his wife a pipe smoker he went off to look for a policeman the policeman asked Daddy what he was doing and told him to move on

Fage   Swim through shoals of fish

Nathalie   Can I come too?

Fage   When you've built up a business with your bare hands

Nathalie   I could look after the goats

Twenty-Two

Wallace   But apart from work and skiing and your home life

Fage   Originally? There's no question that I admired Monsieur Bergognan

Nathalie   This ad Dad look have you written?

Fage   Nathalie your mother found these two bundles in your room

Nathalie   What was she doing in my room?

Louise   Is he starting to smoke again?

Nathalie   How should I know?

Fage   Since when has it been forbidden for your mother to go into your room?

Louise   These two cigarette ends darling are they yours?

Nathalie   Versatile aggressive minimum five years consumer goods marketing experience thirty-two to thirty-eight

Wallace   Can you name the title of the last book you bought? Is that the last book you read?

Fage   It seems to me that your mother and I have given you every freedom

Louise   But it is our house too you know

Fage   It's absolutely out of the question for you to store leaflets in the house

Wallace   Do you ever go to the theatre? A football match? Boxing? All-in-wresting?

Louise   I want them out of here today

Nathalie   Don't worry we're going to give them out this afternoon

Louise   Darling was it you that smoked them it can't have been Nathalie

Nathalie   When I smoke I'm not furtive about it like Daddy

Fage   One needs to admire someone it's only human in the same way that one needs to be admired oneself believed in followed

Louise   The most disgraceful rubbish look at it just look at it to overthrow this society

Fage   At work and in their home life people need to follow and be followed

Wallace   Yes it's important the chain needs to hold come hell or high water

Fage   To overthrow this society there's only one way to fight the heap of stinking shit they call a government the bland fascism that lays its dead hand on our lives the inhuman rhythm of the capitalist factories the glutinous obscenity of a slavering consumerism the brainwashing in a system's schools the proliferation of a pig police force everything which stands in the way of love in all its spontaneity this society which tries to co-opt youth with all the affection of an octopus one way and one way only comrades pull its pants down and let it shit away until it falls apart support the Students Union Action Committee

Wallace   Would you say you were thrifty or extravagant?

Nathalie   Didn't you buy any arrows?

Fage   What's society done to you? Whose pants? That's what I'd like to know

Louise   Tell me you haven't sold them

Fage   Nathalie that experience you had in London

Wallace   Are you in debt at the moment?

Fage   That warm glow

Louise   It seems to me that your generation are actually very fortunate you've got everything you want and you're still not satisfied

Fage   Tell me what it was like

Wallace   Ever had any problems with your health?

Louise   Are you going to take up archery?

Fage   My father was

Wallace   How did you

Twenty-Three

Fage   That's a trick question

Wallace   There's no need to be so suspicious

Fage   Let me put it this way I fix myself a goal and I go all-out which doesn't mean I'm not exceedingly careful this launch I have no hesitation in saying it was believe me the team surpassed themselves in every way working eighteen hours a day for three months weekends as well I'd got Petit Bateau in my sights and I was going to hit them where it hurt merchandising trade incentives supermarket displays consumer offers catch them on the hop jolly them along the only thing I hadn't foreseen was that in so doing I was digging my own grave

Nathalie   That cake's a bit of a disaster

Louise   It's your father's birthday today

Fage   At that speed it's one slip and you've had it I wobbled my skis came apart it was all over in a split second

Nathalie   What are you doing?

Fage   I'm looking for

Nathalie   What slip Daddy?

Fage   Trouble is everything's in such a mess

Nathalie   Your trouble is you tense up you should relax let yourself go

Fage   That makes it even more difficult

Nathalie   We're making anti-matter in physics it's fantastic the teacher keeps tying himself in the most incredible knots

Fage   It's good to see you

Nathalie   You're looking cheerful

Louise   Is anything the matter?

Fage   I'm fine I'll be all right

Wallace   Your lady wife

Fage   She's still moving

Wallace   So what do you do?

Fage   I wait a moment

Wallace   That's interesting so you don't

Fage   Not before I've cut her up

Wallace   I see because you're going to

Fage   Salt her down

Wallace   Like in a fairy tale

Fage   Nathalie told me one but I've forgotten what it was who's that?

Wallace   Monsieur Bergognan

Fage   Tell him to wait

Wallace   He's got his hands tied behind his back he's coming forward his head bowed

Fage   So it's you is it

Wallace   What shall we do with him?

Fage   Where is everybody? I want a crowd a huge crowd

Louise   Relax darling

Fage   In the light of the torches

Wallace   Where are they?

Fage   Everybody's carrying torches there's the smell of slaughtered pigs

Nathalie   You're tired of the old routine

Fage   Strip him

Nathalie   You're a born leader

Fage   Tie him up with barbed wire

Nathalie   Are you the man for us?

Fage   I cut

Wallace   And again

Louise   Out of my first pay packet

Fage   Round the mouth

Nathalie   This belt yes I bought it

Louise   You know perfectly well

Fage   I stick it down no more chatter I cut out a cheek and stick it down Bergognan Bergognan

Wallace   What?

Fage   Didn't I tell you?

Wallace   No

Fage   He has these flabby cheeks well he's only got one now the shouting's getting louder Bergognan

Wallace   In the shower

Fage   In the shower first thing in the morning until my daughter Nathalie

Louise   Do you mind if I put the light out now darling?

Twenty-Four

Louise   You're the one who's going to have to take her to London darling it just wouldn't work with me

Nathalie   Are you all right Daddy? You scared the hell out of me I thought I'd find you smashed to pieces

Louise   What about the passports? Are you sure you've got everything?

Nathalie   It's a miracle

Louise   I'm sure everything will be all right bye then

Nathalie   Daddy's late

Louise   That's a good sign

Nathalie   I'm hungry

Louise   He's not back yet from his interview with
United Cheese I'm keeping my fingers crossed he went off
very confident it's important

Nathalie   Switch from socks and underpants to
Roquefort and Gruyère ugh

Louise   If he's accepted

Nathalie   Mummy I feel sick

Louise   It seems only proper Nathalie that we should
make his acquaintance

Wallace   And then?"

Fage   And then why shouldn't I feel a certain pride

Wallace   Certainly you have a number of achievements
to your credit which are by no means negligible but
fundamentally this complacency of yours

Fage   Would you sooner I despised myself?

Wallace   I didn't say

Fage   My self-confidence if I didn't believe in myself
maybe I've made mistakes they wanted me to go down on
my belly and crawl they thought they could walk all over
me

Louise   Well what are we going to do about it?

Fage   It's quite simple she can't have it and that's all
there is to be said I mean it is a bit much it's not just her
what about us after all it's in her own best interest it's
definitely in her interest it's up to us to look after her it's
all very well her being good academically she's got a
mental age of five anyway there's no problem at all you
just whisk her off to London and it'll all be over before
you can say Jack Robinson

Louise   How did you get on darling? You should try
and eat something just a little

Wallace   What about the other two top people who'd been with Bergognan from the beginning the financial man

Fage   He licked the Americans' boots

Wallace   I see and

Fage   Imagine he wanted to see my papers

Louise   Don't laugh like that eat up

Wallace   What happened to the advertising man? He too

Fage   They kept me waiting an hour and a half in a little cubby hole reeking of Camembert before I was seen by this faceless little bureaucrat he kept going out of the room when I was in mid-sentence and coming back with a pile of files saying do go on he kept on interrupting me saying fine I think we can skip that and leafing through those files while I was trying to get him to listen to me then this woman came in with a bit of rag in her hand I thought it was the cleaning lady she didn't introduce herself of course

Wallace   In other words both of them weathered the storm whereas you

Fage   She asked me how many times I'd been sacked I referred her to my curriculum vitae she said you couldn't always believe what people wrote she looked at me with a smile and added or what they say either the bureaucrat wanted to know what experience I'd had in perishable goods packaging

Wallace   I'm just trying to get this straight there wasn't anything like a general clear out

Louise   I got a chicken you like chicken

Fage   What does this man Mulawa do for a living?

Wallace   You were the only casualty weren't you at least in the upper echelons

Fage   They'll all of them get the chop over the next six months I preferred to hang on to my self-respect and get out right away not everybody has the same

Wallace   Unbending attitude absolutely now the Americans didn't make a clean sweep of the old management they just weeded out one individual who wasn't pulling his weight

Fage   You mean

Wallace   I don't mean anything Monsieur Fage I'm simply asking questions

Twenty-Five

Nathalie   When we were reptiles and we started emerging from the primeval slime

Fage   Start again from scratch

Wallace   After stewing in your own juice for so long

Nathalie   It was a giant step

Louise   The work's not all that interesting but it does me good to get out of the house I feel a different person

Nathalie   Sooner or later it had to happen

Fage   What?

Nathalie   We took the first step

Wallace   And this gaping hole is where we come in this emptiness

Nathalie   The zoology teacher we thought he was a bit of a twit at first but it turns out he's really great he identifies with the species he's talking about

Wallace   Right from the word go our two founders had

the insight that there is no limit to what one can sell

Louise I shouldn't be surprised if I don't get promoted next month the manager took me into his office last night

Nathalie We were doing the brontosaurus yesterday he was standing like this

Fage Oh it's in the blood

Wallace What they've planted are the seeds of a new humanism you've no idea of the numbers of deeply disturbed people who pass through this office it's because it's been so long since the last war

Fage I think I could cope with it frankly

Louise Germaine has explained everything to him she says he's very charming like a great big schoolboy I'm not allowed to tell you his name

Nathalie Is that a dress?

Fage Looks more like a nightshirt

Wallace People need something to mobilise them so that their problems can take a back seat for once

Louise He didn't say yes or no either way first of all he wants to examine her I told him we weren't even sure she was pregnant

Wallace Our idea is to provide a war-substitute why shouldn't leisure have the same sort of urgency

Fage I have a very understanding wife

Nathalie Mind the curve of the slope Daddy

Fage They steamrollered me

Louise All these strange characters coming in and out of the house at all hours her room is like a railway station last night I put my head in to ask them not to make so much noise and found them in the middle of a political meeting and those awful electric guitars you know I found out she's had duplicates made of the front-door key god knows how many and you never say anything we can't go on like this I'm going out of my mind

Fage   To follow a speck of dust all you need is a ray of sunshine to strike it at an angle listen Nathalie answer me when I'm talking to you

Nathalie   What?

Fage   I'm just as appalled as you are

Nathalie   What by?

Fage   Unfair taxes unequal educational opportunities outrageous health conditions in the factories the closing down of the corner shop the destruction of historic landmarks the pollution of the atmosphere the money squandered on atomic weaponry the planes we sold to Libya

Nathalie   Have you finished?

Fage   No I haven't

Nathalie   Well hurry up I've got to go out

Fage   Where to?

Nathalie   I've got a meeting

Fage   Don't go we've got to talk

Nathalie   What about?

Fage   You'll see

Nathalie   I can't

Fage   These pamphlets of yours I wish you'd realise how utterly childish they are not to mention what would happen if the police were to find them here

Nathalie   That would be a shame they cost a lot to print

Twenty-Six

Louise Darling you haven't moved since this morning

Wallace The American tourist is like a great big child and I just wonder

Louise Why don't you do something?

Fage I am doing something I'm thinking about that appointment with Perrier that Nathalie forgot to give me

Wallace It may be that your idea about self-governing groups wouldn't be quite such a good one after all

Louise Can't you think of something for him to do Nathalie?

Wallace What do they want? The illusion of independence the illusion only

Fage Perfectly I'm telling you at Perrier I had every chance

Nathalie There's no need to go on and on about it it's all right for you to say so now

Fage Because the fit was perfect

Nathalie Of course it's all my fault

Fage What do you care you do it on purpose not even that you just couldn't give a damn

Nathalie Don't shout

Wallace You look as if you're chewing something

Louise Darling it's often the little things that matter most

Fage Never felt better in my life

Wallace Open your mouth

Fage In the sale it was a bargain

Wallace   Let me see your teeth

Nathalie   Follow me Daddy

Wallace   Well unclench your jaws

Nathalie   We'll go round the scree

Wallace   Open wide

Nathalie   Careful the snow's crunchy and cut down through the trees

Twenty-Seven

Fage   Good old Captain Bodington

Louise   We'll put it with the rest of the collection but what have you done with them? Darling you're not hiding anything from me are you?

Fage   I've made up my mind not to hide anything any more not to possess anything any more in a few minutes

Louise   Where are they?

Fage   I've got to go out for this crucial interview

Nathalie   He gave them away

Fage   Since they seem so keen to have me here I am shoes well-polished my coat

Louise   Did he say that? He must have been joking

Fage   A clean collar tie neatly tied

Louise   Darling why don't you tell me the truth?

Fage   A knot no wrinkles right in the middle you know what he said to me

Louise   Let's have a look at you

Fage   His wife was holding on to his arm as if she was afraid he might suddenly suddenly he came over well I said go on take it and he said oh no I couldn't I'm treating you I said well in that case and at that moment his wife stepped in we'll soon see about that she said treat indeed

Louise   You sold them

Wallace   Maybe I haven't quite understood

Fage   Then these three policemen showed up

Wallace   There are one or two little inconsistencies in your story which I'd like to try and clear up

Fage   Followed not long after by a fourth oh Place Saint-Sulpice was stupendous bigger than ever the church had been cleaned out the sun was catching the snow-white stone the monument had been put back right in the centre shining white too as if it was new I said I'd buy them all a drink

Nathalie   The police?

Fage   Of course all the policemen hanging round there the police station too had been washed clean come on I said

Louise   Who to?

Wallace   Don't you remember telling me?

Fage   One of the policemen come on I said you've got time for a quick one move along please sir why don't we all go and have a drink mind if I see your identity papers sir? So you were born June 14 1927 in Madagascar? And where did you get these pipes and what exactly are they for? You're not going to confiscate them are you? Not working today then sir? He asked to see my last redundancy pay slip they were all very nice about it what surprised me was that they were so forthcoming they wanted to explain exactly what they were doing and why they were each of them trying to explain everything all at once

Wallace I don't want to belabour the point but is it what you want in life money?

Fage That's not specially important

Wallace Happiness?

Fage Always in pursuit

Wallace Power?

Fage I like to have my own way but I'm not interested in it for it's own sake

Wallace Respect?

Fage Oh yes

Wallace Are you ever ashamed of yourself?

Fage Ashamed?

Wallace Do you ever despise yourself? When you've failed one of your colleagues? Or your wife? Or your daughter? When you know you've betrayed a certain idea you have of yourself? Something that happens to the best of us doesn't it? Used you to chew like that as a child? How about self-control? Any problem? No? Would you like me to open the window a bit? How does intercourse affect you? Does it leave you feeling relaxed and friendly? Are you ever impatient? Tactless? Is your partner's satisfaction as important as your own? Do you withdraw into yourself after intercourse? What gives you the most pleasure? How far do you go? What's your deepest desire?

Twenty-Eight

Louise I asked him how he'd got on at that interview

Fage There was an old workman behind me in the queue a typesetter

Nathalie Do you ever tell each other jokes as you wait

in line?

Louise   He looked at me as if he didn't understand my question

Wallace   I'd like to go over what you see as your own shortcomings that is if you think you've got any

Fage   When the gates opened there was a bit of a scrimmage he got knocked against me he said he was sorry and we started talking

Nathalie   Jokes about people who're unemployed and one of them says to the other

Wallace   You said you're a believer by nature

Louise   We'd already gone to bed

Nathalie   This guy who's unemployed meets this other guy who's unemployed and says to him why are you standing there watching the cars go by? And the other one says what cars?

Wallace   Surely you don't let belief interfere with judgement

Fage   I'll jot them down in case they come in handy for Mulawa

Louise   This man Monsieur Garin what was he like? I just asked him what this Monsieur Garin was like

Nathalie   You can tell him them when he comes to dinner

Fage   I could never be a cynic all the big decisions in my life have been made with a certain ideal in view

Louise   I stopped asking him any more questions

Fage   Leaving Bergognan's for example

Louise   He had his head buried in the pillow

Fage   Marrying Louise both our families were against it but I went ahead

Louise   Are you cross with me? Don't you like me going out to work?

Fage   What does he live on?

Louise   You have a go Nathalie he's not talking to me any more

Wallace   Buoyancy is one thing but how good are you at channelling your energy?

Nathalie   He gets a grant from his government but he gets through an awful lot

Louise   Is there still some hope?

Nathalie   Pushing brings him quite a bit extra

Fage   Is he very extravagant?

Nathalie   He spends on books and he has all these women who live in a sort of commune in his flat

Louise   Yes or no just one word is all I'm asking for

Fage   There are little words that can just swallow you up

Wallace   A decision is never perfect

Fage   Seems quite a lad I'm looking forward to making his acquaintance

Louise   He'll tell us funny stories

Fage   We could do with some of that

Louise   This doctor friend of Germaine's she has to keep the name secret a real stroke of luck it's so difficult in France

Nathalie   I told you he doesn't talk

Louise   I mean it can be awful dirty unhygienic a real nightmare

Fage   This typesetter of mine was saying

Louise   But this time I'm handling it darling I've made an appointment for her for Saturday

Fage   He's a union militant used to be a shop steward

Nathalie   Is this a joke?

Wallace   Is that all?

Fage   A couple of years back he organised a strike something to do with accident prevention he told me the management had been biding their time they didn't chuck him out immediately but two years later they whipped the carpet out from under his feet

Twenty-Nine

Wallace   You'll see it's a fairly rugged enviroment dog eat dog

Louise   Nathalie's been arrested

Wallace   You'll be in the big league

Fage   Nothing to it apparently and yet

Wallace   The jungle world of charters

Nathalie   I'm not saying

Wallace   You'll learn to procure

Fage   Left foot or right foot forward?

Louise   Red-handed

Wallace   Probe

Nathalie   I don't remember

Wallace   Find the weak spots elbow your way in

Louise   Breaking and entering the House of Caviare at the Champs-Elysées

Fage   Absolutely relaxed

Louise   Just her

Wallace   The network of multinational hotel corporations and airlines endlessly ramified

Nathalie   I told you all I know

Fage   String quite smooth

Wallace   All interlocking

Louise   The police phoned up

Wallace   Merchant banks pulling the strings

Louise   The others managed to get away

Fage   Put your thumb here and your index finger there now between them

Nathalie   No comment

Wallace   Here's our chance the level of investment has been such that they're caught in their own spiral they've absolutely got to fill the hotels sell the seats sell the beds

Nathalie   I don't know their names

Louise   They made off with the cash and the stock

Fage   What should we do?

Louise   You'd better go at once

Fage   I haven't shaved

Louise   They said straight away

Nathalie   Why don't you?

Wallace   You've got to keep a cool head nerves of steel

Nathalie   You wouldn't dare

Louise   It'll be in all the papers this evening it would happen now just when they're making up their minds about the job

Wallace Big as they are you'll be dealing with them on equal terms

Nathalie You can hit harder than that you know

Fage What about Red Solidarity?

Wallace Hit them where it hurts

Nathalie If you must but mind my stomach

Louise She's slightly hurt

Fage Where?

Louise In the head

Wallace Let nothing tarnish this burning vision

Nathalie I'd like to help you

Wallace You seem to have pretty well got what it takes

Fage I'm aware of my limits and I'm sure I'll be able to cope

Nathalie I don't know I don't remember

Louise They've taken her to hospital special security she's being guarded no visitors allowed

Fage I'm adaptable when you have faith in yourself

Wallace You keep yourself in trim your muscles look in good shape

Fage You loose the arrow your finger doesn't even feel it go

Thirty

Wallace Your husband's both high-powered and self-possessed not at all I'm very pleased to meet you

Louise Oh yes I haven't come to ask you

Wallace   I can tell you the probability at this stage is about fifty per cent just the two of them left but to what do I owe the pleasure?

Louise   So now it's just a question of chance?

Wallace   Chance?

Nathalie   There's nothing more you can do?

Wallace   I wrote to him this evening here's a copy of the letter are you all right?

Louise   It'll pass I'm sorry

Wallace   Monsieur Garçon whom he's due to have lunch with on Tuesday

Nathalie   I told you everything

Louise   That's next Tuesday is it?

Wallace   One p.m. we like to do the final interview over lunch it's more relaxed yes to what do I owe the pleasure?

Fage   Staring out to sea to the last he was Nelson's favourite lieutenant you know went down without a word

Nathalie   I've never seen him before

Wallace   He talks about you how shall I put it? One gets the feeling that while he's forging ahead you're the one that keeps him on an even keel

Nathalie   I don't remember

Fage   He drained one last cup and closed his eyes he was an artist Bodington

Louise   It was difficult at first then I got a job doing market surveys it's completely changed my life they tell me I'm a quick worker very methodical they're going to make me a supervisor at the beginning of next month

Wallace   What's more striking about him is one gets the feeling of complete commitment

Louise   Unfortunately we're having a bit of trouble with our daughter

Fage   That Peugeot ought never have pulled out

Wallace   I know he told me about how shall I put it this little accident

Louise   Accident?

Wallace   Young people nowadays seem to feel a need to get back to basics hence a certain uncouthness in their behaviour particularly in the sexual field parents don't get much of a look-in I'm afraid however a weekend at Courchevel and everything will sort itself out won't it?

Louise   Oh yes Courchevel but she's been arrested and he

Wallace   Well the police often make mistakes but if you know the right people

Louise   What time did he leave your office yesterday?

Nathalie   You're wasting your time asking me all these questions

Louise   I haven't seen him since

Fage   Not seriously

Nathalie   Yes you hurt my stomach a bit

Louise   I'm sure he'd be very cross if he knew I'd come bothering you

Fage   What are we going to tell your mother?

Nathalie   Put your hand there no lower down

Fage   Until it starts to speak

Louise   Particularly for someone as active as he is

Wallace   Born

Louise   Darling

Fage   Give me that file quick I'm late for my meeting come on girl look alive

Wallace   Obviously

Louise   What time is it?

Nathalie   You can't do this to me Daddy

Fage   The reply to this is no full stop new paragraph our firm has already made contact at the highest level

Louise   You should have called me

Wallace   What were your parents doing?

Fage   A risk? Yes but a calculated one

Nathalie   Look if you force me

Louise   I didn't do your shoes they were all muddy

Nathalie   Daddy answer me

Fage   We could make quite a sizeable profit out of the operation

Wallace   In our firm

Louise   And I was going to give your trousers a press as well

Wallace   You weigh and are how tall?

Dissident, Goes Without Saying

Dissident, il va sans dire

translated by PETER MEYER

Characters

Hélène
Philippe, *her son, aged seventeen*

Dissident, Goes Without Saying was first performed in the UK
in The Room at the Orange Tree Theatre, Richmond, on
6 November 1997, directed by Auriol Smith

One

Hélène They're in my coat pocket

Philippe No not on the table either

Hélène You are kind

Philippe Because you left it double parked?

Hélène Then I must have left them in the car

Philippe One day it will get stolen

Hélène You didn't go for your interview?

Philippe I did

Hélène I couldn't face it I don't know how many times I drove round the block it gets more difficult every time

Philippe I'll go and park it for you

Hélène One more year and you can take your test

Philippe Yes

Hélène Is that a new sweater?

Philippe Yes

Hélène I wonder where the money comes from

Philippe You collect 'em you know

Hélène Someone must have bought it

Philippe Things get passed around

Hélène But whose is it?

Philippe You and your ideas about property

Hélène Things belong to someone

Philippe *goes out.* **Hélène** *makes soup from a packet.* **Philippe** *enters.*

Hélène I wonder if you're telling me the truth

Philippe   I must have been whacked these things happen I never heard the alarm

Hélène   I set it for eight

Philippe   And you made coffee

Hélène   You couldn't care less I'm amazed

Philippe   How many times have I gone for interviews? What's ever happened?

Hélène   Is it good? Lentil soup a new kind I thought I'd try do you like it? Do you? It only needs one Philippe and it could be the right one your father answered an advertisement and eighteen years later he's still there he's made a career of it

Philippe   Good night Mum

Hélène   Where are you going?

Blackout.

Two

Hélène   It worries me seeing you lying there with records all round you you know having no aim in life

Philippe   I want to fight for widows and orphans I want to stroke your hair no let me

Hélène   Seriously Philippe one can do without most things but if one has an aim

Philippe   I have an aim but it's unattainable

Hélène   I'd like

Philippe   That way I know I'll always have it

Hélène   And never get anywhere?

Philippe   I'd like two things for you to stop being alone Mum

Hélène   With you I'm not alone

Philippe   For you to find some nice guy and let me

Hélène   What?

Philippe   You know

Hélène   I'm a burden?

Philippe   It's not that

Hélène   It's ages since I tried to make you do anything

Philippe   Just let me be

Hélène   If you'd only make an effort jobs don't grow on trees another thing that worries me is seeing you so half-hearted about it instead of really trying if I were you

Philippe   You're not me

Hélène   You've let your father down again he'd booked a table

Philippe   His secretary booked a table in one of those nice little local restaurants he keeps a file of I never gave it another thought

Hélène   He rang me at my office this afternoon he waited for you he's so precise about everything he thinks I'm stopping you seeing him that's nice for me

Philippe   I've nothing to say to him

Hélène   He's your father

Philippe   So what?

Hélène   Have you finished?

Philippe   He ought to understand by now

Hélène   For him a date's a date

Philippe   And a son's a son

Hélène   For my sake do tidy up these records they're

collecting dust on the carpet

Blackout.

Three

Philippe You look tired tonight

Hélène I don't no more than usual

Philippe Your hair the usual things do make one tired

Hélène It started to rain and I hadn't got my umbrella

Philippe Well you did your statistics?

Hélène How do you mean?

Philippe As usual

Hélène Well yes

Philippe What's the point of a statistics clerk?

Hélène We analyse invoices by salesmen's areas

Philippe What happens then?

Hélène It means you can follow the development of sales up and down by areas by comparison with the previous year by comparison with the budget soon it will be mechanised

Philippe Meaning?

Hélène It will be put on a computer

Philippe Why?

Hélène To make it quicker and cheaper

Philippe Why are you telling me all this?

Hélène Because you're asking

Philippe You don't ask me anything?

Hélène You never ask questions

Philippe Don't you notice anything?

Hélène What is it? You scare me?

Philippe By asking questions?

Hélène I had to say something to your father it's all settled tomorrow night he's taking you to the cinema

Philippe What's the film?

Hélène You know he's just back from a long trip to Africa don't forget to ask him how he is all this travelling with his diabetes

Philippe Tomorrow night? I can't

Hélène Now listen

Philippe Shut up and look

Hélène But

Philippe It's a surprise go on open it

Hélène Chocolate truffles you're out of your mind

Philippe Aren't they your favourite?

Hélène Yes

Philippe Last time he took me to the cinema it was a film about Chile he's dead set on converting me to his progressive ideas I don't give a damn about Chile tomorrow I'm having a go at night work I've got a job

Blackout.

Four

Hélène I'm so relieved now I can tell you it's true I was upset not so much about the money but doing nothing that's what's so awful for a young lad and to see you worrying

Philippe   You thought I didn't worry enough what's up what do you want?

Hélène   Nothing at all

Philippe   Don't just say whatever comes into your mind

Hélène   Why pick a quarrel? Everything's so nice I'm so happy

Philippe   You only see the good side in other words you see nothing

Hélène   I do try you know my poor Renault 4's beyond repair at least it will cost four thousand francs and the man at the garage says it's not worth that he offered two fifty I took it and as a start with this huge fortune I bought an enormous sausage

Philippe   That will last for centuries

Hélène   Your favourite sort

Philippe   Suppose I go away?

Hélène   When?

Philippe   Next year

Hélène   Where?

Philippe   We're in December

Hélène   You've just got a job

Philippe   I'd like to find a valley

Hélène   A valley?

Philippe   Shut in at both ends

Hélène   I've never had an accident anyway I don't believe in accidents besides you see I'm safe and sound the doctor says anyone can suddenly feel faint I've bought a bottle of wine too the policeman was amazed I sometimes wonder where you get your ideas instead of being interested

Philippe   In what?

Hélène   Well thousands of things everything around you I've decided not to get a new one you can never find anywhere to park and the Metro's just as quick besides

Philippe   You love driving

Hélène   With your money when we've saved and saved the doctor at the hospital was astounded not a rib cracked not a tooth broken when the crash but I can't remember anything either I'll never know what happened

Philippe   With my money

Hélène   You'll buy us another

Philippe   With an engine you can't hear

Blackout.

Five

Philippe   Was it Simon?

Hélène   Your friends never give their name they're in and out of here they don't even say hullo

Philippe   Then who was it?

Hélène   I open the door they don't see me

Philippe   You don't make them very welcome

Hélène   I've told you what I think about their way of life we do exist

Philippe   He said I could drop in at Simon's is that all?

Hélène   I don't understand what you see in these boys

Philippe   Stop it

Hélène   He said Simon's or if Simon's not there
Patricia's

Philippe   Patricia?

Hélène   I think he said Patricia and he said before
twelve

Philippe   I'm off

Hélène   No Philippe first you'll have lunch we'll have
lunch I was waiting for you you know look and before
you sit down listen

Philippe   What?

Hélène   Take off your windcheater your gloves your
hands you might wash

Philippe   I'd rather have a sleep

Hélène   Then you're not going?

Philippe   I don't give a damn

Hélène   Have you been made permanent?

Philippe   What?

Hélène   It's a month today since you started

Philippe   Oh yes

Hélène   Well?

Philippe   Here my pay

Hélène   Oh

Philippe   Take it

Hélène   I didn't ask for anything

Philippe   Shakes you eh?

Hélène   Now you're on the right road I'm entitled to
my dreams aren't I? I wish you'd find a more interesting
job where you can use your brains a little

Philippe   Not so fast

Hélène   Are you going to spend your life eating lettuce with your fingers? You always wrote the best essays in your class

Philippe   I've seen that dress a bit too often

Hélène   You never look at me

Philippe   Buy a new one

Hélène   Philippe

Philippe   Make yourself attractive then my mates will look at you

Hélène   Will they?

Philippe   You used to have a white dress you ought to go to the hairdresser's make him cut off all this to show your face your neck

Hélène   Perhaps I do hide my face but you

Philippe   Show your face

Hélène   You've grown so thin your eyes your temples your cheeks

Philippe   I've never felt better Dad said I was a fine young fellow just like him

Hélène   Aha he wanted to talk to you

Philippe   He did talk to me

Hélène   Well?

Philippe   He said there was a place in his company for a fine young fellow with a future like me how could you?

Hélène   What?

Philippe   Go for a guy like that

Hélène   You upset me

Philippe   I want to know

Blackout.

Six

Hélène   You know Grandma wasn't at all well

Philippe   She's dead?

Hélène   She couldn't go on any more

Philippe   I'm not working tonight we're on strike I'll take you out for a meal then we'll go to a film

Hélène   You weren't listening you do choose the right moment

Philippe   Grandma's dead?

Hélène   Yes she is

Philippe   We aren't

Hélène   Do you know what you're saying?

Philippe   You look lovely today 'madam'

Hélène   Can you imagine it I've been crying?

Philippe   We can still go to a film

Hélène   I didn't love her you think you don't love your mother any more no tonight I think I want it's silly to stay in to pull myself together it's silly

Philippe   You're very lovely

Hélène   And you're funny 'sir'

Philippe   There's a cracking film down the road

Hélène   You've never asked me to the cinema

Philippe   I want to go out with an attractive lady

Hélène   It's time you found a girl

Philippe   And you a man but the right sort

Hélène   When you say things like that I sometimes wonder if you're serious and where you stand with girls

Philippe   Or if I'm gay

Hélène   You never tell me anything

Philippe   I tell you lots of things all the time

Hélène   Yes and I have to work them out

Philippe   I'm telling you to find a guy there are agencies that use a computer

Hélène   I know everything ends up on a computer they've just installed ours in an air-conditioned room

Philippe   Find an attractive operator

Hélène   Perhaps in the next three months they're going to try out the programme we'll go on doing the statistics manually in parallel the machine will do the same figures it's to test if it all works properly after the three months there'll only be the computer programme

Philippe   So

Hélène   Luckily you've got your job

Philippe   Yes luckily

Hélène   What makes you laugh?

Philippe   Three cheers for the Citroën production line

Blackout.

Seven

Hélène   I was beginning to wonder? Yes of course you haven't got me used to seeing you disappear for several days without a word

Philippe   No I'm not hungry I think I'll go and get some sleep

Hélène   With what friends?

Philippe   The foreman's got a house in the country he and two other guys said come I went we had a bit of a party the strike helps you to get to know people at work we don't talk much we can't talk there's so much noise and when the hooter goes we all rush out without a word then next day we're back on the line again

Hélène   I thought you were occupying the factory

Philippe   Yes in turn

Hélène   But you stayed three days in the country

Philippe   Yes you know this strike I don't know the Algerians have taken it over that cheapens it

Hélène   Why are you on strike?

Philippe   To start with it was against the noise level and the speed of the production line then the foreman has a smallholding his parents were farmers

Hélène   I've had a letter from your father listen 'My dear Hélène, I'm writing these few words to tell you I'm going to pay into your account each month the sum of four hundred and fifty francs instead of the three hundred and seventy-five I do now. Justice demands that I should increase your allowance in view of my promotion. You know that although I had not been given the title I was carrying out the duties of export director. Now they have appointed me export director and reviewed my salary accordingly. It is only natural that Philippe and you should get some benefit from this. I am well and hope you are too.'

Philippe   Justice demands

Hélène   He often uses that expression

Philippe   It is only natural

Hélène   Your father has a fetish about being correct

Philippe   To correct me he'd say come here and when he laid into me

Hélène   You never cried

Philippe   I'd concentrate on opening up his skull and twisting his brains between my fingers I never felt the blows at all

Hélène   How silly of me I was automatically looking for the car keys

Philippe   You're going out?

Hélène   I don't know what I'm up to I've forgotten what I was going to do

Philippe   Buy some bread

Hélène   I don't need the car to go to the baker's

Philippe   Don't you ever need a man?

Hélène   You're nearly a man now

Philippe   In your bed

Hélène   That's something else

Philippe   So you're going out?

Hélène   I know I must go and see Madame Tossu she's in hospital

Philippe   What's the matter with her?

Hélène   Brain cancer she's finished

Philippe   Who for?

Blackout.

Eight

Philippe   You're going to look for another job?

Hélène   Not right away there are so many things I've wanted to do for ages and I've put off year after year these records

Philippe . I'll put them away

Hélène   So many things that I don't know what I'll be able to realise my dreams six months' freedom oh you can't imagine

Philippe   You'll be able to stand doing nothing?

Hélène   I'll do something later but first of all long long holidays I'll go for walks I'll visit libraries do you know what worries me most? I never see you with a book

Philippe   My head's too full already

Hélène   What with?

Philippe   My book exists complete in my head

Hélène   What's it called?

Philippe   No title

Hélène   Write it

Philippe   I want to live it

Hélène   What does that mean?

Philippe   If you don't understand

Hélène   Dreaming about it's not enough when you were little you never stopped writing I'm sure that if you'd persevered

Philippe   Stop it

Hélène   You're letting your life slip between your fingers take hold of it make something of it

Philippe   I'll show you my life look

Hélène   I'm looking

Philippe   The part arrives in front of you on the belt

Hélène   Yes

Philippe   I set it like this I put it in

Hélène   Yes and then?

Philippe   There's a pedal you operate with your foot the press comes down plomp I remove the part the belt brings another part

Hélène   And then?

Philippe   Then plomp

Hélène   So that's your life?

Philippe   You've bought the white dress?

Hélène   I never used the hoover yesterday you know I feel I'm changing

Philippe   You've bought the white dress

Hélène   This pair of shoes too

Blackout.

Nine

Philippe   You're crying look it's not important I can tell them to stop coming here

Hélène   Your friends treat our home as their own I've told you

Philippe   We can move somewhere else

Hélène   Who's we?

Philippe   I don't know

Hélène   They're four in your room one of them a girl I gave them a meal they asked me to they say hullo now I mentioned it the other day to the tall one with curly hair

Philippe Simon

Hélène Don't they have jobs?

Philippe They haven't all had my luck

Hélène Two of them have been asleep on your bed since seven they looked worn out

Philippe You're a marvellous mum

Hélène Are they really your friends?

Philippe How do you mean?

Hélène Well they're not like you I was going to tell you I don't like them having a key to the house

Philippe Let me explain

Hélène When I got back from the office I found them there settled in

Philippe By the way I saw Dad he gave me a mammoth lesson in socialism he said he'd met you through socialism

Hélène He'd love to get you to share his ideas

Philippe You still believe in socialism?

Hélène In the old days I fought for it I'm all for the struggle against privileges

Philippe Which ones?

Hélène The absolute power of employers

Philippe He's an employer isn't he he gives the orders? While he was talking I heard nothing I looked at his nose I can't see him again I won't see him again

Hélène You must believe he's sincere

Philippe He walked out on you

Hélène It didn't work any more I'm happier now it's tough but I like my independence

Philippe   You still love him

Hélène   That's got nothing to do with it aren't you going to join your friends?

Philippe   Madame Tossu looked in I told her I thought she was in hospital she was amazed

Hélène   She's been discharged

Philippe   She was never there she said she was passing so she'd taken the opportunity to bring you the lace she said you can pay her next time and she's expecting some new colours she'll show you them next time what were you up to at the hospital? What are you going to make with the lace?

Hélène   A tablecloth for Sundays

Blackout.

Ten

Philippe   That was a disastrous dinner

Hélène   Because you were sulking but what did you think of him?

Philippe   Wet

Hélène   I like him he fits the description I asked for

Philippe   The way he inspected everything as though he owned it already and was making an inventory

Hélène   He likes ideas books country walks

Philippe   He's not good enough for you you'll dominate him and then you'll be more bored than you are on your own

Hélène   Then perhaps I gave the computer a bad description of what I want

Philippe   And you arrived more than half an hour late

Hélène   Without knowing I may have done it on purpose

Philippe   I had to make conversation with the old boy

Hélène   Yes on purpose

Philippe   I was worried

Hélène   For me?

Philippe   After that accident of yours

Hélène   I've no car now

Philippe   These funny turns

Hélène   I've always been absent-minded

Philippe   I know what you're hiding you're going to marry a man like that?

Hélène   You silly boy you don't believe me it's because of that Madame Tossu business? You know I never see anything about this strike in the papers or on the news

Philippe   It's only two workshops that's not enough to stop the factory I can assure you

Hélène   I also rang Citroën

Philippe   They'll say anything

Hélène   I don't know Philippe you don't eat now these bags under your eyes and your father rang he wanted to know why you asked him for money

Philippe   He's stinking rich you're out of work

Hélène   What do we need? I'm on the dole that's enough

Philippe   This is between him and me

Hélène   After all you've said about him?

Philippe Yes I hate his guts

Hélène It doesn't make sense does it? What are you doing? Are you mad? You're not going to hit me?

Blackout.

Eleven

Philippe You've been to the hospital?

Hélène What can I do to make you believe there's nothing wrong with me? You're imagining things and it's beginning to annoy me when I came in your room was full

Philippe What of?

Hélène Your friends lying on the floor and a girl who seemed to be asleep standing up

Philippe Patricia

Hélène You're in love with her?

Philippe I adore her

Hélène She's very pretty but why one girl with all those lads?

Philippe They've their own birds they don't bring them

Hélène What do they all come here for?

Philippe We talk

Hélène You might have a word with this foreman you know you could ask him to get you transferred to another workshop

Philippe Yes that's a good idea

Hélène Now the strike's over

Philippe Yes

Hélène   There are more interesting jobs you've got a good brain

Philippe   Yes

Hélène   If you took the trouble there are lots of ways of making the most of yourself you must simply

Philippe   Have an aim in life is any of that sausage left?

Hélène   One tiny bit

Philippe   That was a good buy

Hélène   You ought to try and write this book

Philippe   It will run into lots of editions you'll bring out the lace tablecloth I'll buy you a sports car Dad will come with the socialist party I'll invite my foreman there'll be chocolate truffles and the telly there'll be the telly

Hélène   I'll buy another sausage

Philippe   And all your fiancés

Hélène   We'll line them up in a row

Philippe   Patricia will dance Patricia's a marvellous dancer

Hélène   The money

Philippe   What?

Hélène   You know

Philippe   No

Hélène   It's not there

Philippe   I forgot to tell you

Hélène   What have you done with it?

Philippe   I'll give it back

Hélène   You've taken it?

Philippe   It's not important

Hélène   You've taken all my savings?

Philippe   A mate's got a problem

Hélène   Without telling me?

Philippe   You'll have it by the end of the month

Blackout.

Twelve

Hélène   Yes I was asleep

Philippe   Sorry to wake you

Hélène   Five in the morning can I get you something to eat?

Philippe   I'm not hungry

Hélène   Have you come a long way?

Philippe   Simon shopped us

Hélène   Your cheeks have vanished they've melted away your eyes are so hollow

Philippe   No letters? What's this?

Hélène   A notice of Madame Tossu's death and your pop magazines three of them I haven't seen you for nearly a month

Philippe   You made a statement to the police

Hélène   Not right away first of all I went to the personnel department at the factory

Philippe   They told you

Hélène   That you'd been on their books for three weeks in all I'll make you a cup of coffee

Philippe   Yes how are things with you?

Hélène   Okay

Philippe   I've brought you some of the money

Hélène   I went to the funeral

Philippe   No one been here?

Hélène   Your friends?

Philippe   I'm cold

Hélène   Wrap yourself up in this blanket I'll get you some woollen socks

Philippe   That's new

Hélène   They threw a farewell party for the three of us the rest of the staff did they gave me this adjustable bedside lamp

Philippe   They knew you like reading in bed

Hélène   Yes

Philippe   Now you're free

Hélène   I'll be able to look after you as long as you're here

Philippe   If I stay they'll come and arrest me

Hélène   They've been several times I expect they're watching the house

Philippe   They haven't bothered you?

Hélène   They took me to the police station to make a statement they've been considerate on the whole though they searched the flat they read all the letters I'd kept they ripped open your mattress

Philippe   What did they tell you?

Hélène   Break-ins at chemists and three of your gang have been arrested

Philippe   What else?

Hélène   Burglary using and pushing drugs

Philippe   Words that hurt eh?

Ring at the door.

Hélène   Already?

Philippe   You'll be able to buy a car

Hélène   You think so?

Philippe   It will make life easier for you

Ringing and knocking at the door.

Hélène   What make do you think?

Philippe   The new Renault 5 you know

Hélène   With lateral reinforcement of the chassis

Philippe   I wanted to see you again you know I knew
they'd come

Knocking at the door.

Hélène   Don't worry about me

Philippe   Nor you about me

Hélène   We'll make them wait a bit shall we?

Philippe   Yes just a moment

Hélène   I'll put on a record?

Blackout.

Nina, That's Something Else

Nina, c'est autre chose

translated by PETER MEYER

Characters

Charles, *aged forty-two*
Sebastien, *aged forty-four, his brother*
Nina, *aged twenty-four*

One
The Box of Dates

Sebastien Want to make me a chargehand

Charles Do tell me

Sebastien I've told you a dozen times

Charles How she opened your knees

Sebastien She opened her knees

Charles Yes *she* did besides nobody refuses promotion

Sebastien I don't like giving orders

Charles You open it this side

Sebastien She had little bells on her bracelets her necklace

Charles I'm afraid for Nina there's lots of room here she'll make herself so small anyway she's only just over five feet

Sebastien Here with us

Charles If they want to make you a chargehand it means they think you're good enough to be a chargehand

Sebastien She had a long necklace it swung to and fro on my stomach

Charles Any day now the boss is going to follow her home he's going to go up to her room last night she enjoyed her food did you see? Rabbit she adores that she had three helpings it would be better if she moved

Sebastien If I don't accept I'll get a black mark and then they'll look for an excuse

Charles If you do accept it's promotion you'll get a rise

Sebastien She told me to lie on my back she got astride me with her little bells underneath the palm tree

her breasts were pointed I had one in each hand now and
then I took my hands off her breasts I put them on her
bottom or I left one hand on her bottom and thrust the
other in between they've had a huge earthquake the
Chinese have did you see? They take it so calmly if it had
been here on the other hand if it had been in England

Charles   They don't have earthquakes in England

Sebastien   No but think if it had been here

Charles   She thinks you're uncommunicative how many
years has it been now?

Sebastien   Well since the French army left Tunisia

Charles   We're in eighty

Sebastien   It was in fifty-four

Charles   She does like you you know and then that
mustard sauce she adores that I told her it's a recipe of
mother's and you'd never cooked before that amazed her
she thinks it's marvellous for a son what do you think of
her? She's interested in everything she's not boring

Sebastien   That makes it the twenty-sixth year

Charles   Twenty-six years she's sent you a box of dates
every year for your birthday

Sebastien   It doesn't mean anything

Charles   It means at lot

Sebastien   A habit

Charles   Never a word inside? Her name and address
always the same? That is something so faithful

Sebastien   After one night not even that I went back on
guard at three she bit my ears till they bled I don't like
dates

Charles   You never thought of getting her over here?
Perhaps she's waiting sitting there in the sand I don't

either

Sebastien Mother liked them we could send them to China for the victims they've issued a bulletin saying they don't need any help from anywhere that's what I call pride the Algerians too they're a proud people not like the Tunisians the chief characteristic of the Tunisians is their flexibility

Charles So you'd agree?

Sebastien They work hard and they don't make a fuss

Charles She'll come and live here *she* likes them dates

Sebastien Oh no

Charles Do tell me what did she do next?

Sebastien The Chinese what I admire about them is that combination of quietness and determination the English and the Chinese have that in common in forty and forty-one they never flinched the English if it had happened here

Charles One of these days the boss

Sebastien In France imagine an earthquake in the middle of Paris

Charles I must have it out with him

Sebastien The chaos would be incredible

Charles So what do you say?

Sebastien The panic every man for himself

Two
The First Spinach

Charles I never said that I said her voice was an alto

Sebastien You said something else

Charles   It's not to take mother's place but a female voice in the house

Sebastien   You think it's sad here?

Charles   Mother never said we ought to live here in a tomb for some time now he's been regularly putting his hand between her legs during work the three juniors who do the shampooing have their share of it it's a normal privilege but Nina that's something else this is real spinach like the old days

Sebastien   The first fresh spinach of the year

Charles   Roast veal with spinach

Sebastien   We used to have it on Wednesdays I chopped the spinach by hand

Charles   Like she did

Sebastien   I used to watch her she'd chop so quickly without any hurry

Charles   Wouldn't we be a lot happier with a pretty pair of legs to look at

Sebastien   If I don't accept

Charles   If you do you'll be climbing up the ladder

Sebastien   We're talking it over in the branch to decide what position to take up

Charles   Even when I was a kid it was my favourite vegetable

Sebastien   To make it really smooth you see I wonder if I used the right saucepan hers were like a feather on the palate you need a saucepan with a thick base

Charles   They wouldn't make anyone a chargehand if he's not capable of being a chargehand

Sebastien   A fitter never gets bored besides you move from one workshop to another you're always in touch by making me a chargehand they've got me I become responsible for a production budget I start being in a small way part of the management it's a trick they often use when there's someone they want to neutralise

Charles There's no security she lives all alone in a little maid's room anyone can climb up those seven floors after her you can give me another helping if you will

Sebastien They want my answer tomorrow

Charles What you're afraid of is the change

Sebastien Chaps who know their job among the fitters there are lots to choose from

Charles He knows she's my girl it turns him on to do that to her when I'm around

Sebastien There must be something behind it

Charles When am I he said yesterday just loud enough for his wife to hear sitting there behind her till everyone heard when am I going to stuff that precious little body of yours? Marie-Dominique and Yvonne the two other juniors collapsed with laughter and he said when am I going to come home with you? Tonight? Old mother Tonton it's a fact she'd have swallowed her false teeth if at that moment a customer hadn't come in and not just anyone Madame Mouchet the wife of the bank manager next door

Sebastien A little more won't you?

Charles She's Polish well she was born Polish a hurricane

Sebastien They are noisy that's because of their history there are lots of them in the factory Poles on the assembly line

Charles You think

Sebastien They've been swallowed up so often in so

many ways through being invaded they've learnt how to get by

Charles   But she

Sebastien   And they're tricky the Algerians we have more trouble with but I prefer the Algerians they're crooks too it's natural for most people who've been trampled on who've let themselves be trampled on if you compare them with the Chinese the day after the earthquake the survivors set themselves up in the street and went on living as if nothing had happened

Charles   It's their political system they've been trained to obey like sheep

Sebastien   You can't train sheep no it's their character the character of these people

Charles   As a chargehand there's nothing to stop you going on

Sebastien   What?

Charles   With union work

Sebastien   It's not so clearcut

Charles   You've more power

Sebastien   A machine when there are problems with it I look after it I live with it till the moment it does exactly what I'm asking of it the whole time I like that then I go on to another machine which needs attention I take my time I talk it over with the lads I don't give orders to anyone you're more independent

Charles   Like us with women's hair you ask them what they want but in the end we decide what suits them

Sebastien   It's fine like this

Charles   Like what?

Sebastien   Like we are

Charles So you'll say no?

Sebastien If I do I risk being sidetracked to some phoney job they did that to Chadex last month .

Charles Nina's coming to dinner tomorrow and she'll bring her things all right? She has such a tiny appetite yet you saw how she kept on asking for more?

Sebastien No

Charles Yes and she'll give you a hand with the housework you'll have lots of time to listen to your records

Sebastien I listen while I'm working

Charles She'll settle you into your armchair she'll put out your slippers customers like Madame Mouchet who've lots of money and never think about what they spend the ones who leave the real tips he keeps them for himself in most places the boss splits his tips among the staff I'm the most senior of the three with twenty-one years there

Sebastien That's what you wanted to talk to him about?

Charles He cleared off when money cropped up never any time for a talk

Sebastien What did the other two say?

Charles Nothing too glad to have a job

**Three
Arriving**

Nina How long ago did she die?

Sebastien Eight months

Charles Yes come on in put down your bag

Nina It's incredible how clean and tidy everything is

here you split the chores between you?

Charles The windows are mine because Sebastien gets giddy all the rest is his

Nina Even the ironing?

Sebastien I've more time than Charles I get home each evening at five thirty

Charles You don't say you leave each morning at five

Nina Oh I couldn't ever

Charles Not like us we've a ten minute walk he has a forty-five minute journey in the morning and an hour and a quarter at night

Nina By underground?

Sebastien I've my bike a Peugeot

Nina Even in winter? And when it's raining?

Sebastien Doesn't bother me

Charles He doesn't like crowds on the way home he stops and does the shopping

Sebastien Do put your things down Mademoiselle

Charles You can call each other by your first names

Sebastien We'll see

Nina You two are so different thank you anyway and if I can help at all

**Four
The Shawl**

Nina It was fine I've really loved these three days I'm going to leave

Charles Going to leave?

Nina   There's no hope of getting on with Sebastien

Charles   Listen

Nina   I like him very much but you know how he is

Charles   He's got nothing against you he's jumpy because he's been made a chargehand and has to maintain the production rate

Nina   You too since I came you buzz about

Sebastien *enters.*

Sebastien   Now look here

Nina   I don't know which of you two is more impossible

Sebastien   You leave your magazines lying all over the place

Nina   You see Charles? It's final

Charles   Nina's going

Sebastien   You're going Mademoiselle?

Charles   I thought you were using first names

Sebastien *(sitting in the armchair)*   Well then Nina off you go

Nina *(settling onto* **Sebastien**'s *knee)*   It won't be as easy as that

Sebastien   What won't?

Nina   Getting used to you *(Sighing.)* to all this dust

Sebastien   Dust?

Nina   I know there's no dust you two you're made of dust oh it's unbelievable

Charles   What Nina?

Nina   He pushed open the door to have a pee he saw me sitting on the pan it could have been the devil he took to his heels I'm not used to shutting myself in

Charles   Well

Nina   Terribly sorry

Charles   You could make an effort

Nina   It's up to me to make an effort? Anyway I'm always making efforts

Sebastien   We all make efforts

Nina   I'm beginning to wonder if it's the right thing to do

Charles   What?

Nina   Make efforts all three of us instead of each doing his own thing like Sebastien for instance suppose you said just something nice to me? Don't you like me a tiny bit? Then why don't you show it?

She takes off her clothes one by one.

Charles   Why are you undressing?

Sebastien   I've an idea she's not going to leave

Nina   It doesn't follow

Charles   You'll catch cold

Sebastien   Yes well I'll leave the two of you together

Nina   No we are together all three of us don't think I need you too you know I can't bring myself to use your first name probably because you overawe me go and get me that big shawl of your mother's wrap me up in it

Sebastien *does so.*

Nina   That's nice did your mother overawe people too?

Charles   She had no cookery book

Sebastien   She didn't write down her recipes either

Charles He's recreated all her dishes

Sebastien Every night I used to sit over there

Charles He'd watch her

Nina It's a way of keeping her alive for the two of you but we could invent little things occasionally for the three of us

Charles I don't know if he'll let you near his stove

Nina Little mice can creep into all sorts of places

Nina *goes out.*

Charles I think you've upset her

Five
The Cinema

Nina It looks quite new

Sebastien Yes

Nina Well it's a lovely suitcase

Sebastien It's better this way

Nina What have you put in it?

Sebastien I've taken a one-room flat at Levallois

Nina I hear Levallois is very pretty it's on the coast?

Sebastien It's near the factory I've been thinking about it for a long time

Nina Oh yes you find the journey tiring

Sebastien When I get back here at night it's too much

Nina Especially now you've these new responsibilities

Sebastien It's so far I can't do my proper share of union work printing leaflets distributing them apart from all the meetings

Nina   Oh good because you look as though you're going on holiday so I thought

Sebastien   What?

Nina   You are telling me the truth?

Charles *enters.*

Charles   Where are you going?

Nina   Sebastien's leaving us he's just explained don't try to stop him

Charles   What does that mean?

Nina   He's right he's made up his mind he's embarrassing you and me and we'd be much better off without him he spends all his time tidying up behind me everything I leave lying about in every room apart from the fact that you and I have no privacy he you know he's methodical he's punctual yesterday I got home late for dinner oh Sebastien the only thing wrong with your reasoning is I couldn't get on without you if you go I go with you

Charles   You go with him? I'm delighted that's marvellous

Nina   I'll commute between you open this case oh look shirts neatly folded handkerchiefs sweaters pyjamas and here's your sponge bag a bit shabby you'll have to buy another one Sebastien we'll put everything back where it belongs then we'll go to the cinema tonight it's on me you mustn't play tricks like this wait a moment while I make myself beautiful

Nina *goes out.*

Charles   That Algerian finally

Sebastien   Not yet no

Charles   You have to sack him?

Sebastien   Nothing's settled yet

Charles   This is the third day running the boss hasn't spoken to me even to give me a rocket

Sebastien   The one thing that's certain is there's a shortage in the stores but for the foreman that's not the point he doesn't give a damn about the Algerian I'm the one he wants to break

Charles   He'd give me a rocket then we'd always have a laugh

Sebastien   There's no proof

Charles   Nina doesn't take all this very seriously but something's up

Nina *enters.*

Nina   Will you do me up Charles?

Charles   Isn't that right Nina? I was entitled to my three rockets a day

Nina   Bloody shit Charlie you're asleep Charlie next customer Charlie fucking shit

Charles   Bloody shit Charlie customers are waiting and you you bloody bastard you're upsetting the customers fucking shit

Sebastien   He says that in front of the customers?

Nina   Bloody shit he whispers it but everyone hears

Charles   Bloody shit Charlie will you never finish you bloody bastard no wonder you lose all the customers fucking shit

Nina   You could do two more customers a day easily you bloody bastard so fucking hell could you or couldn't you?

Charles   It's the final touches are the most important

Nina   That's why they all stick to you that's why they all want you to do their hair

Charles   He's not so bad

Nina   He likes his little jokes

Charles   Putting his hand on the girls' arses for a joke

Sebastien   We tell our girls they mustn't put up with that

Nina   Easy to say they need a nerve if it's their boss

Sebastien   We tell them to report it to their shop stewards it's a fact there are lots who daren't never mind a boss has no right to

Nina   We've no shop stewards how do you expect us to object?

Charles   It's part of the normal working conditions like us getting rockets right and left

Nina   He's not a bad bastard

Charles   No but he's up to something Nina doesn't really think so but for three days now he hasn't uttered a single fucking shit or a single bloody bastard

Sebastien   There are some petty bosses who do that sort of thing we try to stop it

Nina   Yes but us? What can *we* do? You're ready?

Six
The Curtains

Charles   You tell her

Sebastien   It's better from you

Charles   She's more afraid of you than me

Sebastien   She is yours

Charles   I don't know any more now

Sebastien   You brought her here it's your job to do it I mean we could speak to her together

Sebastien   One of us has got to start

Charles   Listen Nina you're much younger than us

Sebastien   Yes

Charles   You've your whole life before you and we've a good bit of ours behind us that's enough

Sebastien   How is that enough?

Charles   I mean Sebastien and I we're not prepared to let you chuck it all away here you can say something too

Sebastien   All away yes our past our habits our personalities

Charles   If you weren't so selfish

Sebastien   If you had a little consideration for the way we live

Charles   If she hadn't got so interested in you it could have worked she and I on the first floor you downstairs like before with nothing changed except we'd have eaten together of course

Sebastien   Man and wife and the general factotum

Charles   You know what I mean

Sebastien   I warned you

Charles   If you hadn't glued yourself onto her from the day she arrived

Sebastien   You're out of your mind

Charles   I say what I think

Sebastien   I kept as far away as I could

Charles As you could

Sebastien She wouldn't leave me alone and you egged her on

Charles We weren't going to ignore you

Nina *enters.*

Nina What a delicious smell it really smacks you in the nose

Charles Sebastien's giving us a little boiled beef

Nina A kiss Sebastien sorry I'm late you want to know where I've been? I've a surprise for all of us you know what we need most in this house? A bath I've found one

Charles What?

Nina On a building site it has four tiny feet Sebastien you don't look your usual self?

Charles He's wrestling with his conscience

Nina It's so deep some of the enamel's missing

Charles He's sacked the Algerian

Nina No job is easy

Charles Sebastien we could have dinner

Sebastien No first of all we've got to talk to her

Charles Right

Sebastien Nina

Nina You know I'm not going to become a fixture

Sebastien Charles has changed since you've been here he's in a bad way he and I we've thought it over

Charles It's Sebastien he can't bear it the way we live

Sebastien No I'm okay but Charles can't stand

Charles I've no worries

Nina   You have both of you I'm going to help you sort them out

She has taken a stepladder and unhooks the curtains which fall to the floor. She opens the window and throws them out.

Sebastien   The covers

Nina   The covers too

Charles   And the chandelier

They tear off the covers, take down the chandelier.

Sebastien   There's mother's room the bed's bigger you can take down the old pictures

Nina   No in that room nothing's to be changed

Sebastien   You'd be better off there

Nina   Or we could turn it into the living-room it has far more light than anywhere else instead of leaving it like that empty the shutters closed we'll clear out all the furniture and I'll make cushions hundreds of cushions

Sebastien   You're not hungry?

Nina   Starving

Charles   Let's eat

Seven
The Coast Is Clear

Charles   So you'll stay?

Nina   I know Charles but we're not going to be out of work both of us

Sebastien   You've fallen into his trap

Charles   Yes the coast is clear for him now

Nina   I won't let him get away with anything don't

worry

Charles You certainly have up to now and I was there

Nina Your being there drove him on

Charles That wasn't just a wandering hand when the last customer had gone he opened his flies

Nina He took my hand and placed it right there I bristled

Charles You called me

Nina I shouldn't have

Sebastien You could take him to a tribunal you could take him to court

Charles Have to prove it

Sebastien The other two girls were there

Charles You think they'd give evidence

Nina Charles hit him he fell the old woman screamed

Sebastien Shouldn't have touched him

Charles Oh anyway you don't think he'll be able to take on a young man at thirty per cent less

Nina There was no harm done I should have let him carry on

Charles And then?

Nina I'd have played with it a bit that's all

Sebastien Oh yes?

Nina But now

Sebastien So he sacked you?

Charles On the spot with no compensation serious misconduct

Sebastien After twenty-one years

Charles   Reason physical assault on his employer

Sebastien   You'd win at a tribunal

Charles   Yes and in the meantime

Sebastien   Maybe it's for the best you know your job you'll find another place where you can do it with dignity

Charles   I can hear Mother saying that

Eight
The Bath

Nina   It's a beautiful bath

Sebastien   It's an antique

Charles   How are we going to fill it?

Nina   With jugs

Sebastien   In Mother's room there's a big one under the dressing-table

Charles   How do we empty it?

Nina   I hadn't thought of that Sebastien's a mechanic he can fix a little pump

Sebastien   Where are we going to put it?

Nina   We'll leave it here

Charles   In the middle of the room?

Nina   A bath needs space all round it so you can move about

Charles   They're usually against the wall

Nina   Our bath is going to be like this

Business filling the bath with jugs, basins.

Charles   What does he say to my customers?

Nina   I don't know

Charles   What do you mean you don't know? Don't they ask?

Nina   He tells them it didn't work any more

Charles   What didn't work any more?

Nina   The old woman thought up the story we have to tell but don't let's talk about it I'll tell you tomorrow today I want

Charles   What?

Nina   Us to be happy

Charles   Tell me what is her story?

Nina   Well Charles you see Madame he'd started drinking a little too much a hairdresser must never have bad breath

Charles   He tells them that?

Nina   She tells them that

Charles   The others say nothing?

Nina   Lips sealed they know how to keep 'em shut and the girls too believe me the atmosphere's no better but some customers do an about-turn they won't have their hair done by anyone but you

Charles   I'll have his skin

Sebastien   There's the law

Charles   I don't believe in the law I'll slaughter him

Sebastien   Two blacks don't make a white

Nina   There our bath's ready

Charles   Form a queue

Sebastien   Not me

Nina   Not you?

Sebastien   No never

Nina   We'll have it together all three of us your replacement started this morning a little Italian

Sebastien   Not me

Nina   Oh yes

Sebastien   I'm off

Nina   I'll undress you

Charles   A foreigner too

Nina   Never stops chattering and sickly so skinny he looks like a matchstick

Sebastien (*letting himself be undressed*)   Italy the home of hairdressing

Nina (*Italian accent*)   Gino my name's Gino I'm from Napoli (*Ordinary accent.*) he'll finish off a haircut in five minutes old Mother Tonton's ecstatic he can do more people his first customer was Madame Bossard's daughter that big blonde with a fringe remember? The one who always asks to be thinned out he took a good half centimetre too much off the sides but she well Charles you're not getting undressed?

Charles   I don't feel like it

Nina   Then undress me

Charles *does so.*

Nina   You get in Sebastien Charles is going to watch us do it maybe get him interested a bath is the greatest pleasure if you do it properly

Charles   I don't see the sense

Nina   No sense just pure bliss you've no idea

Sebastien   It means nothing to me

Nina   Look you have to learn I don't say it will work the first time (*She gets in.*) then there's Madame Barberat one of your oldest customers

Charles   One of my first

Nina   Yes

Charles   I remember when I started she'd talk the whole time about her divorce she insisted I told her whether she ought to get a divorce or not

Nina   You must never tell a customer that it's *her* business

Charles   No you have to give her advice she wasn't that young then and I was a kid her husband used to beat her but you know she said

Nina *is washing* **Sebastien**.

Nina   You know?

Charles   You know I'm so mad about him magnificent hair she had

Nina   Even when it's white today it's still magnificent

Charles   She wanted a very tight perm you know he was a man who'd suffered a lot in his youth he'd never escaped from the clutches of a possessive mother

Sebastien   She got her divorce?

Charles   No talking about it was all she needed ten years later he died of cancer of the throat he never stopped smoking she hated smoke (*He gets undressed; standing next to the bath he washes* **Nina**.) she didn't ask after me?

Nina   Of course

Charles   That hurts

Nina   Rub my back yes harder

Charles   This morning I went to the employment

agency

Sebastien   There are some of them at the factory Italians they become skilled tradesmen real fast

Nina   Then there was Mademoiselle Colin

Sebastien   They're a lively enterprising people

Nina   Have you a lot of Portuguese?

Charles   At the agency I had to see a girl she had curly hair there were two of them interviewing me the other was a fat old woman with glasses she was lame

Nina   When did you go there?

Charles   I told you this morning

Nina *gets out of the bath,* **Charles** *gets in; she washes him.*

Charles   They didn't like it when I told them the job I had

Nina   Why?

Charles   It's overcrowded they made me fill in forms they wanted to know if I'd be interested in being recycled into boilermaking think it over we can send you on a three-month course in Poitiers full pay with board and lodging thrown in

Nine
The Card Game

Sebastien's *head is bleeding. He lets* **Nina** *wash the wound and bandage it.*

Sebastien   You're quite an expert Nina

Nina   I always longed to be a nurse I did a year's training he was waiting for you?

Sebastien   At the factory gates yes

Nina   It's a wretched job shampooing with the tips you do better

Sebastien   You haven't lost your skill

Nina   Then he went for you?

Sebastien   No he wanted to talk

Nina   Don't you talk too much

Sebastien   We walked a few yards together I was holding my bike

Nina   Quiet you'll pass out again

Sebastien   He was walking next to me we were talking calmly Tahar listen I said I had no choice and I knew you wanted to go back to Algeria in two months anyway so two months more or less I know he said he has his wife and two kids back there listen I said this business about a shortage in the stores I don't know if it's you or not I'm happy to believe it's not you I know he said he repeated it twice I know and then I felt the blow I was hampered by the bike when I got up there was nobody there Tahar was a quiet lad not very talkative on the ball technically you never had to touch his machine

Nina   Charles isn't back yet

Sebastien   He gets in later every night and drunker

Nina   You came the whole way from the factory on your bike in this state?

Sebastien   Tahar you've a union card you must understand it's not a decision the lads and I took with any pleasure

Nina   You could have passed out fallen under the wheels of a lorry

Sebastien   I better hadn't

Nina   No but

Sebastien I was determined to get home

Nina In this sort of case you go to the first chemist

Sebastien In this sort of case no you don't

Nina You're not easy to understand

Sebastien The chemist calls the police you're taken off to hospital questions statements you're asked to lodge a formal complaint it's all too complicated

Nina In your mind?

Sebastien In the facts

Sebastien, *lying down, and* **Nina**, *seated, peel the beans.* **Charles** *enters.*

Charles Fifty francs give me fifty francs I need fifty francs

Nina A kiss

Charles Fifty francs

Nina You won't kiss me?

Charles If you drink you don't kiss ladies if you drink you've got bad breath fifty francs or twenty francs

Nina Give me a kiss and come and help us with the beans

Charles What's the matter with him?

Nina It's rather funny Sebastien opened the front door and fainted away at my feet I see I'm making progress with Sebastien he lets me peel the beans with him

Charles Twenty francs

Nina You're going out again?

Charles I'm in the middle of a card game

Nina Stay here we need you

Sebastien Let him go

Nina Not just for the beans

Charles Don't count on me for the beans

Nina *seizes him, takes off his windcheater, his shoes.*

Nina He got beaten up by the Algerian the one he sacked

Charles Why don't we send all these wogs back home where they belong?

Sebastien I can't stand the sight of him let him clear out go back to your bistro

Charles Aren't I in my own home here?

Sebastien Give him his twenty francs

Charles Doing nothing degenerate the lot of them stinking out our country France

Sebastien Give it him

Charles It's not our home any more real Frenchmen of France have no jobs now

Nina *has gone out to get a jug of water: she empties it over* **Charles**'s *head.*

Charles To get a job as a hairdresser the employment agency's useless the bistro's the place to go there might be something in the Avenue Victor Hugo I'm going to have a try there in the morning

Ten
Waking Up

A double bed and a single next to each other. In the double bed, **Charles** *and* **Nina**; *in the single bed,* **Sebastien**.

Sebastien You slept well Charles?

Charles   Yes you slept well?

Nina   Yes and you Sebastien?

Sebastien   Yes today's my last day off work

Charles   Maybe me too it will be settled by lunch

Sebastien   Tomorrow I report for duty

Nina   My two little birds are going to fly away look at me both of you

Charles   Anyway there's a chance

Sebastien   It will be okay Charles

Nina   Look at me oh I shall find it so strange

Charles   Nina it's time

Nina   Get up Nina get up you two stay there tucked up in bed?

Sebastien   Tomorrow morning at seven Leduc his fat little hands behind his back we'll take up the conversation where we left off Pelissier I'm asking you to be firmer with your men there's too much slackness in this team Pelissier

Nina *has got up, washed etc; she gets dressed.*

Sebastien   I'm sorry but I've got my production up twelve per cent over budget is that true or isn't it? If you had proper control of your men Pelissier you'd have done better than twelve per cent you've no authority over your men you tell me how you measure authority I said it's enough to walk up and down the factory he said it's your men who stop most to gossip authority is measured by the quantity and quality of production I said my men have the best results in the whole factory of course he said you've the best machines if I've the best machines I said maybe that's because they're the best maintained

Nina   My knickers Charles

Charles   You left them down the bed

Nina   Clever me

Charles   Who is this Leduc?

Nina   His foreman

Sebastien   An old trade unionist he's the man who formed the first party cell he's got promoted he made me sack Tahar he didn't think I'd do it he wasn't pleased when he knew I had he thought he'd got me

Charles   Now they'll make you sack a few more then they'll make you foreman you've got a future now a fine future a planned future hasn't he Nina?

Nina   Suppose I told you you bore me the pair of you

Charles   As for me they want a young man with one or two years' experience but maybe they'll take me I'll have to accept the pay they're offering that means starting off twenty years behind

Nina *goes out.*

Sebastien   She's gone without a word

Charles   She was going to be late

Sebastien   There's something wrong

Charles   I haven't drunk a drop for over a fortnight it's done with I promise you done with

Sebastien   I know but it's nothing to do with you it's the pair of us

Charles   What should we have done?

Sebastien   We didn't try to find out

Charles   What?

Sebastien   I don't know

Eleven
Leaving

Charles   It's your suitcase it's new

Sebastien   She wanted to borrow it I told her she could keep it

Nina   Charles my sweaters in the top drawer Sebastien my blouses

Charles   I don't believe you

Nina   You don't believe me? I'll introduce you he's five years younger than me he's a baby he has a tiny little crumpled face we can't understand a word the other says my pullovers Charles

Charles   What do you see in him?

Nina   How does one know?

Sebastien   Where's he from?

Nina   Czechoslovakia he's a refugee

Sebastien   Then he hasn't a job?

Charles   She's making the whole thing up

Nina   No I'm not he was standing at the street corner looking lost

Charles   Are you angry with us?

Nina   Oh no I'm very fond of you

Sebastien   You won't come back

Nina   I don't think so my shoes my four pairs of shoes my boots I'll come and see you my slippers

Charles   I can't stand it

Nina   What can't you stand?

Charles   *seizes the handle of the open suitcase, throws it away;*

the contents fly all over the room. **Nina** *collapses in the big armchair and closes her eyes. A pause. She gets up, smiles.*

Nina   You know? I did it wrong first the shoes then the clothes (*Picking up and folding the scattered things; the packing starts again.*) and though he won't get a residence permit it doesn't matter Tonton's given me a big rise

Charles   You've had it off with him?

Nina   Just the opposite he keeps those big paws of his to himself a twenty-five per cent rise the trouble I had keeping a straight face he solemnly summoned me to say he was appointing me first assistant I said Monsieur Fretton you shouldn't do that with your turnover falling every month exactly Nina he said I want you to help me relaunch the place we're going to do it up you have taste

Charles   Too late it's hopeless

Nina   My bottle of lavender water Sebastien I was forgetting

Charles   He's got fifty years to catch up

Nina   In the medicine cupboard and the nail varnish I'm forgetting everything

Charles   He's fifty years behind

Nina   But if I can influence him because it's a fact my head's seething with ideas

Charles   You don't give a damn Sebastien she's ditching us and you say nothing after only two months I'm earning as much as I got at Tonton's after twenty-one years you see we split all the tips and it's a different clientele

Nina   Not to mention your old customers who've followed you that's what I told Tonton I think that's what made him understand well cheerio

Sebastien   Cheerio

Nina   Cheerio Charles

Charles   Well cheerio

Twelve
The Visit

Sebastien, *on a stepladder, is painting a wall; new furniture,*
very modern; **Charles**, *in an apron, is preparing dinner;* **Nina**
enters, shakes her umbrella.

Nina   *You* made the puree?

Charles   Arab sausages puree's not so difficult with
instant packets

Nina   A kiss Sebastien

Sebastien   You're all right Nina?

Charles   He's no time now he gets back late in the
evenings

Nina   You're redoing the place what a revolution

Charles   Every evening or almost he has meetings but
on Sundays he does the cooking you ought to come one
Sunday

Nina   Every Sunday we take a train

Charles   With your refugee?

Nina   He paints landscapes with frightening little people
he paints houses which explode he paints things like that

Sebastien   He's an artist?

Nina   And train interiors he's a dissident released from a
labour camp

Sebastien   He paints in the train?

Nina   He paints train interiors he paints trains that look
like women and animals that look like trains I bought a
camera while he paints I take photographs I photograph

everything he's taught me to look

Sebastien Like you you taught us to see differently

Nina But Sebastien you wouldn't teach me the tiniest little recipe

Sebastien If we were starting again anyway there was this conflict

Charles The management were waiting to get their own back he had to make a definite choice he joined the strikers in fact he's become one of their leaders then the management tried to transfer him he refused the lads supported him that sparked off a new strike the management backed down Leduc leaves him in peace now

Nina Till next time

Sebastien No something's changed now

Nina It's good this puree

Charles I added a spoonful of fresh cream

Nina I can't get over it

Sebastien You see for the first time Charles is recognised for his real worth

Charles In this salon the staff can put their whole heart into it it's the New Coiffure with no gadgets you can invent things and time doesn't count you can spend half a day on a customer if it's warranted

Sebastien For dessert there are dates

Charles A parcel's just arrived

Sebastien The Czechs they're a fine intelligent people they've let themselves be trampled on too

Charles Like every year from Tunisia

Sebastien The Tunisians are too

Nina   That's where they come from?

Charles   Every year

Nina   Yes I remember Sebastien

Charles   Spent a night

Nina   Yes

Charles   Tell us

Sebastien   I've told you

Charles   Oh I haven't mentioned he's got a girlfriend now

Nina   Do go on

Sebastien   She had little bells on her bracelets her necklace

Nina   They melt in your mouth

Charles   We're not very fond of them

Sebastien   So why don't you take them along if the two of you like them

A Smile
on the End of the Line

Les Travaux et les jours

translated by PETER MEYER

Characters

Anne, *a clerk, forty, married with one daughter, Simone*
Nicole, *a clerk, thirty, separated from her husband, with two sons, Antoine and Mathieu; living with Guillermo*
Yvette, *a temporary clerk, twenty, single, with a young brother, Roger; in love with Guillermo*
Jaudouard, *head of department, forty-five*
Guillermo, *a craftsman, checking grinders returned by customers, forty-two, originally Spanish*

The scene is the After-Sales department of the Cosson Company, manufacturers of coffee-grinders, near Paris. It is an open-plan office, the working areas defined by low, metal partitions, with filing and storage units attached to them. Metal furniture, set at right angles, for the three girls, with typewriter and telephone. A device for holding the receiver on the shoulder. A metal workbench with small tools for Guillermo. Standard metal desk for the manager.

A Smile on the End of the Line was first performed in the UK on 13 March 1987 at the Orange Tree Theatre, Richmond, with the following cast:

Anne	Auriol Smith
Nicole	Joan Moon
Yvette	Lucy Durham-Matthews
Jaudouard	Philip York
Guillermo	Andrew Maclachlan

Directed by Sam Walters

One

Nicole Three times already we've changed the motor three times

Yvette I thought I'd die

Nicole A brand new Aristocrat grinder for the price of the Standard one Cosson's exclusive offer to its customers whenever damage is beyond repair

Yvette Yes at the end of the corridor it's silly being beautiful it doesn't mean anything and if I protest

Anne It's breaking her heart she's got to come to terms with it

Nicole Take advantage of it the speed is no greater the reverse in fact but to preserve the aroma the Aristocrat is more efficient you will marvel at the silence of this machine no really and yours is badly dented I have your card in front of me the motor's been changed three times the first time seven years ago

Yvette In love?

Anne With Guillermo

Yvette Yes

Anne Chucked her husband for him

Jaudouard (*leaning over* **Yvette***'s work*) At Beaumoulin they may reply like that at Mixwell they may reply like that

Anne Why doesn't she buy a dog you may ask

Jaudouard You mustn't be frightened when I talk to you

Yvette A phase

Anne I thought

Yvette Of course living all on her own in the country

in the middle of nowhere

Anne   You have to like animals Cécile only likes cats

Nicole   It will be cheaper for you I told her it's not a question of money she said I'm attached to it my husband he's dead he gave it me we didn't earn very much at the time it was crazy

Yvette   Yes another page is turned

Nicole   She's madly in love it's all sighs and whispers

Anne   You believe it?

Jaudouard   At Beaumoulin at Mixwell but not at Cosson

Anne   Could you bear that

Nicole   I swear it's true

Jaudouard   You have to acquire it it can be acquired the house style

Yvette   But where in my letter can you find any apologies?

Jaudouard   I'm not a wolf at Cosson we don't apologise we explain

Anne   You don't feel well?

Nicole   He gave it me for my twenty-second birthday we got married we were twenty we didn't think he was violent never bore a grudge well turn round he'd say

Anne   Do be careful

Jaudouard   And it's too long much too long no need to add all these explanations at Cosson we're brief

Nicole   Everything he could lay his hand on whenever he didn't agree

Jaudouard   We're brief very personalised very attentive and brief

Yvette   Brief yes I see these last two lines are
unnecessary

Anne   Oh yes she lost her head he did too

Jaudouard   It can be acquired a tone that's deferential
and incisive without ever being abrupt the tone the style
of the company

Nicole   But the enamel look she said the enamel's
perfect he threw it at me three four times after a quarrel
it was wonderful we were madly in love and she wanted
to know if I was too and when I told her I was married
also

Jaudouard   At Cosson we don't reply like that Anne my
sweet show her how we reply at Cosson let her see some
examples

Anne   Nicole never stops showing her Monsieur
Jaudouard it's got to grow on her that can't be done in a
month

Yvette   Body and soul body as well as soul

Anne   You make me envious

Yvette   A very old chemist told me

Anne   What's it called?

Yvette   You saw it?

Nicole   The enamel today wouldn't last like that

Jaudouard   What did she say?

Anne   She said that on a machine produced today the
enamel

Jaudouard (*to* **Yvette**)   The enamel would resist in
exactly the same way the method of manufacture has not
changed since the day the house of Cosson started

Yvette   The method of manufacture has remained
exactly the same

Jaudouard　Exactly

Yvette　Yes sir

Jaudouard　You have a temporary contract with us darling which expires

Yvette　The 10th of February if you let it expire I need the job

Jaudouard　If you need the job then well you say you need the job

Yvette　I have to support my family mother earned a good wage I told you she's dead

Jaudouard　You told me yes she's dead if you need the job it wouldn't be a bad idea if you behaved in such a way as to make us want to keep you

Yvette　I don't give satisfaction?

Jaudouard　I won't say that the After-Sales department is the most important department in the company

Yvette　I do my best I look after a young brother

Jaudouard　Monsieur Albert who died eight years ago Monsieur Pierre's father we never see Monsieur Pierre just the opposite of Monsieur Albert Monsieur Albert it was unusual for him not to look in here once or twice a week the After-Sales Jaudouard you see then he'd give me a pat on the shoulder it's the heart I won't say it's the most important part of the body the business needs legs and arms and lungs and a stomach too but when you answer the telephone or when you write to a customer who's in trouble and a customer who approaches us is always a customer in trouble when they approach us it means they need help reassurance and it's the way we answer which will attach them closer to Cosson or detach them to throw them into the arms of Mixwell or Beaumoulin

Yvette　I think I'm polite sir and no customer's complained about me

Jaudouard   There we are we'll have to think carefully

Yvette   You smell of garlic forgive me

Jaudouard   A little piece of dry bread rubbed with garlic in the salad

Yvette   It's malodorous

Jaudouard   Being polite is only half of it there must be the tone a tone which distinguishes us from our competitors a tone of courtesy and firmness the customer must feel that we're certain our quality is superior to all others at the same time that we're ready to give him a service tailored to his needs and personalised

Yvette (*to* **Guillermo**, *their fingers entwining and untwining, all the gestures of desire*)   He called me darling he pressed up against me, he told me I'd just under a month to show if I'm able to pick it up I'm in love

Guillermo   It will come

Yvette   What will?

Guillermo   One day the habit

Yvette   He made speeches at me it was your voice I heard Guillermo say something

Guillermo   You'll manage

Anne *is munching an apple;* **Nicole** *is flat on her stomach on a desk.*

Nicole   No I won't put up with it

Anne   What name?

Nicole   Raguet from Bordeaux she shut me up I couldn't get a word in

Anne   Raguet last year or the year before

Nicole   You had to cope with her?

Anne   He's just having a little fun Nicole it's sheer

cruelty remember he's a Spaniard it won't go any further because Guillermo oh you're in a bad way (*She massages her neck.*) because you sit in the wrong position when you type everyone forgets they've only one spinal column making people suffer is in their blood

Nicole   I saw him trembling

Anne   Because Guillermo's a sensible chap anyway Jaudouard won't stand for it

Nicole   You noticed too?

Anne   Yes and the girl's only a temp

Nicole   He rubs up against her

Anne   It makes me laugh

Nicole   With his sermons about how to build up the Cosson image he'll make her permanent you'll see

Anne   Let this muscle go relax since he took over from Monsieur Benin

Nicole   Monsieur Benin was much more human

Anne   He particularly doesn't want any trouble with Monsieur Célidon's promotion coming up

Nicole   You think there's a chance he might be appointed?

Anne   To Monsieur Célidon's job?

Nicole   That skirt of yours it's real Scotch tweed oh I like the colour it's a breath of summer

Anne   He won't get it Nicole I was talking to Cécile about it they'll never want to move him up into management but Monsieur Célidon says it's a foregone conclusion they'll put him in Sales they want to widen his experience I said to Cécile that if they shift Jaudouard because there's talk of him being moved to another department

Nicole   If Jaudouard's transferred and they don't appoint you then I say any other solution's unfair and I won't accept it

Anne   Except that appointing a woman you know that would never enter their heads

Nicole   Maybe it's up to us to force it into their heads and not just that yes quite a few other things too

Anne   This idea of a union here nobody would understand it you'd be burning your wings relax you feel this shoulder how knotted it still is

Nicole   I think the only way to make them understand is to go and do it

Guillermo *has entered.*

Guillermo   You haven't seen Monsieur Jaudouard?

Anne   Well what does Guillermo think about it?

Nicole   What would your father have thought Guillermo? You think differently Guillermo thinks

Anne   Well let him say what he thinks

Guillermo   You haven't seen Monsieur Jaudouard?

Nicole   You see?

Guillermo   What makes you talk about my father?

Nicole   Wasn't he killed because of his ideas?

Guillermo   It's Madame Serge, she's asking for Monsieur Jaudouard

Nicole   Died in Franco's prisons

Guillermo   To give him a memo from Monsieur Bataille

Nicole   After fathering this little boy

Yvette   Cosson After-Sales at your service hullo yes

what is your reference number?

Anne   I don't know yet

Nicole   Well when's it for?

Guillermo   A little party

Anne   Yes I hope

Yvette   Three weeks is the usual time our factory's in the Vosges repairs are done at the factory with the time for transport you have to reckon

Nicole   Guillermo and I we don't share the same views Guillermo thinks the management must know what they're doing so they're always right

Guillermo   What matters is not looking for trouble

Anne   Guillermo's so wise

Guillermo   We've problems enough already

Jaudouard *has entered.*

Jaudouard   I'm asked to read you an internal memo please inform your staff that the management invites head office staff to have a drink with their chairman and managing director Monsieur Pierre Cosson to congratulate him on winning the Five Continents golf tournament the party will take place in the entrance hall on Tuesday next at five thirty p.m. the half-hour's work thus lost will not have to be made up later signed Charles Bataille administrative and financial director

Two

Jaudouard   Hay fever? No it's not

Anne   Even so this hot toddy will do you good

Yvette   It could be caused by any number of things we'll have to dismantle it to see

Anne Under your shirt in winter you ought to wear one of those anti-bronchitis flannel vests

Yvette In the Vosges you can rely on us being as quick as possible

Anne It happened like that? Suddenly?

Nicole Photographic goods didn't pay any more he became a heavy-goods driver I never saw him with Guillermo I've made a new life

Yvette That's normal especially if you drink a lot of coffee after four or five years the motor

Anne Like taking a corner he actually used those very words

Nicole With those margins he couldn't struggle on any longer he does those long international runs I couldn't either

Yvette What Nicole?

Nicole I couldn't react any more I was standing still in the middle of a whirlpool

Yvette Nicole how can I help it?

Anne You look better already it's your sinusitis you get it every winter

Jaudouard You do have an opinion even so?

Anne She's a sweet girl sensible quick has to earn a living like most young people she couldn't care less about what she does absent-minded anyway not cut out for this kind of work it does seem to have cleared your nose you're breathing now

Yvette Even when you set it in the extra-fine position?

Guillermo It started with the little tour he made round the office after the party

Nicole I tell you we can't accept it we're not cattle

Jaudouard   A customer on the line

Anne   Feels when the person answering isn't really concerned

Guillermo   It's more than a year since he set foot on this floor

Anne   Sweet but foreign to the spirit of the department that must be what you were looking for

Jaudouard   What?

Anne   A change of air it won't take her three months to destroy a climate that's been created by dozens of years of effort maybe it's for the best who am I to judge?

Yvette   You're not giving me an answer

Nicole   You think you like things to be clear-cut but then you adjust don't you? Cosson After-Sales at your service hullo

Yvette   And Monsieur Célidon?

Anne   Jaudouard did try to get him to have a word with Madame Serge

Nicole   Célidon's feeble he's not going to get involved never

Jaudouard   This girl does have abilities if only we can manage to train her

Anne   You'll manage seeing how you take her in hand mind you I'm not sure she wouldn't rather be taken in hand by Guillermo

Jaudouard   You're not being objective Anne

Anne   No I'm a woman aren't I

Jaudouard   Talking about another woman

Anne   And I'm forty and she's twenty so much the better as we've got to take a corner you've heard that little phrase

Guillermo   He said when you approach a corner
Monsieur Albert's father Monsieur Martial he was the
grandson of Monsieur Théophile who founded the
business and his son Louis was the father of Monsieur
Martial

Anne   I don't know if Célidon's feeble anyway why
should he get mixed up with the problems of junior staff
he's a business school graduate he knows he's launched up
the promotion ladder and even Jaudouard

Yvette   He doesn't listen to Jaudouard

Guillermo   When Monsieur Martial lost his right leg in
1915 and was condemned to death in his absence in 1945
two weeks later Monsieur Albert came back from his
Oflag he took the business in hand rebuilt the factory
there was nothing left after the American bombing I had
my back turned I'm not sure exactly what he said

Nicole   He said I thank the staff for their efforts which
have allowed me to win this golf tournament whose
prestige at the international level rebounds on the
company which bears my name but which belongs to you

Anne   It's thanks to the devotion of the entire staff that
Cosson has attained this world-wide dimension

Guillermo   Has achieved this impressive growth

Nicole   Which naturally leads to questions about the best
way to approach the future

Anne   A future heavy with uncertainty

Guillermo   He said heavy with threats

Nicole   He said we have to take the corner

Anne   He was mumbling it was pitiful

Jaudouard   Hadn't rehearsed it enough Monsieur
Bataille wrote it

Nicole   You saw the face Madame Serge was making?

Anne   She was obviously hating every word she heard

Nicole   Hasn't she got a photo of her family hanging on her wall

Guillermo   In a solid silver frame Monsieur Albert gave her for her twenty-five years service it was the year before Monsieur Albert fell off his horse in 1969

Yvette   On your guarantee there should be the retailer's stamp with the date you've no stamp with the date? She says it's started making a noise like a jet plane and the retailer didn't date her guarantee

Nicole   There's nothing in the office regulations to forbid you decorating your area is there?

Anne   Célidon won't do anything

Jaudouard   The order comes from high up it comes from the top it comes from Monsieur Pierre

Nicole   Monsieur Jaudouard you're a friend of Madame Serge suppose you have a word with Madame Serge direct?

Jaudouard   So that Monsieur Célidon finds out I've short-circuited the official channels?

Nicole   But you do agree we can't accept?

Guillermo   When he was crushed against a rock that was a loss Monsieur Albert he had a head on him two years after the opening of the new factory he brought out the first prototype of an electric grinder

Anne   Monsieur Bataille's much more flexible *he* could speak to Monsieur Pierre

Nicole   But how can we approach Monsieur Bataille?

Anne   I could say a word to Cécile

Yvette   A noise like a jet plane what answer do you

give?

Nicole   Ask Monsieur Jaudouard

Yvette   Doesn't grind any more it produces lumps

Guillermo   He'd drunk several glasses of champagne he
went round the offices his glass of champagne in his hand
till he finds himself facing the poster of Johnny Halliday
that's a good four or five feet high and Odile said she
didn't like Johnny so Monsieur Pierre turned round he
said he didn't either he didn't like Johnny he said these
aren't offices now they're Arab bazaars you'd think you're
in the kasbah get it all cleaned up Monique said she was
entitled to like anyone she wanted to and it was her desk
Odile who'd have done better to hold her tongue but had
had a glass too much said looking at Johnny gave her a
headache and she and Monique work on the same
customer files impossible to split them up

Yvette   I've nothing else to say to you I love him I want
him

Nicole   And he?

Yvette   Ask him I can't make him say

Anne   If I talk to Cécile and if Cécile mentions it to
Monsieur Bataille Célidon will never know that might be
the way

Jaudouard   Célidon will guess

Guillermo   With Monsieur Albert this sort of thing
would never have got blown up like this because
Monsieur Albert kept in touch with the staff he had a
word for everyone he knew the children's names and any
illness they'd had

Yvette   Sleep with him he smells of garlic all the same I
think I'll have to

Guillermo   What?

Yvette   It's simple Guillermo come down from your cloud escape from your past to get myself made permanent

Guillermo   No

Yvette   What right have you to say that?

Nicole   We'll make it as good as new

Yvette   I want you so badly

Nicole   And when you get the machine back

Anne   One afternoon in sixty-eight he passed through the office he slipped me an envelope it doubled my salary your smile goes down well over the phone he said

Yvette   From there to outlawing the smallest postcard

Guillermo   All because some people always have to go too far

Nicole   Words don't say much Guillermo

Guillermo   Listen

Nicole   But we have to use them I imagine it's not easy for you

Guillermo   Wait I won't be a moment

Nicole   Anyway I can tell you it won't make me lose any sleep kill myself maybe but not lose any sleep

Three

Yvette   The chaps I've slept with before you

Anne   I'm sorry

Yvette   They were schoolfriends then friends from dancing from cycling

Nicole   Anne he hates me that man like he hates

Guillermo

Anne No you must understand he has a lot on his mind

Nicole I'd like to know what

Anne But we've no repair service in Paris any more not even for the simplest cases all repairs are done at the factory in Vosges of course I understand you insist for your part you must understand

Yvette Anyway friends we got on well and then less well and sometimes very well

Guillermo In the flea market on Sunday morning in the middle of a pile of old iron without the drawer and the handle the remains of an old grinder it gave me a shock

Anne But we can only do what it's possible to do she says she's the wife of the French ambassador in Russia and she's only in Paris for a week

Guillermo I recognised it ten yards away before I saw it I felt it I felt I was caught in a magnetic field

Yvette I've decided that you'll be my master I'll be your servant Guillaume the Lionheart I'll never be your lady

Jaudouard If she's the ambassador's wife let her sort it out with the embassy they'll send it in the diplomatic bag

Yvette The lady of your dreams is Cosson you've given yourself up to her service

Anne She thinks it needs a simple adjustment the ambassador makes his coffee himself in his office at crack of dawn to grind it he must have his Cosson he's never used anything but a Cosson

Yvette They might be able to afford a second machine

Guillermo Like a dream that's so beautiful you're afraid of waking up the first Cosson model designed by

the founder Monsieur Théophile in 1869 how much is it?
Twenty francs twenty francs this old wreck? Twelve francs
twelve francs? On your way sixteen francs

Nicole   Guillermo could repair it

Guillermo   If Monsieur Jaudouard gives permission no
one need tell Monsieur Célidon

Nicole   In a case like this better appear to be a little
flexible everyone knows Guillermo's the best man at
Cosson for repairs

Jaudouard   He should have accepted that transfer to
the Vosges

Guillermo   The miracle is that five years ago in the
attic of a farm in Normandy I found a handle from the
same model the only complete example known is in the
national museum

Nicole   All the same it's a waste of talent Madame
Serge says so herself

Yvette   We're not made the same way Guillermo have
you thought of that? We've nothing in common it's like
oil and vinegar when they're mixed together

Nicole   Another year or two and he'll have lost his skill

Guillermo   The drawer's missing

Jaudouard   Another year or two? The problem could
be put differently in a year or two

Anne   Monsieur Jaudouard

Jaudouard   I tell you this my dear you personally his
job checking inward deliveries is sheer duplication

Guillermo   Finding this particular drawer? A chance in
a million

Anne   The customer's on the line Monsieur Jaudouard

Jaudouard   I've studied the problem from every angle

whichever way you look at the matter it would be
handled just as well in the Vosges

Anne Monsieur Jaudouard I can tell her it's okay?

Guillermo It could take a thousand years so I'll end up
making it myself

Nicole There might be a foreign body in your coffee
you haven't checked?

Jaudouard With my budget I can't justify keeping him
on

Nicole A piece of grit yes that can happen you say the
screw broke all on its own?

Jaudouard I mentioned the point to Monsieur Célidon
when it's a question of cutting expenses he's all ears he is

Nicole But it was you who offered him the job and I
know for a fact that the factory will be more efficient if
they don't have to check them the grinders will go straight
onto the repair line

Anne I can tell her

Jaudouard Tell her to jump in the sea fuck it we can't
carry on like this everyone does what they like in this
department and mark my words it's going to stop it's
finished do you hear? There's a rule we're obeying it tell
her

Guillermo What Yvette?

Yvette You know my name now?

Guillermo Yvette

Anne I have to confirm unfortunately after consulting
the head of the department

Guillermo You're the air I breathe

Yvette You're the sea I swim in

Guillermo   Your tongue tastes of nuts

Anne   I'd have liked to have helped you

Guillermo   What Yvette?

Yvette   What you're going to do about Nicole

Guillermo   You're not going to let him touch you

Yvette   If I have to to be made permanent

Nicole   He hates me

Anne   He's frightened

Guillermo   No

Yvette   What does it matter?

Anne   Yesterday he went to see Monsieur Célidon

Nicole   It hurts

Anne   Your neck

Nicole   It hurts all down my back now if you knew
Anne I'm thinking of the children if it weren't for Antoine
and Mathieu

Anne   Poor Jaudouard

Nicole   The bastard the lunatic

Anne   No Nicole

Nicole   I know *you* like him

Anne   He got ticked off by Célidon listen he marched in
last night with a demand for additional staff he'd worked
himself to death producing pages of figures to prove that
with the present staff and a load of correspondence and
telephone calls growing steadily in view of the growth in
the numbers of machines in use on the market our
present delays can only increase and be reflected in the
time taken for repairs which already average three weeks

and two days and he'd worked out the backlog which
adds up to two hundred and fifty hours a month i.e.
ninety per cent of one additional employee from which his
report demonstrated the need to recruit a fourth girl
Célidon demolished the whole thing piece by piece he
disputed the basic premises for instance the average length
of a phone call he asked for the statistics in real time ah
there are no statistics in real time? How Jaudouard can
you claim to be responsible for a department like this if
you have no statistics for the average time spent by each
girl on each job? And Guillermo? What use is he?
Jaudouard came out livid he'd never had such a
resounding flop in his whole career

Nicole   *He* didn't tell you that

Anne   I had lunch with Cécile

Nicole   Something's brewing then

Jaudouard   I'm sorry darling

Yvette   It's not serious you know

Jaudouard   I was sharp with you it's my nerves work's
not always a piece of cake

Yvette   Anyway you don't smell of garlic now

Jaudouard   I've been thinking about you

Yvette   You're going to make me permanent?

Nicole   This car we've just bought

Guillermo   What's changed?

Nicole   Everything

Yvette   That's no answer you know Monsieur
Jaudouard?

Jaudouard   Have you seen *Marathon Man*? You never go
to the pictures? We might go and see it together?

Anne   Disaster total and absolute

Nicole   She still hasn't come home?

Yvette   It's a good film?

Nicole   You've no news you'd rather not talk about Simone? You're wrong you know do talk even if it does seem pointless

Yvette   My tastes are I love stories with happy endings and torture

Nicole   It helps

Jaudouard   You've no idea the things I like

Yvette   We'll take Roger my young brother?

Anne   Célidon who had never up to now shown any interest in this department

Yvette   I can't leave him on his own how many children have you got? Cosson After Sales at your service hullo yes give me your reference number I'll check

Nicole   Makes you wonder if there hasn't been a change in the plans for his promotion

Anne   Cécile hasn't said a word about that

Yvette   The problem is the speed? In the filter position the Aristocrat model if you fill the holder to the brim

Anne   We ate at that Chinese place the case went all the way up to Monsieur Bataille he made Madame Serge come down he didn't say anything to Madame Serge but there she was listening to her protegé being torn to shreds without being able to say a word

Yvette   That's unusual we reckon fifty-five to sixty-five seconds no with the Standard you have to reckon eighty seconds the Aristocrat is more efficient

Nicole   She's an elephant

Anne   Yes she'll get over it

Nicole   But Jaudouard

Yvette   Apart from which it's quieter and besides it preserves the aroma better

Anne   I'm wondering if before leaving the job he didn't mean to leave his mark behind him

Nicole   And get Jaudouard into trouble

Anne   And make life difficult for Madame Serge anyway it's all going to fall on our heads make no mistake about that

Jaudouard   You always take your young brother along? Even when you go out with Guillermo?

Yvette   He gets frightened all alone at night he adores the cinema Roger does

Jaudouard   In this department everyone's private life is their own affair I won't allow anyone to stir up trouble Nicole's reliable you can depend on her

Yvette   I get on well with Nicole you know

Jaudouard   It would do you good to listen to her it would stop you talking nonsense to the customers the Aristocrat is the more efficient? Really? You haven't yet understood that the Standard is the machine that requires the least time, the machine for people in a hurry? The screw makes the bean explode whereas in the Aristocrat there's a grinder like in the old mills which crushes gently without overheating for the discerning coffee-lover almost three months here three months and still not understood a thing?

Nicole   The partition Monsieur Jaudouard have you managed to see Monsieur Célidon? You've spoken to him about the partition?

Four

Jaudouard   Every picture the word every is underlined
every picture of whatever kind in the office however at
the discretion of heads of departments one picture per
person at the most will be allowed of a size not exceeding
twenty-four by thirty-six signed Charles Bataille
administrative and financial director Madame Serge tipped
the balance now you know what you have to do you've
till twelve o'clock to clean the place up Monsieur Pierre
may look in at lunch-time he's let it be known there's to
be no delay what's this?

Anne   The letter from the ambassador's wife with a note
in Monsieur Pierre's writing

Nicole   Simply crazy to feel happy but I do I don't
know why

Yvette   A surprise for you

Nicole   Stockings?

Yvette   A miracle they stand up to the claws of a cat it's
not eleven yet and I'm hungry

Nicole   Here taste

Yvette   Paysan biscuits yes I saw the ad they've a
slightly smoky taste put them on try them out

Nicole   I'll never believe that

Yvette   I have more than once you know I used to run
away from home you get over it she'll get over it I got
over it when I knew my mother was done for riddled with
cancer

Nicole   If you're saying that to make Anne happy

Yvette   Dad decided the best thing to do was buy
himself a sailing dinghy

Anne   At their discretion that means one head of a

department can refuse while another

Yvette   The management's so lunatic they drive me mad the higher up they are

Nicole   Not a fold it falls perfectly

Anne   Cut it out sewn it the lot on Sunday

Nicole   In the top left corner there's a reference number

Yvette   I'm hanging two photos eighteen by twenty-four side by side that takes the same space as one photo twenty-four by thirty-six

Anne   One picture they say one

Yvette   Wait or eight photos nine by twelve that takes the same space I'll cut out eight photos of guys in the nude and stick them together that makes one picture just one

Anne   That's arguable

Yvette   Monsieur Pierre steps in

Anne   And Madame Serge

Yvette   Let's see Jaudouard hm hm tell me Jaudouard

Nicole   Don't make me laugh my back

Yvette   I'll hang eight photos of Monsieur Célidon full-frontal profile three-quarter view with a hard-on I'll cut out Monsieur Célidon's head

Nicole   Stop it

Yvette   This dress you know I think it ages you it gives you a serious look you don't need that and the armholes aren't quite straight are they? Three times I ran away the second time with Mum's jewellery the third time

Nicole   You send it back to us the repairs are free naturally

Anne   Simone's not a thief

Yvette   Wait suppose you shortened it like this?

Anne   It's the second time she's run away in six months
I decided to make it when I was at home alone after the
session at the police station

Nicole   He's made you permanent?

Yvette   Still temporary he gave me a three months'
extension what about you I've a feeling he's ignoring you
do you know why?

Nicole   We'll do our best to please you to start with I
shouldn't have started an affair with Guillermo then with
Guillermo we shouldn't have bought a Citroën DS I went
out of my way to tell him it was in a poor condition it
had done more than a hundred thousand kilometres we
got it for less than the price of a new deux chevaux but
he'd just bought a Peugeot 304 to replace his Simca

Anne   Even a new 304's not a DS

Nicole   I did tell him Guillermo spent half our Sunday
under the chassis

Anne   For ten years now he's been talking about a DS
you should have thought now he's talking about a CX

Nicole   For when he gets promoted

Anne   Illusions help you to live

Yvette   I haven't any

Anne   You say that

Yvette   Some men live wrapped up in their illusions
Guillermo for instance maybe it's because he's a man they
won't allow themselves to see that a boss is a boss and
he'll exploit you up to the hilt

Nicole   It's not jut a rumour?

Anne   No doubt about it now Monsieur Pierre's
negotiating

Yvette Not with Mixwell?

Anne The Beaumoulin people visited the factory
yesterday Mixwell offered a better price but he'd rather
Cosson stayed in French hands

Nicole Beaumoulin are bargain basement rubbish

Anne Mixwell's much the same the ambassador's wife
wrote to him direct he replied oh yes we've an excellent
repair man here

Guillermo He came down in person can you do a
good job on this for me my dear fellow? Monsieur
Jaudouard was waddling along beside him yes Monsieur
Pierre we'll do it for you Monsieur Pierre

Nicole A devoted couple they understood nothing

Yvette Who?

Nicole Anne and her husband

Guillermo One day Monsieur Albert brings me a
machine I was learning the job with Monsieur Duclos the
only repair man in the place at the time all repairs were
done in Paris then and Monsieur Duclos was on sick leave
he suffered from renal colic in the end he died of liver
trouble then we knew it wasn't renal colic but an abscess
in the liver

Nicole And I'm not prepared to let him go I'll fight I'll
kill you

Yvette If necessary

Nicole And the partition?

Jaudouard Been moved down the list of priorities

Yvette When you talk you've completely stopped
snorting your sinusitis is finished apparently?

Jaudouard It starts in the spring darling every year

Nicole Sales Administration have managed to get theirs

Guillermo   It was in fifty-five hey son would you be able to do a good job on this thing? It was a machine from the thirties in burr walnut with gilt bronze decorations made specially for the Maharajah of Baroda the Maharajah was on a three-day official visit to Paris

Nicole   Between them and Purchases and it's been put up in three months though there was less reason than between us and Sales Administration

Anne   It's not just the noise of their machines the girls squeal and chatter that department's a farmyard and we've been asking for it for how long?

Nicole   It's been promised it's been budgeted for has it or hasn't it?

Anne   Yes or let them come out and say there's no difference between their work which is automatic with no need to think and ours

Nicole   That's exactly what they will say or they'd show the difference in our salaries which they don't

Jaudouard   Try to win all battles at the same time darling and you'll lose them all

Yvette   You've always been like this?

Guillermo   How?

Yvette   Meek

Guillermo   I was a woodworking craftsman Monsieur Albert took me on as a cabinet maker I'd just finished my apprenticeship when my boss went broke I was nineteen from the day she arrived from Spain my mother had been doing housework with her arthritis I wanted her to stop working

Nicole   Perhaps we're wrong to believe it

Yvette   But why is he selling?

Anne   She lives at Le Vesinet

Yvette   On her own?

Anne   I said to her Cécile buy yourself a dog some nights you can hear strange noises

Guillermo   When Monsieur Duclos died Monsieur Albert placed his trust in me

Jaudouard   Monsieur Pierre will be able to play his golf every day

Nicole   He doesn't do much else now

Yvette   What difference will it make?

Nicole   How much is he getting for it?

Anne   She of all people anything frightens her

Nicole   Perhaps we're not properly looked after

Jaudouard   Is that addressed to me?

Nicole   You're the boss aren't you? In Sales Administration under Monsieur Boyançon they're looked after all right

Anne   He didn't need that to feed the family

Jaudouard   At your level you see things from daisy height at my level you have to see things in a certain perspective

Nicole   Seen from the summit our partition gets lost it's not even a speck on the horizon

Jaudouard   It might be better if we did a little work

Nicole   Are you saying that to me?

Yvette   If your machine is more than six years old we strongly advise you to take advantage of our exclusive offer the Aristocrat for the price of the Standard the grinding speed is slower

Jaudouard   When we've caught up the equivalent of the
fourteen days' arrears we've accumulated since September
in April we've handled a daily average of fifty-five claims
the target was fixed by Monsieur Célidon at sixty-six but
to catch up with the backlog we'll handle seventy-five
cases a day without overtime the arrears will be
eliminated by an improvement in productivity

Yvette   The aroma is better preserved what we've done
is to adapt the most advanced technology to our long
established process

Five

Jaudouard   The choice is yours Guillermo if I were you
as they're offering you this job in the Vosges once again
and for the last time

Guillermo   If I don't accept

Jaudouard   You know the company thinks highly of
you you'll be able to carry on with your real job there

Anne   He accosted Yvette in the lift

Nicole   Célidon?

Yvette   There was just him and me in the lift

Jaudouard   Monsieur Célidon thought of giving you a
job in Paris as a messenger I told him no in that case it's
best to choose the clearest solution let's give him a
generous nine months' notice three of which are to be
worked

Guillermo   You're sacking me?

Jaudouard   In three months you'll get a half year's
salary

Nicole   It's Madame Lebarrieux from Poitiers

Yvette   Yes

Nicole   I told her to write she won't stop phoning

Yvette   From Poitiers?

Nicole   She works in the Post Office

Yvette   What do we say? My Cosson packed up the other day when my husband threw it at my head I'm sending it back to you all the same as it was working perfectly see if you can't do something even if it costs me as much as a new one I'd rather keep this

Jaudouard   Think you've nine months to look around a good craftsman like you will easily find

Guillermo   A lifetime

Jaudouard   At forty-two you're young and a change will make you younger if that frightens you you've the option of transferring to the factory of course I understand your hesitating the factory's not the same factory any more the spirit there has changed this morning I hear their row's started again the moulding shop's closed down

Yvette   I was surprised he knew my name I blushed absolutely scarlet

Anne   She thinks he's that handsome?

Nicole   Listen to her

Yvette   Ideal beauty objectively it does exist you Guillermo objectively you're not handsome but that doesn't prevent a flow between two people

Anne   Then Célidon's your ideal

Yvette   Christ that man's terrific

Anne   What did he say to you?

Yvette   I didn't hear a word he said

Guillermo   Yvette

Yvette   Guillermo nobody can tell you anything why are you looking so miserable?

Jaudouard   This newspaper article?

Anne   Let me read it to you merger in the electrical household goods industry Mixwell withdraws Beaumoulin the winner Cosson the hundred-year-old firm famous for its high quality coffee grinders is passing under the control of the Beaumoulin group which is vigorously pursuing its acquisition policy and is on the way to becoming one of the three leading companies of its kind in Europe the decision to look for a partner Monsieur Pierre Cosson chairman and managing director of the Cosson company told us was taken because of the continued success of our product it had become necessary to move into top gear we are proud Monsieur Francis Baignères the dynamic young chairman of the Beaumoulin board explained to us to welcome Cosson into our fold they have a superb product which is part of the national heritage and we shall strive to give them a new impetus the French directors of Mixwell the American giant have refused to make any statement will this operation have the beneficial effects which the parties anticipate? In the last decade Cosson has profited from the return of a substantial percentage of consumers to a certain mystique about coffee-making as in the good old days however it has not been able to enlarge its base by diversifying its range of products or to rejuvenate its management it remains to be seen whether its take-over will not lead eventually to a vulgarisation of the brand

Nicole   That's the limit

Yvette   Keep calm

Nicole   If it's true I can't believe it

Yvette   He must know Monsieur Jaudouard should

Jaudouard It's a management decision an exceptional bonus of two hundred francs granted to the staff in Sales Administration as a reward for the extra effort they have made to handle the increase in orders due to the promotion of the Aristocrat

Nicole While we sit here twiddling our thumbs I presume? Though I'm getting bloody well used to injustice it's not the two hundred francs I don't give a damn about that but I do know how things are run in that department they're brainless little things who spend the whole day gossiping except when Monsieur Boyançon walks down the room then they all begin typing away like galley slaves but they don't care a fuck for their work

Yvette Not surprising it's no job for human beings

Anne I'd rather be a cashier in a big store

Yvette Or a washer-up in a restaurant

Anne They could at least have made an internal announcement before we read it in the paper

Yvette How many has she?

Anne Cats? She's no idea her house is full of them

Yvette Your stockings I'm waiting to hear?

Nicole I haven't been near a cat

Yvette You mustn't think the Standard is inferior in quality you see there are two distinct technical principles if it's important for you to gain a few seconds every morning

Anne Not that I'm discouraged

Nicole But it's hard

Anne Yes

Nicole Not knowing how to get through to her

Anne   Yes you know she hasn't opened her mouth

Nicole   Since she came back? That was Saturday?

Anne   Yes at four in the morning

Nicole   Anyway she is back that's a relief she looked all right?

Anne   But doesn't say a word the psychiatrists tell us this silence is like an appeal that's addressed to us an appeal we have to decipher to be able to reply

Yvette   You say nothing Guillermo I'd like to know what happened to your father was he tortured?

Anne   Don't be afraid to surrender to your child be simple get down to the deep levels of your authentic self and then perhaps contact will be obtained I tell you I'm through with psychiatrists

Guillermo   First there was Monsieur Théophile then Monsieur Louis then Monsieur Martial then Monsieur Albert then Monsieur Pierre the young Monsieur Nicholas who's eighteen showed promise but there won't be a sixth generation

Yvette   You never talk about it you know I'm curious

Anne   All they succeed in doing is make us feel guilty *I* say when she wants to talk she will talk

Guillermo   Mother crossed the Pyrenees with me in her arms I was one year old father stayed behind

Yvette   How did they kill him? Did your mother never say?

Anne   We've tried everything more freedom more discipline

Nicole   Guillermo doesn't bother much about them but Antoine and Mathieu adore Guillermo they'd follow him to the end of the world

Six

Anne   Cécile gave me carrots and cucumbers from her garden

Nicole   Anne you're a chum

Yvette   For me too? Did you know I'm almost a vegetarian?

Nicole   It's her day of triumph she's at the top it's happened

Anne   She grows them organically without fertiliser that's why they're so good I don't know if I dare offer you any Monsieur Jaudouard she's not all that interested in her career you know her tablecloths her cats saving the Parthenon she has a cupboard full of embroidered tablecloths all from different countries

Nicole   Now Monsieur Bataille's appointed managing director

Yvette   Monsieur Pierre's completely dropped out?

Anne   She's always followed Monsieur Bataille

Jaudouard   Here's your chance to show what you can do he told me

Anne   Every year for the whole of September in Athens she scrapes away she puts her cats in one of those animal homes and sits there scraping

Nicole   Monsieur Bataille himself?

Jaudouard   If you fail there's the door he said that's a language I like but if you succeed

Anne   She's no children so there's nothing to stop her taking her holidays in September people flock there from New York Moscow

Yvette   What's the matter with these columns?

Jaudouard   But a boss can't succeed on his own you girls and I are on the same raft there's a new wind blowing through the company up to now people who care people who are on top of their job haven't been rewarded

Anne   And think of Madame Serge being given early retirement she's always been fair to you hasn't she?

Nicole   An active woman like her

Jaudouard   A forceful woman these last few years I must say she wasn't thinking quite so straight

Anne   It's the carbon monoxide from motor vehicles and the sulphur in factory smoke when that mixes with the oxygen it sticks to the marble and forms a layer of gypsum which crumbles when it rains

Yvette   A strike how long do you think it might last?

Nicole   They say surroundings have an influence on people this factory in the middle of the meadows in a clearing in an immense pine forest

Jaudouard   It only takes a handful of agitators to sway a whole workforce the world is full of sheep and who's going to suffer? Us lot here

Yvette   And Monsieur Célidon?

Nicole   Ah that interests you does it?

Jaudouard   He's taking over from Madame Serge

Anne   And in his place?

Jaudouard   Nobody they're reducing the hierarchy I want fewer generals and more soldiers more initiative and less waste I'll be the captain of a tight ship with nothing useless on board he said

Yvette   Her tablecloths what does she do with them all alone in that house?

Jaudouard In the competitive environment in which we operate

Yvette She invites all her lovers to enormous orgies? In the middle of the pines they run naked through the meadows?

Anne She doesn't like men

Yvette Her girlfriends then

Anne Men or women

Yvette Hasn't she got a little hole between her legs?

Anne She never feels lonely I envy her without her Monsieur Bataille would never have

Guillermo Monsieur Bataille you remember when he joined the company or don't you?

Nicole Cosson After-Sales at your service

Anne All I remember is he joined the same year as me

Guillermo Yes from Beaumoulin

Yvette Guillermo's waking up

Guillermo When Monsieur Albert took him on he thought he was making a good deal little did he know he was introducing the worm into the fruit it took Monsieur Bataille ten years to achieve his ends and Célidon do you know where he came from? Beaumoulin of course Madame Serge was the only one to realise what was being plotted for Cosson it's the end now everything's fine the gravediggers are standing by when you think that Monsieur Bataille's always said his heart was on the left in the factory the unions call the tune that's the way it is in Monsieur Albert's time they didn't exist now it's burn the place down that's what makes Monsieur Bataille's game so easy it'll be the old gang's fault he'll be able to finish his clean-up and the Beaumoulin people will go through Cosson like a piece of cheese

Jaudouard   It's not easy for you Guillermo I understand but do stop demoralising these ladies especially as you're interested in at least two of them and two is one too many I just mention it I'm worried about Nicole her output's down and you know this is not the right moment I must succeed in reviving this department they're waiting to see how we do it makes you laugh does it?

Nicole   Really? In that case we're terribly sorry

Anne   At the heart of the damaged columns

Nicole   The company hardly ever makes a mistake like that

Anne   They inject titanium the public aren't allowed in now

Yvette   Where exactly is the Parthenon?

Nicole   Send it back to us we'll have another look for yours it might still be at the factory the factory is occupied we must ask you to be patient

Anne   The feet of two million visitors a year have dug trenches in the marble they're waging a vast campaign before it's too late she's chairman of the Île de France section they're studying a plan to cover the whole site with a giant glass dome

Guillermo   It's disgusting

Nicole   You can rely on us

Jaudouard   A pretty little bottom like a couple of ping pong balls

Nicole   Immediately

Yvette   Saving old stones while the Cambodians are being massacred in thousands they string them up by the feet if they don't work enough

Anne   No

Nicole If she hadn't told me herself

Anne She told you to fool you

Nicole She told Guillermo too

Anne She told you because she told Guillermo she told Guillermo to make him lose his temper

Nicole Poor man he needed that

Anne Poor man? Too bad if I'm hurting you he deserves everything he's getting

Nicole You're wrong

Anne I love you I love her too it's so easy to drift along the girl's harpooned him because of his job anyway he should have realised what was brewing ages ago and reacted accordingly with his seniority and fine reputation in the company but no a young manager who's still learning the job says this way to the slaughterhouse and off he goes like a lamb to get his throat cut

Nicole Anyway she has slept with Jaudouard

Anne I don't believe a word of it

Nicole It's never the right moment for you Monsieur Jaudouard to talk about grading I'm sorry you must give me a few minutes you've avoided this conversation twice already

Jaudouard Not happy?

Nicole You know perfectly well

Yvette At your service hullo

Anne After she got an extra three months?

Yvette If it's something wrong with the safety device you'd better send it back to us

Jaudouard You know what to do if you aren't satisfied?

Nicole You do what I'm doing speak to my boss

Yvette   Repairs are taking rather longer than usual at the moment

Anne   I'd have more respect for a prostitute

Nicole   The job? I like the job it's just that I don't have to tell you I'm still classed as a second grade shorthand typist

Guillermo   Nicole

Nicole   Wait I'm busy

Yvette   This programme

Anne   Which one?

Yvette   About the Cambodians

Anne   Maybe I'm not interested

Nicole   I'm not complaining about my salary look I don't know if I'm well paid or not all I want is to be paid for the job I'm doing

Jaudouard   All salaries are frozen my sweet till Beaumoulin's Personnel Department can make their comparative analyses

Nicole   I'm telling you

Jaudouard   You're wasting your time

Nicole   It's also a question of dignity

Jaudouard   Your dignity will have to wait

Nicole   Will it? Then let me tell you

Jaudouard   But without getting excited about it oh you're going? Tears the floodgates are open?

Anne   It's true that in the last two years there aren't many people like her who haven't had a single merit increase and I don't think you can say Nicole doesn't do her job like a real professional

Jaudouard   There's something the matter with the girl all I know is we're nowhere near the seventy-five claims a day

Nicole   Yes Guillermo I'm sorry

Jaudouard   There'll be trouble at the end of the month

Nicole   What's the matter?

Guillermo   I'm transferring to the Vosges

Seven

Jaudouard   Well? What do you say? Your partition

Nicole   Yes at long last our partition why your partition? You get the benefit of it too

Anne   It certainly is a change not just the noise in fact my ears still find it hard to get used to it

Nicole   Having a place of our own at last I confess I find it hard to believe

Yvette   Cosson After-Sales at your service will it soon be over? I can't tell you the management is doing its utmost to end it as quickly as possible the management is concerned about the nuisance to its customers

Anne   You were able to convince Simone

Yvette   The management cannot surrender to blackmail by a handful of people manipulated from outside if we surrender this time

Jaudouard   Well my dear fellow everything's going like a bomb? Our friend Guillermo's fantastic good God when you think that the average output per man day at the factory is twenty-four well yesterday he managed thirty-five today he's all set for over forty

Nicole   Cosson After-Sales at your service some delay is inevitable but the management is concerned about the inconvenience suffered by its customers and has taken the necessary measures

Anne   You got her to talk? She told you something?

Nicole   Yes repairs are being processed normally the channels are rather clogged

Anne   Cosson After-Sales

Nicole   When will you understand?

Anne   They've put up the partition haven't they?

Nicole   I'm talkiing about the grading we must have a representative body there's no other way to get these things discussed we must force them to listen

Anne   You're not the only person in this situation our company is dealing with the matter you mustn't be impatient

Nicole   To make them hear the voice of us girls in the front line who know what it's all about take the output statistics it's a lot of humbug in a department like this so much an hour doesn't mean a thing

Anne   Cosson After-Sales you're calling from Cannes? Our lines are congested you keep on trying to call us? Yes they are people from outside the company who have infiltrated

Yvette   She poured it out in a flood I promise you she didn't draw breath I was splitting my sides hell it went on and on with the story of her parents who think they love her who think they love each other a classic case

Anne   I'm jotting down your reference number

Jaudouard   A nice little detachment of mobile police with tear gas to get the bastards out but first of all we've got to let it ripen

Nicole   Or rot

Jaudouard   That wouldn't be a bad thing

Nicole   That partition it's taken two years to get it

Yvette   Cosson After-Sales at your service yes it's gone on for one month and one week production's been stopped now for thirty-eight days so we hope yes luckily

Anne   She doesn't believe we love her

Yvette   The management has made all arrangements

Nicole   Cosson After-Sales but do let me explain now you're getting upset

Anne   We appreciate how patient our customers are

Nicole   In the lift?

Yvette   He waited till I came out onto the landing

Anne   With a bunch of flowers?

Jaudouard   To launch the PIP the Profit Improvement Plan Monsieur Bataille held a meeting yesterday of directors and Heads of Departments the PIP will only succeed if it becomes a GIM a Great Ideas Mill every employee male and female down to the most junior is invited to submit his or her suggestions so that we can bake a good loaf which will benefit the entire staff I want everyone to add his or her measure of flour he appointed an interdepartmental committee the RSCC to study the working of every cog in the organisation

Yvette   Mindful of the interests of its customers the management cannot consider surrendering to the actions of a handful of lunatics

Nicole   Anne

Anne   Nicole

Nicole   Makes me feel sick

Yvette   The things they make us say

Anne   We're between the hammer and the anvil

Yvette   I'm exhausted

Jaudouard   Our little treasure's tired?

Yvette   For a start you stop being so familiar

Anne   I simply can't carry on

Guillermo   Faced with the blind obstinacy of a rapacious and distant management obsessed with increasing profits who for over a month have refused to negotiate the strike committee once again states its determination to stand firm fraternally united in the fight to achieve their legitimate demands the workers will not submit to squalid manoeuvres of division and intimidation in order to assure the victorious outcome of their struggle they appeal to the solidarity of tradesmen and the whole population an open day will be held on Saturday from noon to midnight bring your wives and children a jumble sale and picnic await you for the benefit of those families hardest hit with a visit to the factory and a ball followed by a great debate with the work-force who are defending their standard of living as well as the autonomy and integrity of their company this conflict concerns you it affects the prosperity of the whole district long live the unity of the Trade Union movement we shall never lower the flag I received this copy at home PS handwritten blacklegs will get beaten up if the cap fits wear it

Yvette   She was phoning from Deauville I'd rather do without it however long it takes provided the management won't give in and then I hope they hang the lot of them you wouldn't by any chance be able to lend us the gallows I asked?

Anne   What's obvious is that deliveries are being halted we're losing sales every day for whose benefit? How much longer can it go on? Yesterday Cécile told me Monsieur Bataille was ready to make a concession these Beaumoulin people vetoed it the meeting was rather lively voices were raised

Nicole   One less Cosson sold means one more Beaumoulin sold

Anne   Exactly what I mean

Nicole   They'll keep our head under water for as long as they need

Yvette   What'll remain of Cosson

Anne   There's one man who's happy look at him

Nicole   He's been threatened Yvette's seen Simone? *I've* seen the labour inspector I asked him how to start a union branch nothing to it at two then at four a.m. last night they phoned him from the factory

Jaudouard   The RSCC the Reduction In Structural Costs Committee set up to implement the PIP consists of one representative from each department

Anne   In her eyes it was when she came home last night she kept her teeth clenched but there was something different a light

Nicole   All that's needed is a letter to the management from the central union committee stating who they appoint as their representative

Yvette   Wait

Jaudouard   Will analyse existing structures will propose any change in structures capable of leading to a reduction in costs and at the same time an improvement in efficiency

Nicole   Anyone can put themselves forward as the representative

Anne   Something's happened

Nicole   It's clear to me we'll never succeed any other way

Anne   Is that so? Well let me tell you I'm utterly opposed to it it's putting the wolf into the sheep fold go ahead and everything will happen here the same way it did in the factory exactly the same

Nicole   Not if it's us

Anne   The same it won't take long before you're thrown out and they take over

Eight

Nicole   Anne he's not going to the Vosges after all

Anne   I never thought he would that's cheered you up

Yvette   My flat's so small you know Guillermo you've made up your mind?

Nicole   He's becoming a restorer with a second-hand dealer who goes to fairs and markets he sells old copper saucepans kitchen utensils and antique tools you can still find them in the country there are more and more people who collect that sort of thing Anne Guillermo's leaving me

Yvette   Still you will need a tiny corner you won't be able to live without your workbench to mess around at on Sundays

Jaudouard   Monsieur Bataille told Monsieur Célidon it was amply deserved and as Guillermo has finally decided to leave us

Yvette   Cosson After-Sales at your service you can send it to us you must allow three weeks yes everything's back to normal now

Anne   I don't believe a word of it

Jaudouard   Monsieur Bataille is adding a further three months' salary to his redundancy payment he'll be going

with a full year's pay in his pocket and for you darlings
an exceptional bonus of three hundred francs it's a
personal decision of Monsieur Bataille's

Nicole   You can tell him he can keep them

Anne   Yes at last she's gone off to do her scraping she
took the plane for Athens yesterday morning one week
late Monsieur Bataille didn't want her to go before the
strike was over

Jaudouard   Monsieur Bataille insisted on rewarding the
staff of the department for rising to the situation I didn't
have to ask him for anything

Anne   One day last week normally she'd have been in
Athens by now I say one day it was the middle of the
night a man appeared in her garden she was scared out
of her life you'll never guess it was her nephew from
Sweden she didn't recognise him she hadn't seen him
since he was a kid and the day before I was invited to
dinner we dined the three of us she used an embroidered
tablecloth from Bessarabia just think if there hadn't been
this strike I told her you'd have missed him

Yvette   Miles from anywhere in the country like that

Anne   Listen I received her end of term report she's
above average in every subject and top in French takes an
active part in the class

Yvette   Our three hundred francs apiece if we put them
together we could have a little party

Nicole   The union branch needs funds why don't we
give it to them?

Anne   I have to buy some dusters I'm afraid

Nicole   Anne Guillermo's moving out tomorrow

Yvette   Monsieur Théophile's grinder too?

Guillermo   Yes Monsieur Théophile's too

Yvette   You've sold it?

Guillermo   I've sold my whole collection the lot I sold it to *him*

Yvette   Who?

Guillermo   My new boss that's how we got to know each other he's the leading specialist in France for old kitchen and table ware he's had a stall for ten years at Montreuil and another at Clignancourt he used to sell a lot to the Americans now most of his customers are Japanese Arab businessmen too

Yvette   And Nicole?

Guillermo   What about her?

Yvette   I like her

Guillermo   Monsieur Célidon too you like him

Yvette   That's right we do like each other

Guillermo   And Monsieur Jaudouard you throw yourself at every man you meet

Yvette   Not Monsieur Jaudouard

Guillermo   You hop from one branch to the next

Yvette   I am faithful you're stupid jealousy's the stupidest thing

Guillermo   I wonder if there's anything in your head

Yvette   There's you just you

Guillermo   And all the rest

Yvette   You

Guillermo   And the rest

Yvette   That doesn't prevent

Guillermo   I wish I understood

Anne   And she's talking to us now

Yvette   To you loving always means excluding you want to exclude Nicole why exclude her?

Guillermo   I'm letting her have my flat

Yvette   The least you can do

Guillermo   I'm coming to yours

Yvette   You're coming to mine to set up a tyranny I'll be the first piece in your new collection well no I hate collections in our home anyone will be welcome anyone can help themselves take what they want

Nicole   That does me good Anne what you're doing now

Anne   And if you want to know what logistics are they're Monsieur Bataille's new hobby-horse the whole reorganisation revolves round the installation of a logistics department Célidon's been promoted he'll be the logistics manager Monsieur Boyançon's leaving Sales Administration for training at Beaumoulin Cécile thinks it's the prelude to merging the two sales forces Sales Administration will come under Logistics together with Purchases Shipping Data Processing

Nicole   And us

Anne   Us? Us no not us

Nicole   And Jaudouard? He's not being moved?

Anne   Yes

Nicole   Tell me Anne why won't you tell me?

Anne   He's going to replace Boyançon

Nicole   I don't believe you

Anne   Yes

Nicole   He's going to Sales Administration? That's

impossible he can't accept

Anne   It ranks as promotion for salary purposes

Nicole   Supervising those brainless little things and that ranks as promotion you're joking

Anne   You know how long he's been waiting for it

Nicole   He'll buy a brand new Citroën CX a white one

Anne   In fact it's a step down they're throwing him a bone he's an old servant

Nicole   But us? You're not saying who's replacing him Anne it's you?

Anne   No it's not me

Nicole   Then I say there's no justice simply because you're a woman is that it?

Anne   The question didn't arise

Nicole   Then who'll take over the After-Sales Service?

Anne   There won't be an After-Sales Service

Guillermo   Thank you I don't want any favours

Jaudouard   But you're one of the longest serving employees in the company you're not going to refuse a small farewell present

Guillermo   You see these hands? They've worked hard they're empty they'll stay empty I'm sorry

Jaudouard   A small thing really but you won't stop the management and staff as a sign of their appreciation of your excellent service my colleagues and I simply wanted

Anne   The duties will be split between Data Processing and Sales Administration most claims will be handled by Data Processing but for special cases one girl will be transferred to Sales Administration yes under Jaudouard the RSCC has analysed all cases handled by the

department over a three-month period they have classified
them into sixty-four different categories for each category
there will be a standard letter which will be produced by
the computer all phone calls will be switched to an
answering machine which will tell the customers to write
you see

Nicole   Yes I see

Anne   The PIP

Nicole   The PIP yes the measure of flour

Anne   They've worked out that eighty per cent of the
cases will fit one of the sixty-four standard letters for the
remaining twenty per cent they're going to keep one of us
do you see? Cécile who never drinks the other night she
let herself go she had that young nephew to entertain she
swore me to secrecy he doesn't understand anything but
Swedish she'd bought a bottle of Muscadet Simone went
out last Sunday with Yvette and young Roger

Nicole   It is a beautiful partition

Anne   Jaudouard doesn't know anything yet don't
breathe a word

Nicole   Guillermo's moving in with Yvette

Guillermo   He's got several hundred coffee pots in stock
about a hundred and fifty coffee grinders

Yvette   That girl Simone is unbelievable it was pelting
with rain what do we do? Let's go rowing she said so we
go to the Bois she Roger and me not a soul on that lake
except us suddenly she stands up and starts imitating you
Anne and your husband Roger was doubled up laughing
so was I the parental speech went something like this
Simone my own darling you know that what means most
in the world to your daddy and me is your happiness I
mean real happiness the one you construct not the one
you think you find on motor-cycle pillions or in
discotheques

Nicole   I don't know if I've thanked you enough Monsieur Jaudouard

Jaudouard   For?

Nicole   This partition

Jaudouard   When a request is reasonable it gets dealt with in the end I'm still thinking about your grading problem my sweet

Nicole   Yes *I'm* thinking about the two boys

Jaudouard   Which ones?

Nicole   Antoine and Mathieu I imagine you are too Guillermo

Anne   What about my husband?

Yvette   What about him?

Anne   What did she make him say?

Yvette   You know Simone my dear how you've made your mother suffer those first white hairs you know where they come from and those bags under her eyes we exist too

Nicole   Cosson After-Sales at your service

Yvette   So we've thought it over Mummy and me tomorrow you and I we'll go together I've made an appointment with a man whose job is helping children who have problems I'll leave you alone with him you can tell him everything

Nicole   Don't mention it it's our job to point out the different alternatives yes we can repair it for you but in view of its age you should consider Cosson's special offer to its faithful customers an Aristocrat at the same price as the Standard will save thirty per cent and you'll have a machine which does not merely grind in the first place it's the quietest machine on the market but above all if you care about preserving all the aroma contained in the bean then I tell you you mustn't hesitate

Nine

Yvette   It's important the bed in a home

Nicole   More important is the table

Yvette   No the bed

Anne   You learn to believe in certain things and one day you're told

Jaudouard   Our customers aren't the same any more

Nicole   First the table a huge table you can do everything on

Jaudouard   What people want from us now isn't what it used to be they don't care so much about feelings

Yvette   Madame Fondevaux from Grenoble

Nicole   I understand you're being fond of it but we've examined it carefully it's a matter of general wear and tear after fourteen years you know

Anne   It's not just a matter of exchanging the motor go ahead and send it back to us

Jaudouard   Some bridges must be crossed

Nicole   For putting your elbows on for eating preparing the food writing sewing ironing

Anne   Bridges? There's such a tumult inside me at night I often wake up with a start I try to work out the reason for it all I try to comfort myself I can't help feeling appalled

Nicole   It's quite easy you send it by registered post

Anne   I think people are still human beings life's so hard for them

Nicole　With the best will in the world we can't do it any quicker

Anne　In their jobs in their family relationships there are so many things that don't work they ring us not so much about their complaints

Nicole　For reading aloud the things you like for them to do their homework

Yvette　And Anne what will happen to her?

Nicole　Her massage usually I don't have to ask her she sees when my neck hurts this morning I asked her she behaved as though she hadn't heard

Guillermo　There's a farmhouse table he's just picked up in the Alps solid walnut the top's a single board we could have it for next to nothing the feet have been eaten away

Anne　A smile on the end of the line a little warmth someone who listens who understands doesn't that mean anything any more?

Yvette　First a bed a huge bed we can dive into all three of us

Nicole　And have a conference

Yvette　And sleep and have fun all three of us

Nicole　All over the bed

Anne　Our factory's in the Vosges you must reckon three weeks including the delivery time you Monsieur Jaudouard you find it easy to dismiss it all I find

Jaudouard　One can disagree with some of it but the main thing is the impetus Monsieur Bataille he does get things moving which doesn't mean for instance that choosing Yvette was the right decision I told him so

Anne　Yvette?

Jaudouard   Monsieur Célidon had made up his mind about Yvette hasn't she got the best statistical results? Maybe I told him but when it comes to handling the difficult cases the cases that don't fall into one of your categories then we need a girl who really has experience the one who's best at dealing with customers

Anne   Yvette?

Nicole   Who?

Yvette   Célidon himself called me into his office to inform me I couldn't believe it Anne is much better qualified I told him or else Nicole anyway it's a crime it's a decision he said

Nicole   That's what comes of having little chats with future directors in the lift

Yvette   What about Anne I asked him

Anne   And Nicole?

Jaudouard   I'm disappointed with her I'd never have believed it she used to be sensible at least she did her job now she leaves it all to you and spends her time sowing discontent never mind she'll get her notice quickly and correctly due to reorganisation it's a kindness we're doing her so that for one full year she'll get the special state benefits

Yvette   I'll sleep between the two of you

Nicole   We'll all take turns in the middle

Anne   I've tried to tell her Nicole I said I can understand you're trying to save your home

Jaudouard   I never thought I'd see a human being fall so low

Anne   You can't possibly accept that Yvette and you will tear each other to pieces I can't even repeat what she said it was so ghastly it's against nature and your children I told her

Jaudouard   The example they're going to have before their eyes they'll end up in prison or the asylum someone will have to pay for their food and I know who the taxpayer people who work who try to maintain a few principles in their life

Anne   Yes I'm afraid for Simone Yvette's acquired an influence over Simone

Nicole   For the occasion he stood up when I came in Nicole the decision I have to transmit to you he blew his nose he said of all a manager's duties this is the most painful

Guillermo   He refused to drink his chocolate this morning

Yvette   Roger's a dreadful child he teases him and Mathieu's unhappy because Antoine laughs

Guillermo   I wouldn't want Mathieu to feel rejected

Nicole   The RSCC has decided that two jobs should be made redundant and yours is one of them so I asked him what job the firm was offering me he said for me there was nothing you are not unaware I imagine that a union representative cannot be dismissed out of hand these details will be settled in the proper manner he said you will see the Personnel Department and what's happening to Anne I asked him

Jaudouard   Quickening the pace of consumer demand that is Monsieur Bataille's master plan when a world market is in recession if you want to improve sales you must increase turnover and for that you need products with a shorter life you must put a brake on repairs by new purchase incentives

Nicole   It's true she's been transferred to the Personnel Department?

Jaudouard   It's a solution that will suit you so well a change of horizon

Anne   I don't know I'm lost I'm all confused so perhaps

Jaudouard   That I can tell you is what Monsieur Bataille thinks with this increase in employment legislation which is designed to paralyse business the Personnel Department must be filled with more experienced people who have tact I shall miss working with you Anne we'd got used to each other

Yvette   Let's say on Saturday we'll finish painting the bathroom and the living-room

Nicole   And we'll hang your father's photograph now you've found it

Anne   We'll meet around the building

Nicole   You don't mind?

Guillermo   In nineteen thirty-six my mother's brother he gave Dad's name under torture they arrested him in Bilbao

Jaudouard   You'll come and see me?

Anne   Where?

Jaudouard   In my office and then

Guillermo   There were three of them locked up together in this cell years afterwards we heard the guards finished them off fifteen years later I joined Cosson like joining a religion

Jaudouard   At home with my wife it's always much the same I was thinking we know each other pretty well

Anne   You're not serious

Jaudouard   We've a lot in common

Guillermo   For a long time I tried to imagine it then I swept it all out of my mind

Yvette   Father cleared out when Mother was ill and I was beastly to her and the doctor said we'd better be prepared

Jaudouard   Once or twice a week after work we need to change our ideas

Anne   You're not serious Maurice

Yvette   I don't give her more than a month he said I didn't understand right away then suddenly I did understand she saw I'd understood and she understood at once herself

Nicole   Guillermo you wouldn't care for a child of your own?

Yvette   Or two?

Nicole   One with each of us?

Anne   My husband and I all the problems we've had with Simone should have brought us together

Yvette   Three plus two will make five

Nicole   If you include that dreadful Roger

Jaudouard   I've been thinking about it

Anne   Since when?

Jaudouard   My sinusitis in February

Anne   Cécile warned me she said watch out that man's wicked Cécile knows me she knows I don't get involved casually

Yvette   Cosson After-Sales

Nicole   That is why we're supreme the method of manufacture has not changed the enamel has resisted

Anne   You think I should accept?

Jaudouard   It would suit you there

Anne   It's quite a bridge to cross

Yvette   We'll be safe from the big bad wolf

Jaudouard   And it never hurts to have a friend in the Personnel Department

Nicole   Monsieur Jaudouard how do we answer a case like this? We've written to her three times already

Anne   Not at all I've no resentment Yvette the reverse I think it's all for the best

Jaudouard   Nonsense you're joking Guillermo's joking

Yvette   A little advice perhaps Anne yes I'll come and see you every now and then

Guillermo   It's done Nicole Monsieur Jaudouard's talking to you

Methuen World Classics *and*
Methuen Contemporary Dramatists

Methuen Modern Plays

include work by

Jean Anouilh

John Arden

Margaretta D'Arcy

Peter Barnes

Sebastian Barry

Brendan Behan

Edward Bond

Bertolt Brecht

Howard Brenton

Simon Burke

Jim Cartwright

Caryl Churchill

Noël Coward

Sarah Daniels

Nick Dear

Shelagh Delaney

David Edgar

Dario Fo

Michael Frayn

John Godber

Paul Godfrey

David Greig

John Guare

Peter Handke

Jonathan Harvey

Iain Heggie

Declan Hughes

Terry Johnson

Sarah Kane

Charlotte Keatley

Barrie Keeffe

Robert Lepage

Stephen Lowe

Doug Lucie

Martin McDonagh

John McGrath

David Mamet

Patrick Marber

Arthur Miller

Mtwa, Ngema & Simon

Tom Murphy

Phyllis Nagy

Peter Nichols

Joseph O'Connor

Joe Orton

Louise Page

Joe Penhall

Luigi Pirandello

Stephen Poliakoff

Franca Rame

Mark Ravenhill

Philip Ridley

Reginald Rose

David Rudkin

Willy Russell

Jean-Paul Sartre

Sam Shepard

Wole Soyinka

C. P. Taylor

Theatre de Complicite

Theatre Workshop

Sue Townsend

Judy Upton

Timberlake Wertenbaker

Victoria Wood

For a Complete Catalogue of Methuen Drama titles
write to:

Methuen Drama
Random House
20 Vauxhall Bridge Road
London SW1V 2SA